Magic Lantern Guides
Proof of Purchase
Canon EOS Rebel
X/XS

Heiner Henninges/Bob Shell

Canon

EOS Rebel X S

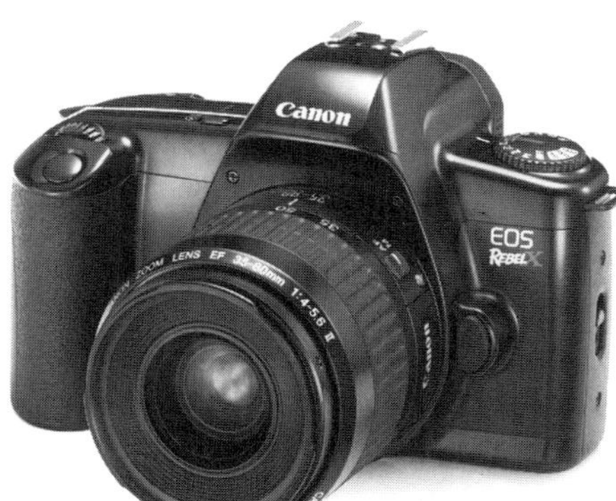

Laterna magica

Magic Lantern Guide to
Canon EOS Rebel X/XS
(International Designation EOS 500)

A Laterna magica® book

First English Language Edition April 1994.
Published in the United States of America by

Silver Pixel Press
Division of The Saunders Group
21 Jet View Drive
Rochester, NY 14624

From the original German Edition by Heiner Henninges
Translated by Phyllis M. Riefler-Bonham
Edited by Bob Shell
Editorial Assistants: Mimi Netzel, Lynn Love
Production Coordinator: Marti Saltzman
Printed in Germany by Kösel GmbH, Kempten

ISBN 1-883403-09-X

All product photos courtesy of Canon, all others
unless specified are by the author.

Contents

Introduction

Canon has produced many innovative cameras in its EOS series. The first REBEL cameras (the EOS 1000 series in other markets) were probably more responsible than any other for introducing autofocus SLR photography to a broad range of people. The REBEL series is significant because Canon designers reduced the number of internal components, creating small, lightweight, easily operated cameras. Canon also introduced intregal image programs with five subject programs and five creative programs.

The Canon EOS REBEL X/XS (or the EOS 500, as it is known in markets other than North America) is the smallest and lightest of

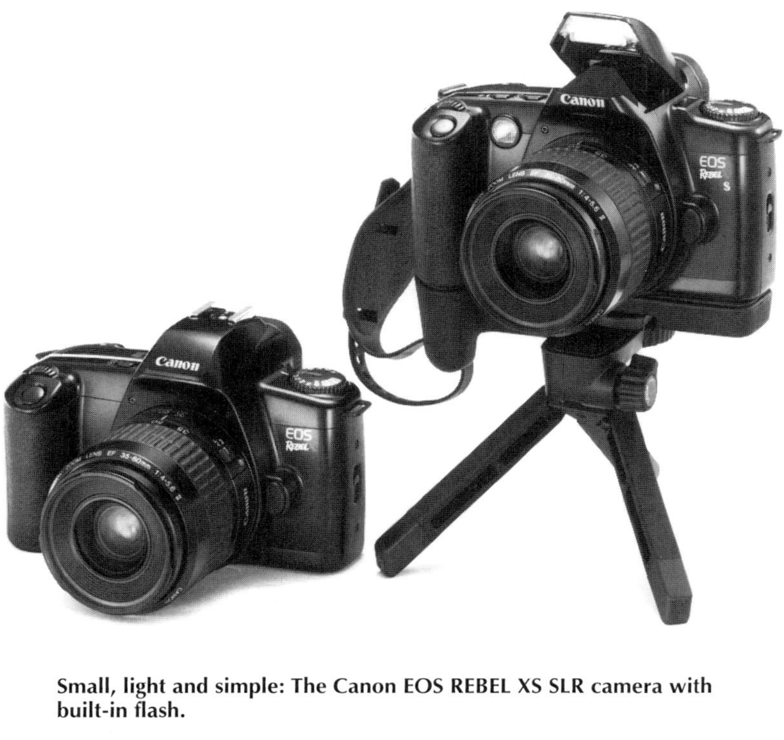

Small, light and simple: The Canon EOS REBEL XS SLR camera with built-in flash.

all the AF SLR cameras to date. It is also the quietest of its class. Still, it offers everything one might want in a modern autofocus SLR camera: three types of exposure measurement, two types of flash metering, 6-zone or 8-zone exposure metering, four programs for artistic expression and four image control programs. Super-sharp pictures are guaranteed by the new 3-point wide-spectrum autofocus sensor. Because of its fully automatic functions, the EOS REBEL X/XS prevents shaky pictures and even masters fill flash modes.

Additional practical features of the EOS REBEL X/XS include automatic multiple exposures, self timer and, as an accessory, a grip with a collapsible table-top tripod. The Canon EOS REBEL X/XS allows the photographer to concentrate solely on the subject, mood and composition when it is set on the Green Zone program. Together with the standard EF 35-80mm f/1.4-5.6 zoom lens, the Canon EOS REBEL X/XS weighs just 18 oz. (520 g). With this camera a photographer is well equipped for most picture-taking situations ranging from landscapes, close-ups or portraits to high-speed snapshots. Its portability and picture-taking ease make the EOS REBEL X/XS fun to use while taking great photos.

And there is even more! This book is intended to show how all of the REBEL series' innovative technology can be utilized for personally creative and technically perfect shots. The following pages will describe the basics of these exceptional cameras and their comprehensive line of accessories as well as provide information on how this technology can be translated into maximum photographic success.

Rebel X/XS Operation

Handling

The Canon EOS REBEL X/XS is the world's smallest and lightest autofocus SLR camera featuring built-in flash. It is as easy to handle as a fully automatic compact camera and, in addition, may be used in conjunction with the entire line of Canon EOS lenses and accessories. Preliminary adjustments required to take a picture may be reduced to a minimum. In fully automatic mode the subject may be selected and framed and the camera is ready for shooting. There are fewer switches and buttons on this model than on other EOS models to suit amateur photographers. All relevant function displays are constantly visible on the external LCD panel or in the viewfinder.

For high-speed snapshots and experimenting with interesting situations, the photographer can master this camera and override the fully automatic setting by utilizing the many options offered by the EOS REBEL X/XS for extended creative composition.

The Command Dial

The Command Dial on the upper left side of the camera offers a total of 14 different settings. These are divided into three sections: the function setting zone (providing individual function adjustments); the creative zone (providing individual control options); and the image zone (offering subject-specific programming).

The L in the red box on the Command Dial stands for Lock. In this position the camera is switched off. The green rectangle below the L, called the "Green Zone" by Canon, indicates that the camera is programmed to be fully automatic. In this setting the EOS REBEL X/XS controls all functions automatically. Aperture and shutter speed are determined by the camera, with flash added if necessary. An acoustical signal activates the focus, which is also indicated by a green LED in the viewfinder. If the required shutter speed is too slow, a warning will appear in the viewfinder to indicate the risk of camera shake. This feature also applies to the subject-specific programs for portrait, landscape, close-up or action shots on the image zone of the Command Dial.

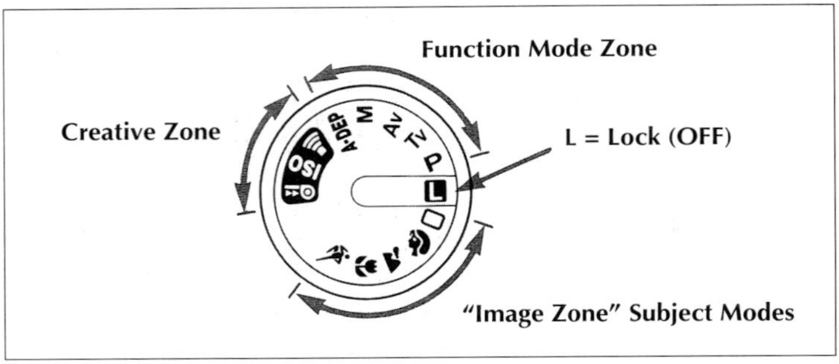

The Command Dial with the three segments for function modes, creative modes, and "Image Zone," subject modes.

Above the L mark of the Command Dial are five more adjustment marks. They allow the selection of program (P), shutter priority (Tv), aperture priority (Av), manual control (M) and the automatic depth of field (A-DEP) settings.

Above these five, in the silver segment of the Command Dial, three more settings provide creative and technical choices. With these modes the photographer may activate or deactivate the acoustical warning signal, set the film speed manually and rewind the film before the end of the roll.

Four icons below the green rectangle on the Command Dial can be utilized under certain conditions when the photographer knows what the subject will be. Those settings include portrait mode, landscape mode, close-up or macro mode, and sports or action mode.

Shutter Release

The EOS REBEL X/XS has a two-stage shutter release button. Just a slight touch of the shutter release button activates the camera's entire electronic system. The autofocus system automatically focuses the lens; a short beep and a green light in the viewfinder verify that focusing has been successful.

Simultaneously, the exposure setting is indicated as a speed/ aperture combination on the LCD panel. When the Command

The controls on the Canon EOS Rebel X/XS are clearly marked and positioned for quick recognition and operation.

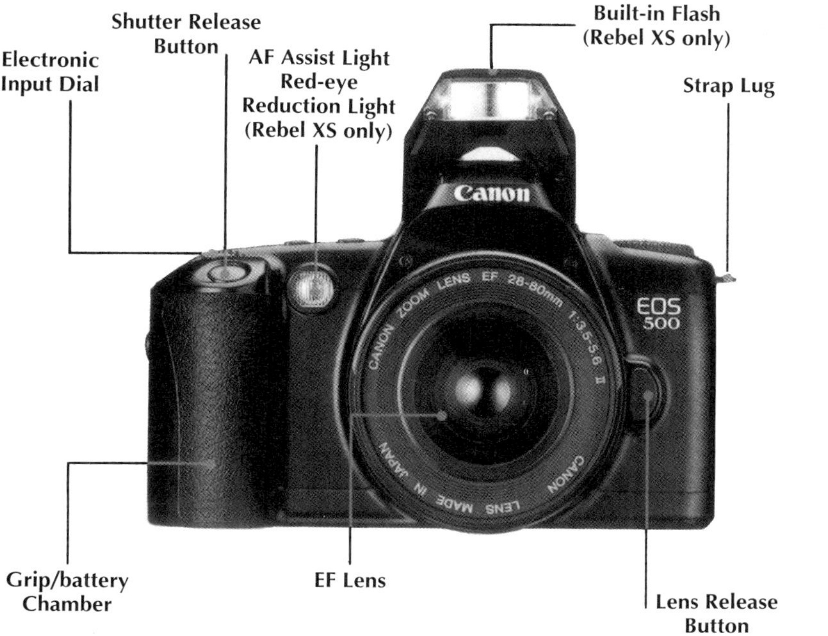
Shutter Release Button
Electronic Input Dial
AF Assist Light Red-eye Reduction Light (Rebel XS only)
Built-in Flash (Rebel XS only)
Strap Lug
Canon
EOS 500
Grip/battery Chamber
EF Lens
Lens Release Button

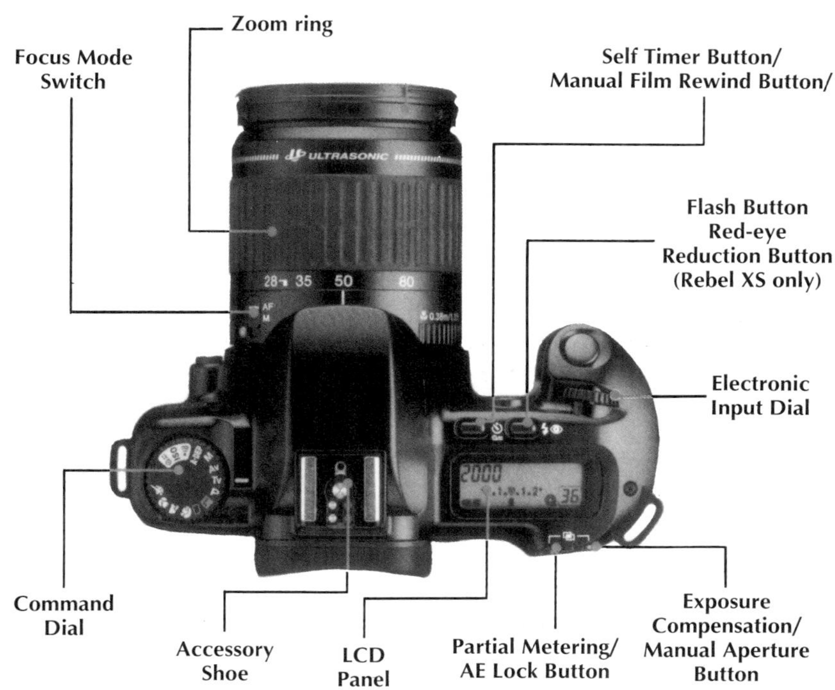
Zoom ring
Focus Mode Switch
Self Timer Button/ Manual Film Rewind Button/
Flash Button Red-eye Reduction Button (Rebel XS only)
Electronic Input Dial
ULTRASONIC
28 35 50 80
AF
M
Command Dial
Accessory Shoe
LCD Panel
Partial Metering/ AE Lock Button
Exposure Compensation/ Manual Aperture Button

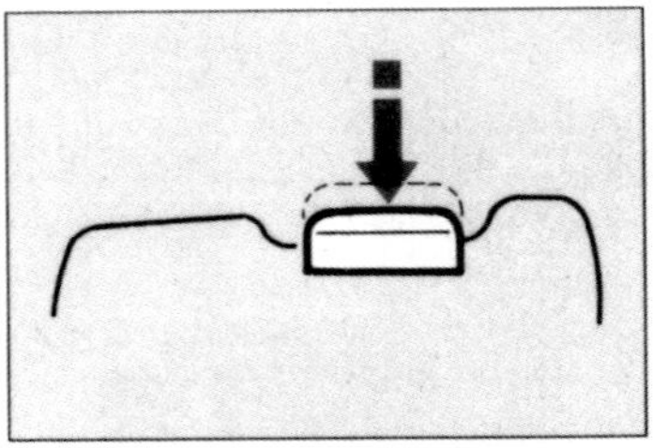

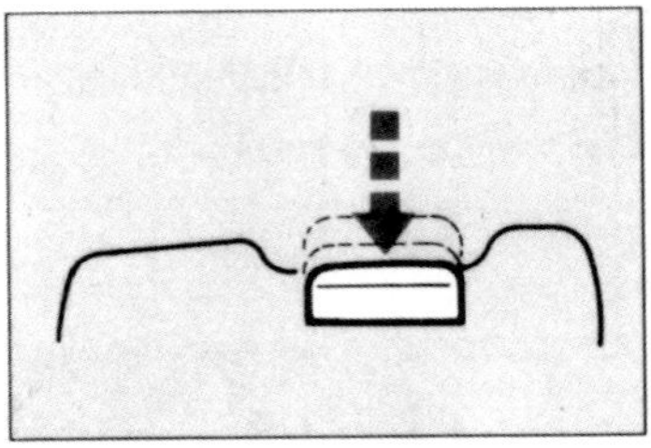

Light pressure on the shutter release button activates the camera's electronics. Continued pressure trips the shutter.

Dial is on the Green Zone or various subject-specific programs in the image zone, the flash will automatically flip up and fire if needed. The camera's AF control (continuous autofocus or one shot) and the film advance system (series or individual frame) are functions of the EOS REBEL X/XS's selected exposure program. For example, one shot AF mode is activated in portrait, landscape, close-up and A-DEP (depth of field) programs. In other programs the switch from one shot to AI-Servo with continuous focus adjustment is automatic, based on the system's sensing of subject movement. In both AF operating modes, a picture can only be taken if the autofocus system is able to focus on the subject.

The Electronic Input Dial

The Electronic Input Dial is typical of Canon EOS cameras and may be considered a truly practical invention. Depending on the selected exposure function, the dial (located directly in front of the shutter release button) may be turned to produce a desired setting. This input dial may be used by itself or in combination with exposure settings. In the manual setting it may be used to input the shutter speed or aperture value. An adjustment of the shutter speed requires only a turn of the input dial. An aperture adjustment requires that the Av button on the camera's Command Dial be selected.

If the P program has been selected, turning the Electronic Input Dial shifts the automatically selected time/aperture combination either toward higher shutter speeds and greater apertures or to slower shutter speeds and smaller apertures. In shutter priority mode (Tv) the Electronic Input Dial allows a change of the shutter speeds, and in aperture priority mode (Av) a change of the aper-

The Electronic Input Dial allows the user fast control of the active variables in the function modes.

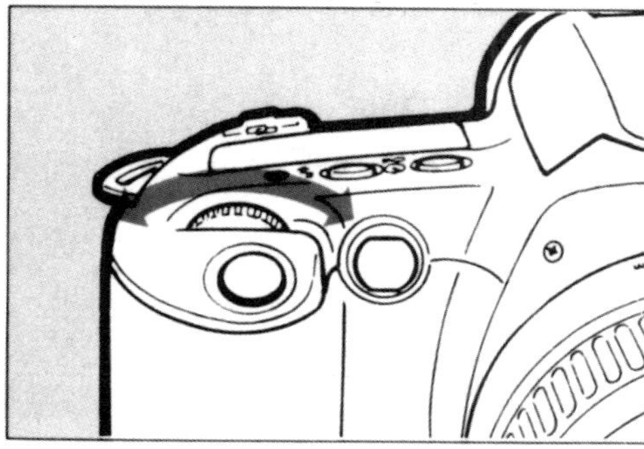

ture. In conjunction with the exposure compensation button (Av +/-), the Electronic Input Dial is used to select the exposure correction. If this button is pushed at the same time as the partial metering button this input dial may be used to designate the number of desired multiple exposures. When the Command Dial is on ISO, the input dial sets the film speed. Additionally, the acoustical focus signal can be deactivated with the input dial in conjunction with the appropriate setting of the Command Dial.

Flash Button (REBEL XS and EOS 500 only)

Should lighting conditions require it, the built-in flash may be erected and will fire when needed in subject-specific programs with the exception of the landscape setting. Creative programs which are indicated above the L on the Command Dial require that the photographer press the flash button next to the LCD panel in order to utilize flash light. When the flash button is pressed, the flash unit is automatically raised and becomes activated. To avoid red-eye in shots taken of people in a relatively dark environment, the krypton lamp on the front of the camera will light up for about 1.25 seconds before the camera shutter fires. This bright light causes the subject's iris to close and, therefore, the red retina of the eye will not show in the picture. When the camera is in a subject-specific program setting, pressing the flash button is sufficient to avoid red-eye. The eye symbol will be displayed. When creative programs are used, the flash button must be pushed a second time to activate the red-eye reducing function.

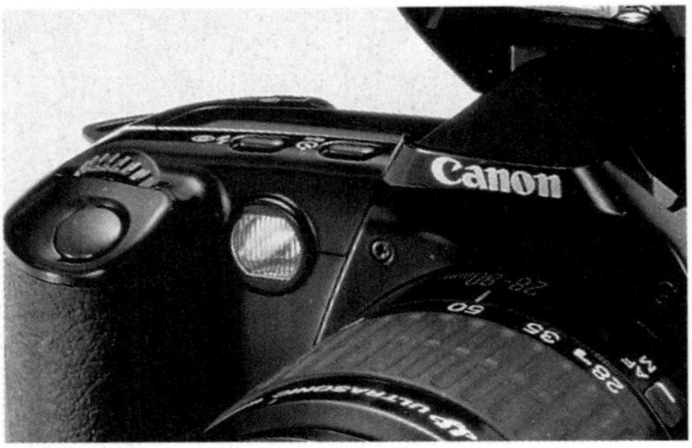

The built-in krypton lamp assists the camera's autofocus feature in low light or low contrast situations. It also doubles as a red-eye reduction light.

If lighting conditions are such that autofocus is not possible, the AF auxiliary lamp (the same krypton lamp which acts to reduce the red-eye effect) emits a light beam to allow the camera to focus. The beam reaches about 15 feet (5 m). External Speedlite flash units take over this function when used, through their integrated IR (infrared) sources.

Self Timer
The self timer is activated by pressing the button above the LCD panel next to the flash button. When pressed, the self timer symbol is displayed. When this setting is chosen, exposure takes place 10 seconds after the shutter button has been pressed. The self timer may be used with all programs. In the portrait program the krypton lamp lights up for the last 2 seconds; otherwise the end of the timer period is signaled by a different frequency beep. The self timing cycle may be interrupted by pressing the self timer button a second time.

Lens Release Button
By pressing the release button next to the camera bayonet the lens may be rotated counterclockwise (to the left) and taken off.

Back Cover Latch
The camera back is opened by pushing up on the latch located on the left side panel.

Battery Compartment
The battery compartment is opened by moving the battery cover latch at the bottom right of the camera's handgrip. The EOS

The button to the right of the lens mount is the lens release.

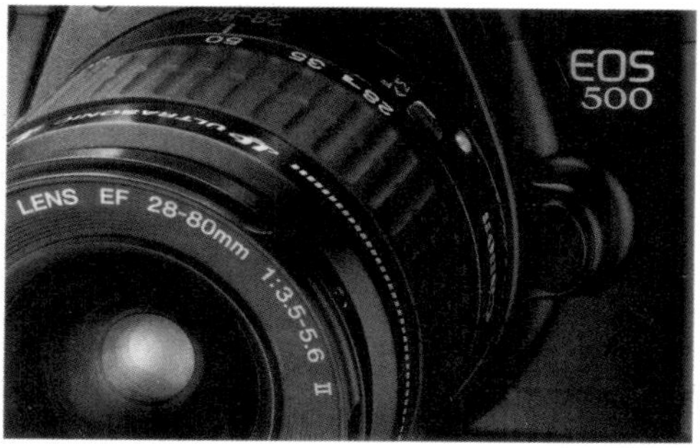

REBEL X/XS is the first of the EOS family to use two lithium batteries of the CR123A type.

Remote Control Jack
A jack for remote release by cable (available as a special accessory) is located on the handgrip below the Electronic Input Dial. The remote cable release is Canon's product number RS-603E3 (see Accessories Chapter).

Partial Metering/AE Lock Button
The partial metering button allows "spot" metering of about 9.5% of the image area. A circle in the viewfinder indicates the measured area. A green star in the viewfinder tells you when partial metering is in operation. The partial metering button must be pushed first and then the shutter released.

Av(+/-) Button
In the manual exposure setting the Electronic Input Dial is turned to adjust the aperture while the Av(+/-) button is pushed. This button is also used for +/- exposure compensation in creative programs. The exposure may be corrected in half steps up to +/- 2 EV steps.

LCD Panel
The EOS REBEL X/XS's LCD panel is the data display of the camera. At a glance the photographer can check exposure values, exposure correction, multiple exposures and, the number of available shots. The battery level is also indicated.

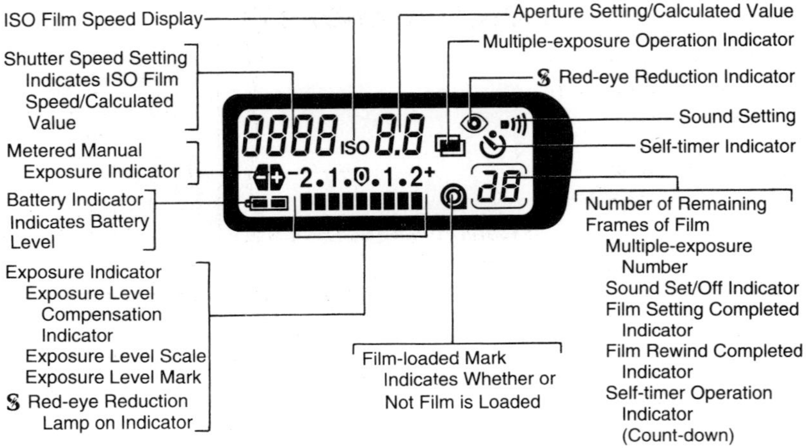

The LCD panel on the top of the camera displays all relevant exposure data, as well as camera function information.

Viewfinder

The displays in the Canon EOS REBEL X/XS viewfinder are extremely clear. All the LED indications are easy to read and are located at the bottom of the image frame. Only three measuring fields and the partial metering area are marked on the viewing screen.

Rewinding

A film cassette symbol with two arrows is located at the very top of the silver section of the Command Dial. If the dial is set to this symbol, pressing the film rewind button rewinds a partially exposed roll of film.

ISO

The ISO indicator is also found in the silver segment of the Command Dial. This setting permits the manual input of the film speed by means of the Electronic Input Dial. Normally the film speed is set automatically via DX coding throughout the range from ISO 25 to ISO 5000. By using manual speed control input, film speeds ranging from ISO 6 to 6400 may be set. Manually set film speeds are retained for only one roll of film and must be reset each time film is changed.

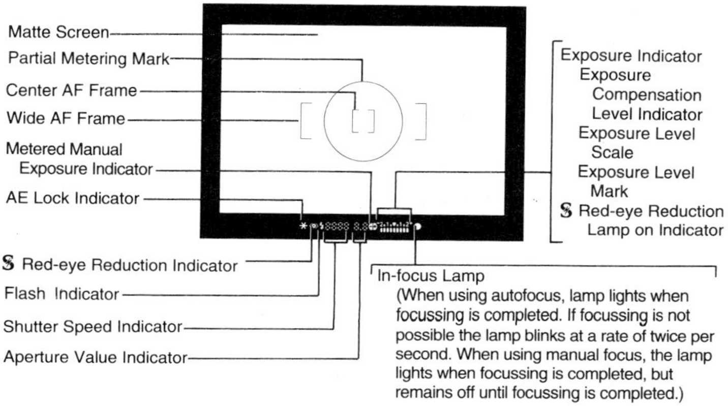

When you look into the camera's viewfinder you will see the indicators for the autofocus sensors, the circle denoting the measuring field for partial metering, and an LCD panel beneath the viewing screen which displays exposure data.

Loading the Camera

After opening the camera's back the film is slipped into the cassette compartment. This process is most easily done when the bottom of the cassette (the end with the protruding spool) is inserted first, making sure that the small red pin inside the compartment fits into the hole in the film cassette spool, and then the entire cassette pushed inside. The film leader is pulled up to the red mark on the opposite side of the camera's compartment. The camera back is then closed by applying gentle pressure. Before the first roll is inserted, the protective foil on the pressure plate on the camera's rear inside panel must be removed. Also, care must

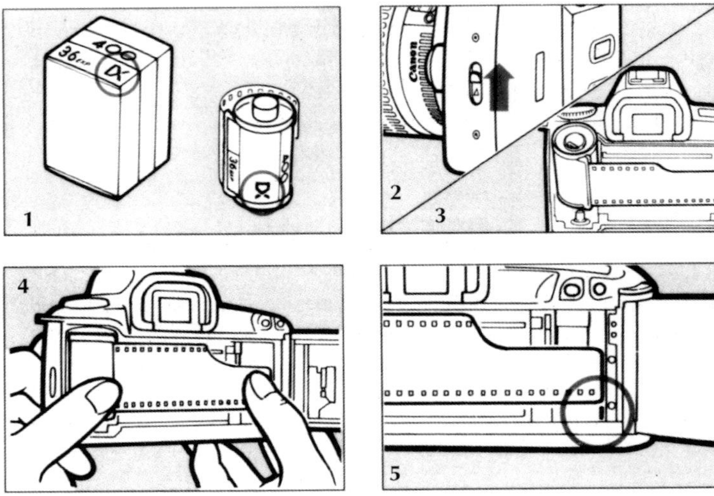

Loading REBEL series cameras is very simple. With DX coded film, (1) the camera will automatically set the correct film speed. Refer to the text for details on the proper loading procedure (2-5).

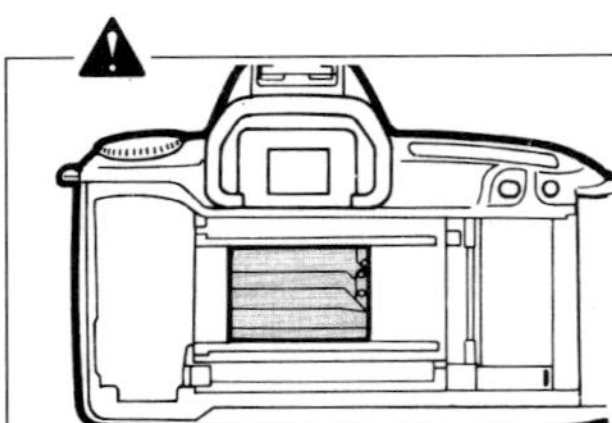

The camera shutter is a very precise mechanism and can be damaged easily. When you are loading film, be very careful not to touch any part of the shutter.

be taken that the delicate shutter blades are not touched by fingers or the film leader. Once the rear panel is closed and the camera is switched on, it will automatically wind the entire roll of film forward into the take-up chamber. This is normal operation for the EOS REBEL X cameras, which then rewind the film one frame at a time as the pictures are taken. The only disadvantage of this system is that the film frame numbers will always be in the reverse order from the order in which the photos were taken.

The frame counter of the LCD panel indicates the number of available frames. After all frames have been exposed, the camera will then automatically wind the short remaining leader into the film cassette. A partially exposed roll may be rewound any time using the Command Dial and the film rewind button. If there is no film in the camera, the film-loaded mark on the LCD panel will be absent. Otherwise the film-loaded mark is visible even when the camera is switched off.

Film Advance

An integrated micromotor advances the film automatically for individual or series shots, depending on the selected program. For series shots the EOS REBEL X/XS transports one frame per second. To achieve this, the shutter release must be held down continuously; for individual shots the release must be pressed once for each shot. In the Green Zone, the landscape, close-up and A-DEP (depth of field) programs, continuous exposure is not possible, and photos must be taken one at a time. In all other programs the release may be held down continuously for frame-by-frame series shots.

Because the Canon EOS's motor is extremely quiet, pictures may be taken with this camera in situations where transport and release noises would be disturbing.

Earlier Rebel Models

Prior to the Rebel X/XS, there have been two previous generations of Rebel cameras. The original Rebel was offered in versions without a built-in flash and simply called REBEL (EOS 1000 in some markets). It was introduced slightly later with a built-in flash as the Rebel S (EOS 1000F). Operation of these cameras is almost identical to the REBEL X/XS models, with the exception that the DEP mode is not as automated as the Rebel X/XS. Because of this, the authors recommend that all owners of earlier REBEL cameras read the previous chapter in addition to this one.

The original REBEL was replaced with the REBEL II, without built-in flash, (EOS 1000N in some markets) and the REBEL SII, with flash (known as EOS 1000FN). Except for the added soft focus mode and the addition of music during the self timer count-down, these cameras are generally identical to their predecessors.

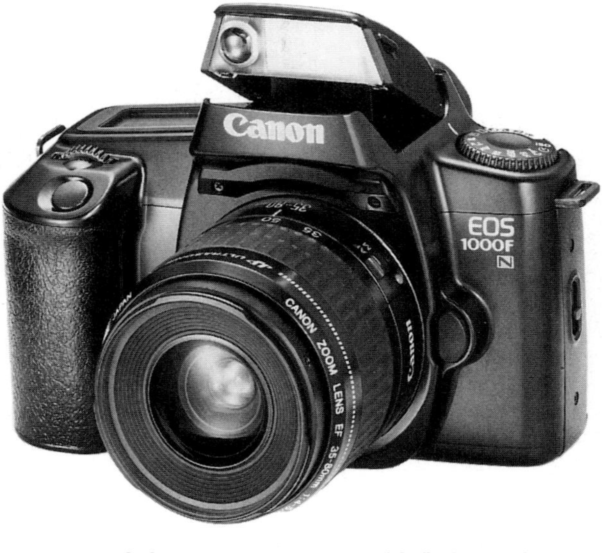

The Canon EOS Rebel SII (or EOS 1000FN) with flash raised.

Autofocus and Metering Systems

Both original REBEL versions have only a single central autofocus sensor which is not of the cross-base type and responds well only to vertical contrasts. When a difficult subject is encountered, it often will help to achieve focus by switching the camera from horizontal to vertical (or vice versa) to enable the sensor to find focus. In addition to this simplified autofocus sensor array, these cameras use a simpler three zone metering system, far less versatile than that of the REBEL X/XS. In spite of their simplicity, the authors have found these cameras to be very functional and practical, producing a high percentage of properly exposed photos.

Battery Type

Unlike the REBEL X/XS, the earlier REBEL cameras are powered by a 6-volt lithium 2CR5 battery.

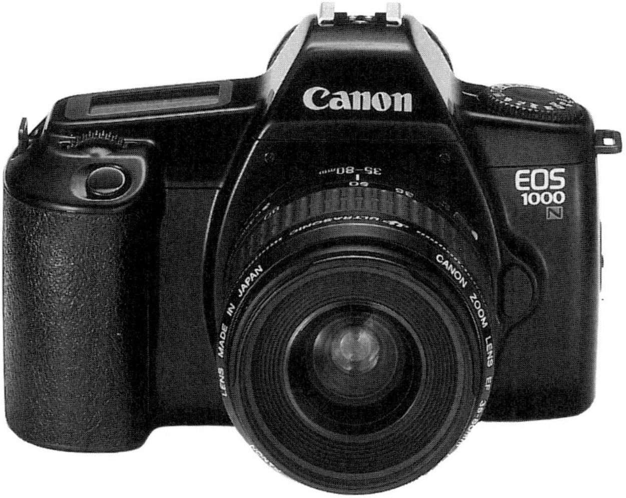

The Canon EOS Rebel II (or EOS 1000N).

Automatic Depth of Field (DEP)

The depth of field mode in the original generations of REBEL cameras operates as it does on other EOS models. To operate this mode the Command Dial is set to the DEP position. Next, the photographer places the autofocus sensor in the viewfinder on the area desired to be the closest part of the depth of field range. Once this is targeted in the viewfinder, the photographer presses the shutter release button all the way down. The LCD Panel and the viewfinder will display "dEP-1" as confirmation. This step is repeated for the farthest limit of the range and the camera will display "dEP-2". At this point, with partial pressure on the shutter release, the aperture which will yield this depth of field is displayed and the lens will automatically be set for the hyperfocal distance for the desired depth of field range. A third pressing of the shutter release takes the photo. It is important of pay attention to the shutter speed displayed as it will often be too slow for handholding when great depth of field is desired. In this case, a tripod or other camera support should be used.

Musical Self Timer

The REBEL II and SII feature a mode on the Command Dial which is indicated by a musical note symbol. When set to this position the Electronic Input Dial is used to select a number from 1 through 4 on the LCD Panel. These correspond to musical compositions by Vivaldi (2), Beethoven (3), or Bach (4). The first setting, (1) is a simple beeping tone. By setting the desired number, the photographer can select which short melody plays during the countdown of the self timer. Or if no music is desired, the beeping tone may be selected. This music is certainly more pleasant to people's ears than the beeping tone and can be previewed at each setting by touching the shutter release button.

Soft Focus Mode

The most useful mode, to one of the authors who specializes in glamour photography, is the soft focus mode on the REBEL II and

SII. It is sadly lacking on the REBEL X/XS. This unique mode allows very nice soft focus photos to be taken with any Canon EF lens. To operate it, the photographer sets the Command Dial to the SF position and uses the Electronic Input Dial to select either a 1 or a 2 on the LCD panel. This corresponds to two different degrees of soft focus.

Once the desired soft focus effect has been set, the photographer then simply composes the picture and shoots. The camera then fires two shots in rapid succession on the same frame of film. The first exposure is taken in normal sharp focus, the second is made with the lens thrown out of focus at its closest possible focus. The overlay of sharp and soft images produces a wonderful soft focus effect which can not be obtained in any other way. The camera also automatically adjusts the two exposures so that they combine to properly expose the image. Because the two images are taken in rapid succession, but not instantaneously, it is best to use a tripod or other camera support and to work with subjects who can hold still for the short time it takes to complete the two exposures (about one second at most shutter speeds).

It is unfortunate that this mode has been omitted from the REBEL X/XS models since it is highly useful and makes the REBEL II and SII the ideal glamour photographer's camera. Bob Shell has enthusiastically recommended this camera to aspiring glamour photographers since it was introduced.

All REBEL cameras are remarkably agile and versatile cameras belying in picture quality their very reasonable price. While not as rugged as the more professional EOS cameras, they can take pictures every bit as good as those taken with other EOS cameras when used with Canon EF lenses.

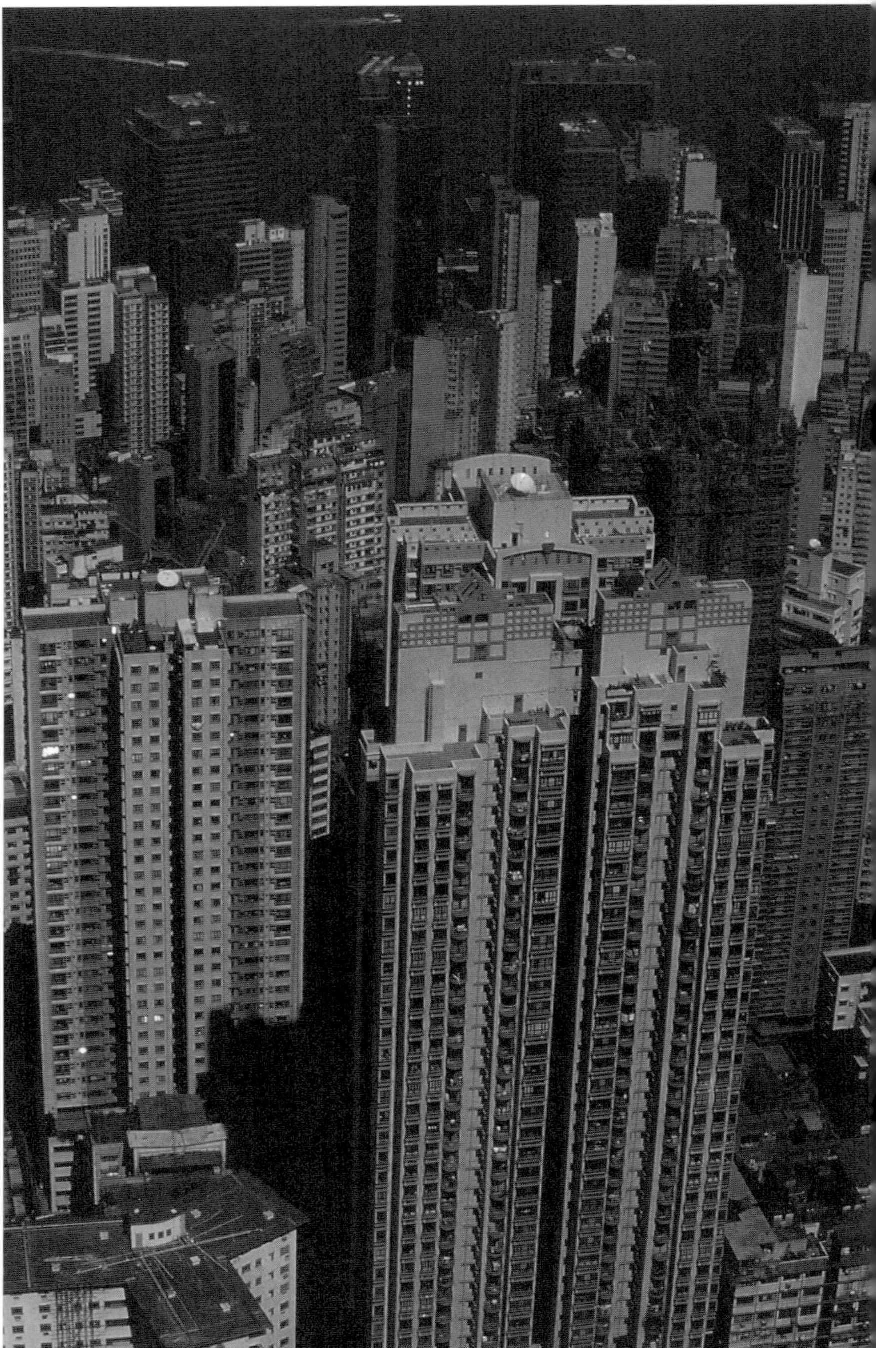

Autofocus Operation

Autofocus in General

For automatic focusing, the Canon EOS REBEL X/XS camera uses the same system as the EOS 10. This multi-base focusing system uses the TTL-SIR (Second Image Registration) principle: the focus is determined by performing measurements through the lens with a special "BASIS" sensor (Base Stored Image Sensor). It detects phase shifts of two partial images similar to earlier split-image indicators. The deviation between the partial images is used by the AF microprocessor to compute the direction and order of magnitude of the required adjustment. Located to the right and left of the central cross-focusing sensor, the camera has two other sensors. This configuration produces a three-part wide-range autofocus frame which makes it easy to hold even moving subjects within the AF frame. The wide-field AF sensor offers decisive advantages in many picture-taking situations. On one hand, important image details need not necessarily be located in the image center in order to be in focus; on the other hand, the AF system recognizes and follows subjects moving parallel to the film plane.

The camera automatically selects the focusing point. Optionally, a central focusing point may be selected for special picture-taking situations. To do this, the partial metering/AE lock button is pressed for selective metering. The light metering and flash-exposure measuring is then done from the same area as the focusing sensor.

The operating range of the AF sensors built into the camera is between 1.5 and 18 EV at ISO 100. At the low end, this corresponds approximately to an exposure time of 1/6 second at f/1.5. Even under conditions of very low light the EOS REBEL X/XS is still capable of automatic focusing. In darkness or in a low-contrast situation the built-in krypton lamp will turn on to assist the autofocus system. This allows automatic focusing within a fo-

Because it uses Canon's exclusive cross-based sensor, the AF feature of the EOS REBEL X/XS can easily focus on subjects in which either horizontal or vertical lines predominate.

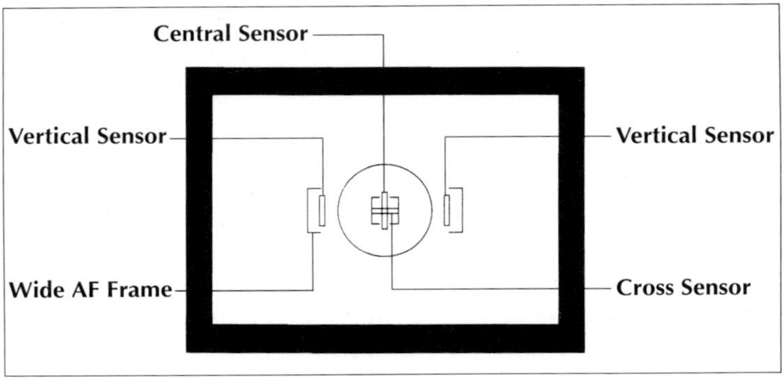

The three AF sensors together provide the large measuring field of the REBEL X/XS, enabling it to focus on horizontal and vertical contrast lines.

cal length range of 35 to 135mm and distances of 3.3 feet (1 m) to about 15 feet (5 m). With this system automatic focusing is possible even in complete darkness. When the built-in flash unit is switched off and an external Canon Speedlite or an SCA systems flash unit with infrared AF auxiliary flash is used instead, the flash unit's infrared light is activated instead of the camera's built-in krypton light. This increases the range to about 30 feet (10 m). and cuts drain on the camera batteries. The Canon EOS REBEL X/XS automatically chooses between two different focusing methods. Depending on the picture-taking situation, it switches between one shot and AF/AI (servo) autofocus modes.

Autofocus Modes

AI Servo Autofocus

AI-servo refers to a constant focus update on moving subjects. When the shutter release button is pressed halfway down the AF mechanism is activated. The measuring system is activated continuously and automatically recognizes the movement of a subject in the measuring field. Multiple measurements are taken by the Canon EOS more frequently than by other systems, allowing the AF microprocessor to pre-calculate the speed of motion and the position of the subject at the moment the shutter is opened. Therefore, even subjects which move rapidly in a direction oblique to the camera can be photographed perfectly in focus despite the delay between the time the release is pressed and the actual exposure. AI-AF may be called an intelligent autofocus which decides automatically whether the focus value should be stored or updated due to the subject's movement. In any event, the EOS REBEL cameras include a focus default which allows the camera to be fired only when the focus is correct.

One-shot Autofocus

In one-shot mode the focus is adjusted and stored for one subject in one of the three measuring fields when the release button is pressed lightly. Normally, the subject need only be in one of the three autofocus frames. The exposure value is stored at the same time. Even in partial metering mode the EOS REBEL X/XS's autofocus system performs well. Here, the automatic focusing precision may be coupled with exposure manipulation.

Manual Focus

If the AF system is incapable of automatic focusing due to the special make-up of the subject (for example, extremely low contrast, monochromatic or very light surfaces, uniform horizontal structures, very strong backlighting, reflections or subjects at different distances in the AF measuring field), the green AF indicator in the viewfinder will blink. Usually, autofocus is possible even in these instances by focusing on another subject at the same distance from the camera and holding this focus by maintaining light pressure on the shutter release button while recomposing the photo. Therefore, manual focusing will be necessary only in exceptional cases. To set the camera for manual focus the AF switch on the lens will be moved from AF to M. If a lens is equipped with a USM motor or a Micro-USM, it is not necessary to switch to M. Lenses with these types of motors may be focused manually at any time. To do so the focus adjustment ring on the lens is turned until the subject appears in sharp focus on the viewing screen. The focus may be evaluated on the viewing screen or by referring to the green focus indicator LED, which will light to confirm focus. However, some EOS EF lenses (the less expensive ones with a single A designation) do not have the capability of manual focus.

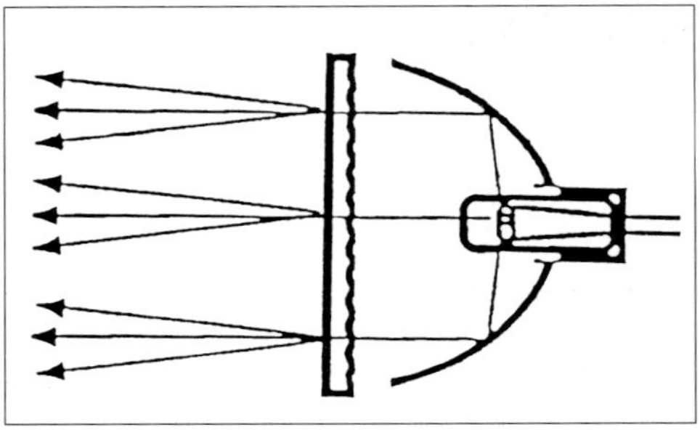

The drawing shows the spread of light from the camera's built-in krypton lamp.

Autofocus Measurement and Lens Control

Distance measurement takes place in the camera itself. This is true of all EOS REBEL models including the EOS REBEL X/XS; however, the lens is adjusted by a motor housed in the lens. Currently, Canon lenses use four different types of drive motors: the Ring-type USM, Micro-USM, AFD, and standard small electric motor. Mounting the motor in the lens has the enormous advantage that the best motor may be selected to match the characteristics of each lens. The fastest drives in the Canon line of lenses are ultrasonic motors (USM). The high-end lenses which use the Ring-type USM mainly include high-performance zoom lenses and telephotos, and will satisfy the most sophisticated professional demands. The original EOS lens motors, the AFD (Arc Form Drive) motors, are now used only rarely and will be found even less frequently in future EOS lens systems as they are all replaced with Micro-USM motors. A standard small electric motor is used in only one lens, the 100mm macro. The advantages of individual drives will be discussed in detail in the chapter on lenses. At this point it should be noted that the speed of the autofocus system also depends on the lens motor drive. The Canon system allows an optimal adjustment of the drive to the components of the lenses to be moved.

Exposure Metering

Rebel Series Exposure Control

Thanks to the EOS REBEL series camera's well-conceived exposure metering and control system, correctly exposed pictures are not hard to produce. Correctly exposed means that precisely the right amount of light reached the film producing an image which corresponds as closely as possible to the photographic scene. This principle applies to authentic color reproduction as well as to correctly perceived tonal differences in black and whites.

In order to be able to produce correct exposures, light intensity must be measured. To this day there is no integrated light meter which will produce a perfect metering result under all conditions. Because different subject details exhibit different degrees of reflection, an exposure meter detects the sum of all brightness readings which it views as an average value based on its calibration. Conventionally, based on the meter's calibration, this brightness value corresponds to neutral gray (about 18% reflectance). Today's light metering systems have been greatly improved by the use of microprocessors and special sensors in the Canon EOS models.

In addition, the Canon EOS REBEL X/XS features two metering methods and offers five variations of modern exposure metering:

1. 6-zone autofocus-based metering using three main fields activated in all programs except M.
2. Selective metering by pressing the Partial Metering Button, including spot autofocus in creative programs.
3. Center-weighted integral metering in M mode.
4. Canon's exclusive A-TTL 4-zone flash metering with Canon 300 EZ, 420 EZ, 430 EZ flash units, as well as with the SCA 3000 System such as the Metz Mecablitz 40 MZ-2 flash units.
5. TTL 4-zone flash metering using the built-in flash unit and other TTL flash units.

Left AF-Sensor is active

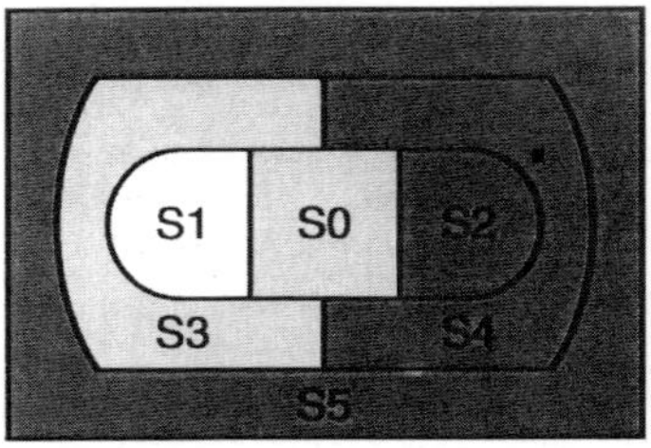

Central Cross Sensor is active

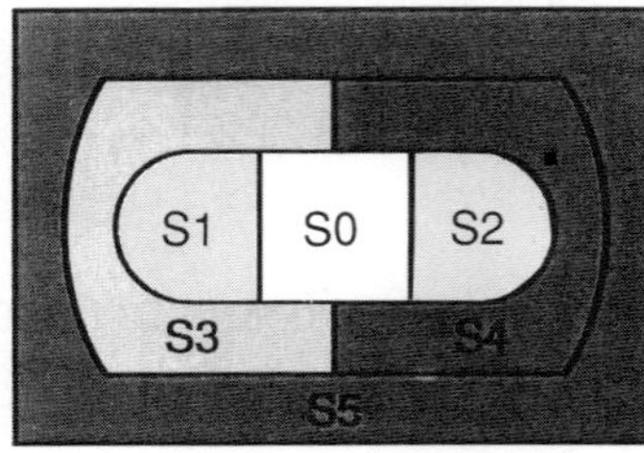

Main Exposure Field

Intermediate Fields

Right AF-Sensor is active

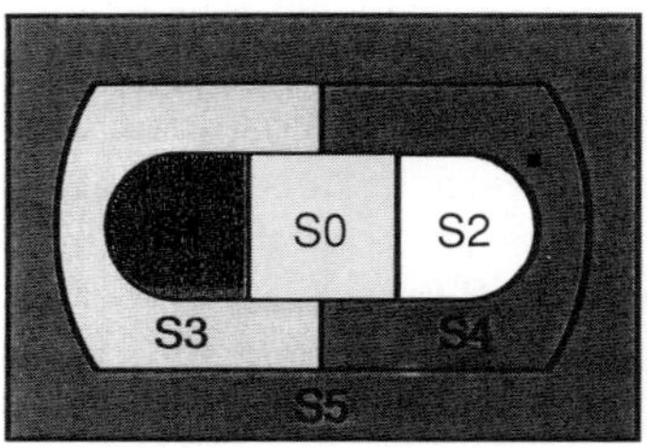

The light meter control circuitry of the REBEL X/XS cameras automatically activates the proper sensors to deal with the contrast range and illumination of the subject, emphasizing at all times the area closest to the active autofocus sensor.

Peripheral Fields

Multi-Zone Metering

Multi-zone metering is the simplest and most reliable metering method for all occasions. Even in critical lighting situations this mode automatically provides the most appropriate exposure values. Those who work with color negative films may completely trust this method. Those who use slide films may want to change the exposure values suggested by the camera in some instances due to creative considerations.

Basic problems concerning all exposure metering and control systems are related less to metering accuracy than to the analysis and compensation of differences between light and dark image areas. After all, films have a more or less limited exposure range

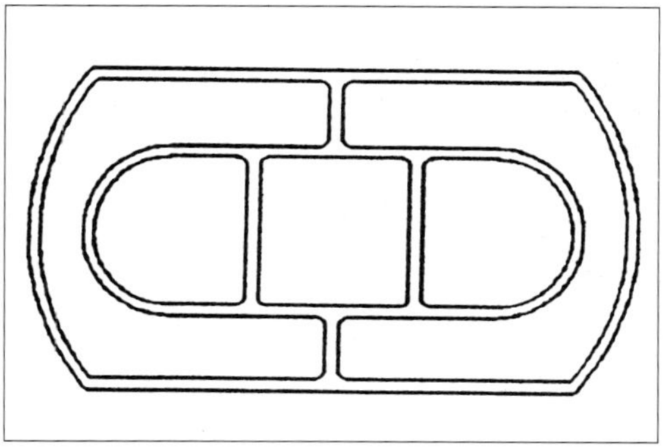

The multi-area metering of the REBEL X/XS cameras is attained by dividing the image area into six separate fields which are measured independently.

which must cover the lightest and darkest zones of photographs so the picture will be reproduced with sufficient detail and gradation.

In Canon EOS REBEL X/XS multi-zone metering, the image area is divided into six different zones (other REBEL models have three metering zones) which are measured individually. Now, as opposed to when photographers determined an average value based on multiple measurements, the EOS REBEL series camera's microprocessor compares the order of the distribution of light and dark zones in the image with 1,000 stored subject situations and adapts the exposure based on these reference values. This metering method produces perfectly exposed pictures almost every time.

Partial Metering

Technically, correctly exposed may mean (especially to the photographer using slide film) that the exposure is still not perfect. In certain situations multi-zone metering, which tends to be programmed for compensation, still does not produce the desired image effect. Selective metering is useful, for example, when a photographer wants to emphasize a detail in a high-contrast scene while deliberately sacrificing normal contrast in the rest of the picture through over- or underexposure.

The REBEL series cameras feature a measuring field for partial, or selective, metering which is indicated by a small circle in the center of the viewfinder. The circle's range is only 9.5% of the en-

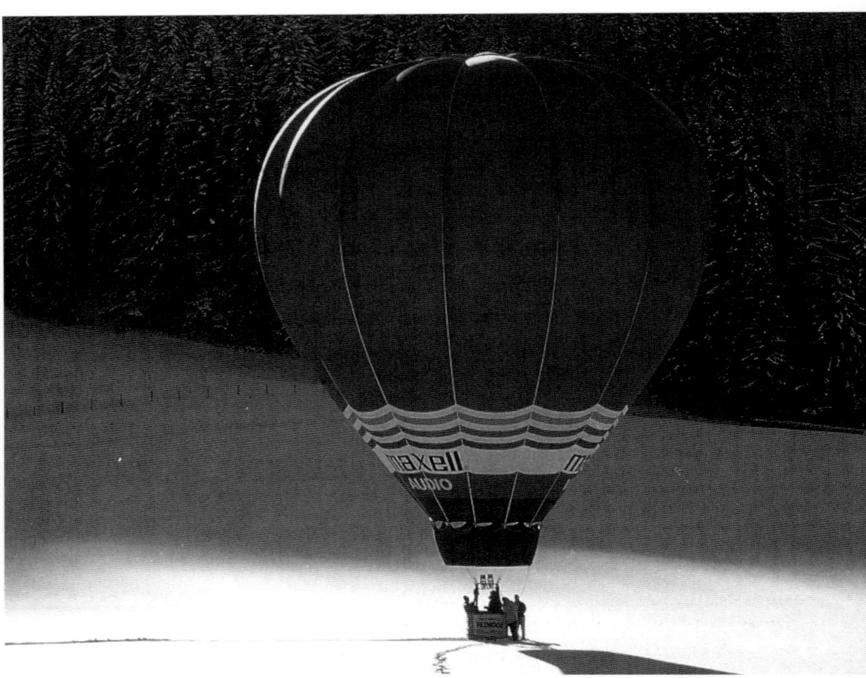
maxell
AUDIO

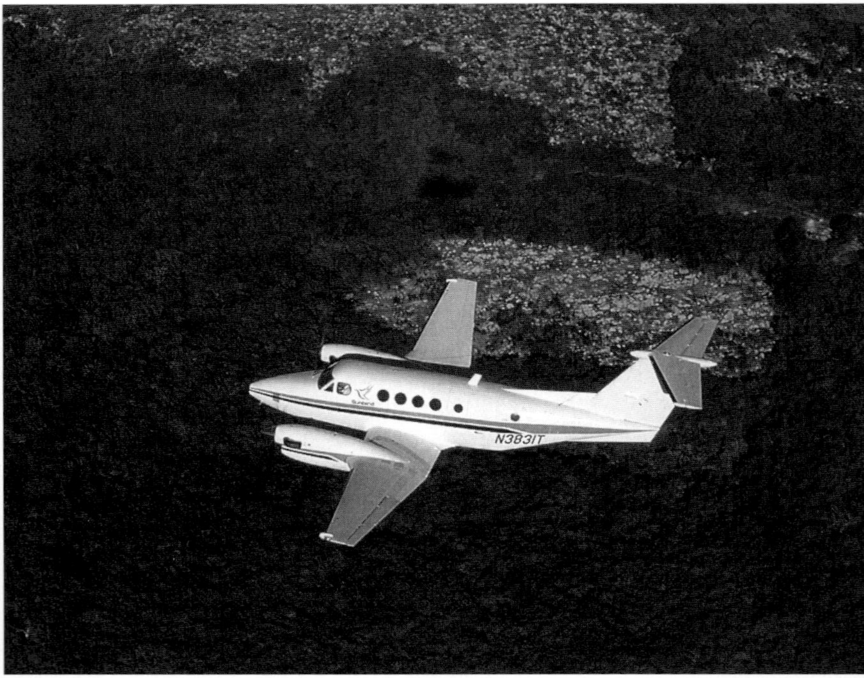
N3831T

tire image area. Partial metering refers to the method whereby the photographer interprets the lighting situation with regard to a specific mood or intention. This method, accessed by the Partial Metering Button, does require practice.

Partial metering is appropriate, in particular, when the brightness differences in the scene may lead to the over- or underexposure of important image details. This method is often employed in creative image composition.

A Partial Metering Example

A portrait is to be shot at sunset. The red sun is at an intensity level where it is possible to be viewed with the naked eye. If the camera's portrait program is activated, the aperture will open widely. Due to shallow depth of field with an open aperture, the sun will be out of focus. The brightness differences in the image can be reduced to a technically desirable level by flash. For snapshots this is certainly the most satisfactory solution; however, this may not be absolutely true for a professionally or creatively composed image. In this case the photographer may take certain steps to compensate for the conditions. If the partial metering field is aimed directly at the sun, the exposure will be shorter. The portrait in the foreground will be underexposed and reduced to a silhouette. This technical manipulation guarantees a mood-charged image. A touch of flash, possibly during the second exposure, will provide detail in the shadow areas. Quite a different mood is attained when the photographer points the partial metering field at the darkest image area, in this case a person's face. The face is exposed correctly while the pastel colors of the sky and the sun are subdued through overexposure. In this way a very romantic picture is obtained, albeit without any indication of the drama of the sunset.

The trick in most cases is to provide a touch of detail in the lightest (or darkest) area of the picture. Between these two de-

The multi-area light metering system of the EOS REBEL X/XS cameras can provide correct exposure in a variety of difficult lighting situations.

scribed extreme situations lie a great number of combinations and brightness levels which may be achieved by an experienced photographer by targeted selective or partial metering. Hence, this is a creative metering technique which allows the photographer to interpret or enhance an existing mood. Those who want to use their EOS REBEL camera to creatively compose pictures should first take pictures using multi-zone metering and then experiment with partial metering.

Summary of Partial Metering

Multi-zone metering is suitable for all picture-taking situations and always provides (specifically with color negative films) an exposure producing a technically perfect, printable negative. Slide photographers may also trust this exposure technique, even when dealing with critical lighting conditions such as backlighting and severe brightness gradients in the scene.

Center-Weighted Metering

In the manual exposure setting the EOS REBEL X/XS's metering system is set on center-weighted metering. In this mode the entire image area is measured but more emphasis is given to the image center.

Exposure Control

Normal exposure metering in the case of the Canon EOS REBEL X/XS is 6-zone metering, (with other REBEL cameras it is three zones). If one of the two peripheral metering zones of the large AF metering area is activated, the lighting in that area is given greater consideration in the determination of the exposure. This prioritizing makes sense because the camera focus is always related to the most important part of the subject, and this location is where the emphasis of exposure metering should be. As a result, the surrounding area of the activated AF sensor is of particular importance. The exposure, in turn, results from the combination of shutter speed and aperture. Both factors offer important creative opportunities. Correct automatic exposure, aperture and shutter speed as creative tools used separately or in combination, as well as using one's imagination, are available via the EOS REBEL series' different operating programs, divided into creative and subject-specific programs.

The photographer may decide whether to use the camera in fully automatic mode, or as a creative tool. All that is required is a single turn of the Command Dial.

The black L (for "lock") in the red square setting locks all functions; the LCD panel does not display any symbols other than the number of available shots. A turn to the left or right on the Command Dial will reactivate the camera. This turn should be considered carefully because it decides the complexity of techniques used by the photographer.

Creative Programs

The REBEL series cameras feature the following exposure programs. These can be selected depending on picture-taking requirements and will produce the correct exposure:

P Automatic programming (fully automatic, no shooting techniques) - no automatic auxiliary flash, can be modified by Shift function (turning the Electronic Input Dial), the camera selects both shutter speed and lens aperture for proper exposure.

Tv (Time value) Preselected exposure time with shutter priority - time (shutter speed) is selected by the photographer and the camera selects the appropriate aperture for correct exposure.

Av (Aperture value) The photographer selects the lens aperture and the camera selects the shutter speed for proper exposure, aperture priority.

A-DEP (Automatic depth of field adjustment, REBEL X/XS) The depth of field range is defined by three AF metering points, automatic exposure time and aperture setting by the camera. Or **DEP** (Depth of Field adjustment, earlier REBEL models)

M (Manual input of shutter speed and aperture) These parameters may be selected freely or based on the camera's exposure meter readings.

Subject-Specific Programs

In order to make full use of the subject programs which are indicated in the "Image Zone" on the Command Dial below the L position, the photographer must have a basic knowledge of photographic technology. Conversely, there are many common photographic conditions that can be accommodated by a few well-designed picture-taking applications. These applications each involve similar technical prerequisites. Canon developed its own exposure programs for these common applications. With subject-specific programs, even photographers who do not deal with photographic principles on a daily basis can experiment creatively while leaving the technical problem-solving to the camera. The EOS REBEL series cameras feature four subject-specific programs and one fully automated standard shooting mode.

Programmed Image Controls (PIC)

Many different configurations of automatic subject-specific controls, called PIC system (Programmed Image Control) by Canon, are available. They are amazingly capable of automatically controlling all important camera functions in practically encountered situations. These programs are ideal for photographers who do not want to practice the fine art of photography on a daily basis but do want optimal results. PIC options are: Green Zone (green rectangle on Command Dial, fully automated standard mode) Portrait, Landscape, Close-up (macro), and Action or sports program.

Easily recognized icons, or pictograms, on the Command Dial facilitate fast selection of subject-specific programs. After an appropriate setting has been chosen, the photographer need only compose the image and take the picture. The programmed control system automatically adjusts the ideal focus, exposure metering method and the film transport selection for the chosen picture in a subject-appropriate manner.

Green Zone

The green rectangle on all EOS REBEL series camera's Command Dial has exactly the same purpose as a green traffic light which signals the driver to go. It demarks the REBEL series' standard program which is fully automatic. Technically, it is identical with the P program found on the creative side of the Command Dial (above the L). However, unlike P it offers no overrides or adjustments. In the Green Zone, the camera determines the best combination of exposure time and aperture for a given picture.

Using the Green Zone when taking pictures will result in capturing more than 80% of all normal subjects in a technically perfect manner. Canon describes this Green Zone program as "intelligent automatic programming." One "intelligent" aspect of this is that Green Zone programming functions as aperture priority in low light. The automatic programming feature kicks in only when the largest lens aperture has been reached with a shutter speed corresponding to the inverse value of the focal length of the lens in use. As a result, the largest aperture is selected along with an applicable shutter speed. Additionally, with longer automatically adjusted shutter speeds the REBEL series camera signals the risk of a poor exposure by a blinking shutter speed indication which (where available) simultaneously activates the built-in flash unit. The intelligence rests in the information which, for example, is passed from the zoom lens to the camera's central microprocessor.

In the Green Zone, the camera works with a continuous autofocus. When the shutter release is pressed lightly, the camera will attempt to determine the focus based on all three AF fields. Based on the distance parameters in the image areas, the camera decides ultimately which metering field is to be considered for adjustment. The shutter is allowed to fire only after the focus has been achieved and the flash (if in use) has signaled its readiness. A green flash symbol in the viewfinder blinks under conditions of extreme backlighting or low light. In almost the same instant the flash unit is activated. The film transport is in the fully automatic programmed individual image mode. The multi-zone metering feature with analytic capability assures correct exposures even in extreme situations such as snowscapes in sunshine.

The Zone's green rectangle represents the optimal selection for

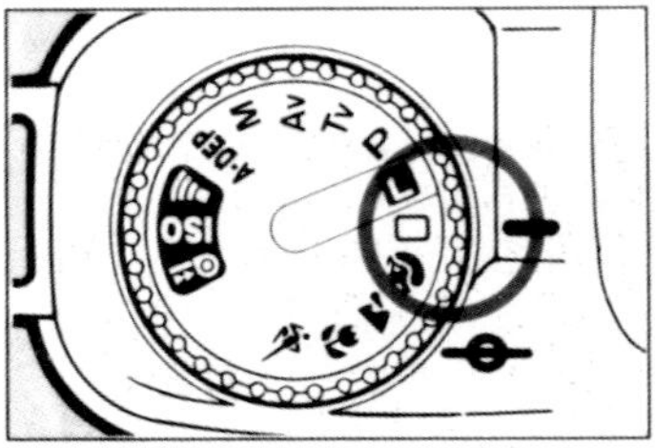

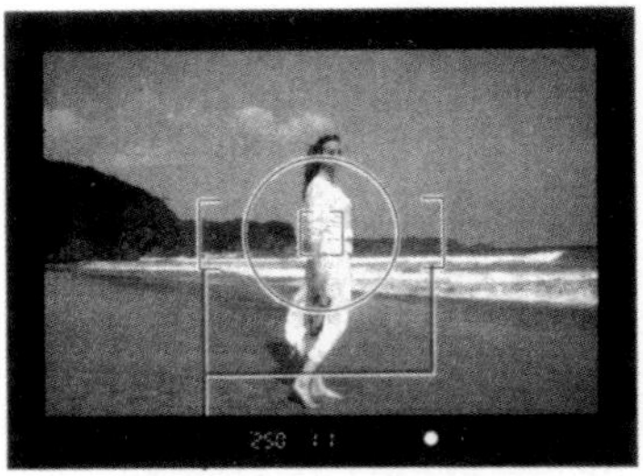

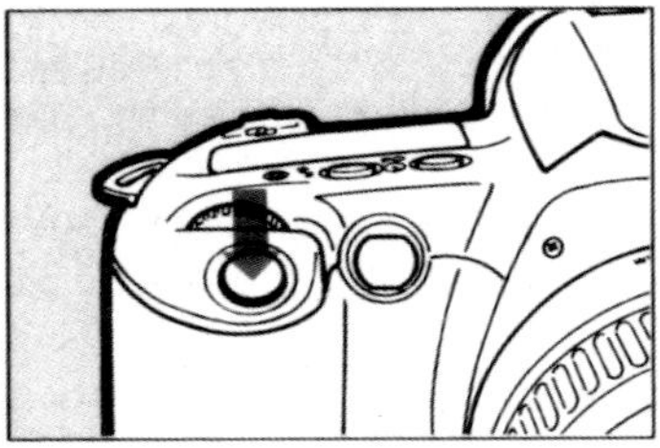

The Green Zone, indicated by the green rectangle on the Command Dial, allows you to quickly capture most subjects with a press of the shutter release button.

standard subjects - simple snapshots and keepsake pictures which do not require complex photographic techniques. In case of doubt as to what program should be used, the fully automatic mode ensures the highest percentage of successful pictures. And it does not matter what focal length is used because any Canon EF lens may be used in this mode. In the fully automatic Green Zone program mode, the LCD panel indicates the combination of exposure time and aperture and, as in all other program modes, the frame number and the battery status.

Portrait Program

This setting is designed for use with telephoto lenses. With zoom lenses the longest focal length is recommended. The program was adapted to two typical types of pictures: the head-and-shoulder shot and the full portrait. When the photographer is close enough for the subject's head and shoulders to fill the frame in the viewfinder, the autofocus frame should be directed at the subject's eyes, the release button pressed lightly, and then pressed the rest of the way only when the subject has been framed as desired.

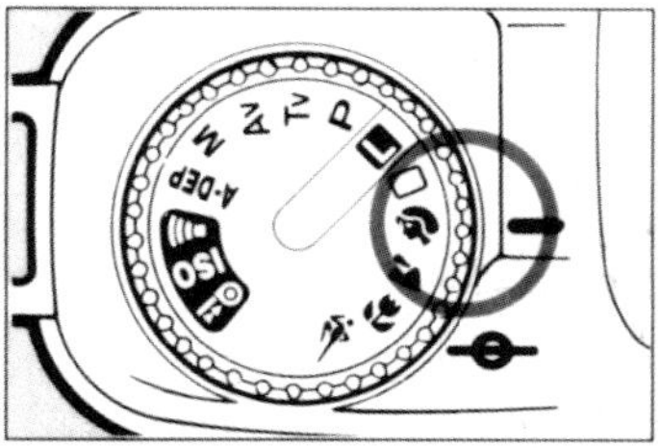

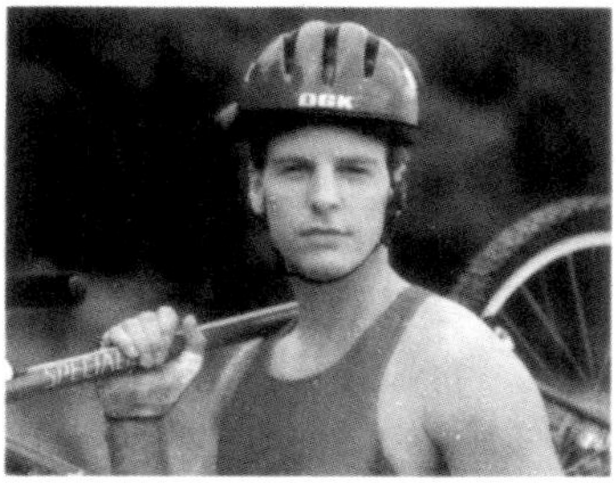

An example of a perfect subject for the portrait mode.

This procedure must be followed, otherwise the base of the neck will frequently be in perfect focus but the eyes will not. After each shot the focusing field must be positioned again on the eyes and the setting locked in with gentle pressure on the shutter release button. When USM lenses are used, which feed distance information to the camera's microprocessor, the range is started at f/11 to assure sufficient depth of field. The aperture will open to f/5.6 and remain at this setting only from distances which correspond to five times the focal length up to distances which correspond to 10 times the focal length. Very fast shutter speeds will result in an incremental closing of the aperture. When using EF lenses which do not feed distance information to the camera, the lens will always be set to 2/3 of a stop from its widest aperture, and only stopped down further when the camera runs out of shutter speeds at 1/1000 second. The advantage to using this wide aperture lies in selective focus, which dissolves even a highly distracting or annoying background to a pleasant blur. This is usually desired in most portrait photographs.

Landscape Program

One-shot autofocus and individual frame advance are designated by the camera when the Command Dial is set on the landscape symbol. After all, taking pictures of landscapes is rarely a fast-paced endeavor.

An analysis of many thousands of landscape pictures has shown that nature scenes are usually located in the infinity or

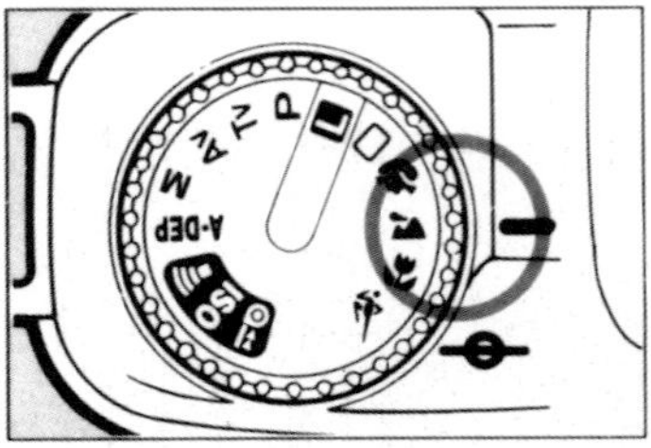

For subjects such as this, use the landscape mode.

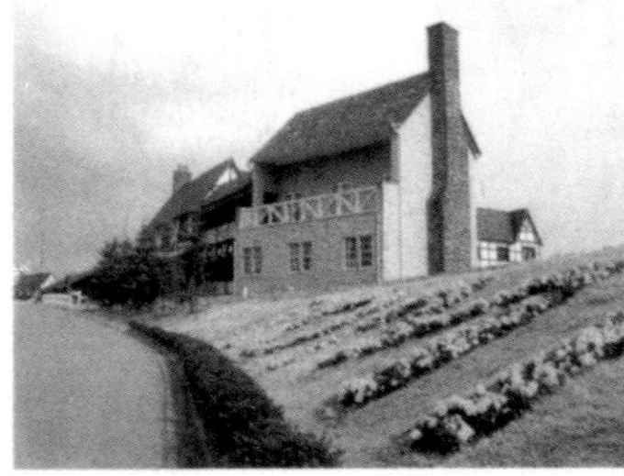

close-to-infinity distance range. Amateur photographers shoot almost exclusively panoramic views. When there is much in a picture it should be in focus from front to back. Therefore, this program provides a small aperture opening for an extended depth of field range. This is why extreme super-wide-angle lenses as well as zoom lenses starting at a focal length of 28 and 50mm are highly suitable in landscape program mode. Telephoto focal lengths greater than 200mm are not recommended when the setting is on the landscape symbol. Considering the described conditions it may be assumed that more than 90% of landscape scenes will be captured as correctly exposed pictures exhibiting impressive spatial sharpness. Super-wide-angle lenses make image composition more difficult; considerable experience is required to prevent a gaping void in the foreground and a few details in the background.

Designed for a wide-angle view, the concept of landscape refers to a subject-specific program which reduces the exposure by closing the aperture and increasing the shutter speed in equal increments once an aperture of f/5.6 and the reciprocal value of the focal length are reached.

Those who like to place people in the central foreground of a picture, such as, members of the family in front of the Grand Canyon, Niagara Falls, or the Eiffel Tower, should switch to the A-DEP program in the REBEL X/XS or DEP in earlier REBEL cameras (see the Automatic Depth of Field section, below). Buildings and cities may also be captured very successfully in landscape program mode.

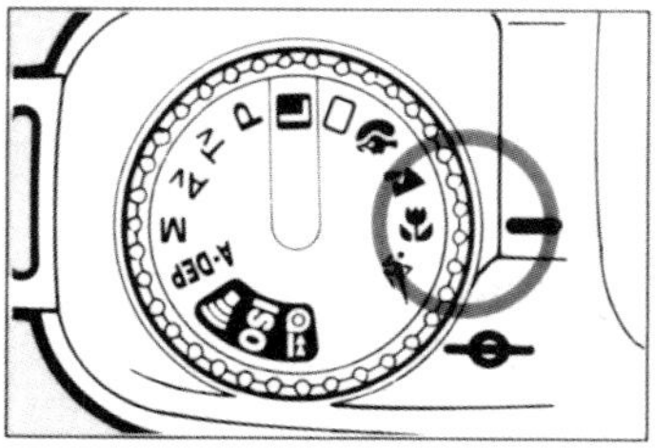

A perfect subject for the close-up mode.

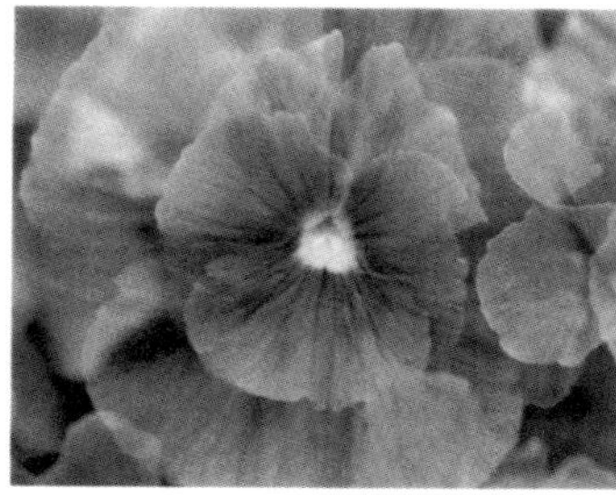

Close-up Program

In this subject-specific program, the photographer very quickly reaches the limits of existing light. This is why the close-up program has been designed for shots in existing light as well as with flash, which will be added automatically (where applicable). Of course, if necessary, any Canon Speedlite may slipped in the hot shoe. The main advantage of using a Canon flash unit is that the camera's electronic setup and the flash unit are fully compatible and may be coordinated precisely. For example, the EOS REBEL X/XS automatically adapts the flash unit reflector setting to the lens focal length, thereby maximizing the unit's guide number. In addition, A-TTL or TTL flash control may be used optionally. In this case, the flash initially just has a fill function; however, it becomes the main light if there is not enough ambient light. In close-up program mode f/5.6 is the largest available aperture opening. Smaller apertures are given preference by the program so that depth of field will be as great as possible.

Without additional flash the automatic process is the same as that of the landscape program which also uses an aperture of f/5.6. Multi-zone metering is activated in order to achieve an optimal exposure of all the details in a close-up shot. As long as the release continues to be pressed, focus and exposure values in the close-up range remain stored automatically. Problems presented by photographic range limits in the close-up mode may possibly be solved better (but by no means easier) with one of the creative programs on the "upper" side of the Command Dial.

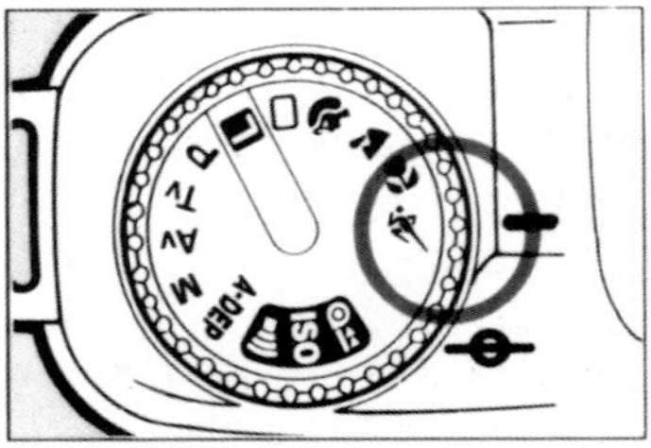

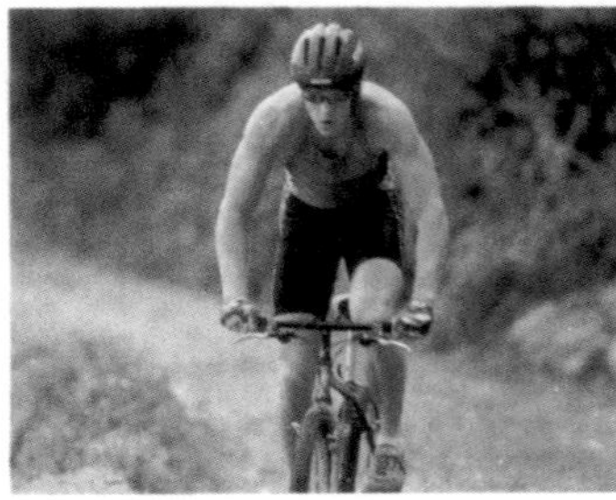

An ideal subject for the sports/action mode.

Sports/Action Program

The sports and action program is the ideal automatic mode when pictures are still blurred despite all the fully automatic features. This program produces super sharp pictures of all normal fast moving tourist or family events. Therefore, it is the ideal program for snapshots!

Of course, it is also possible to obtain sharp sports photographs using the sports program. The emphasis is on "it is possible!" Anyone going to a Formula-1 race without first trying out the sports program should not be surprised if success is limited. It is just not possible to pull out a camera (maybe with a long telephoto lens) at the last moment, press the release and obtain a complete roll of spectacularly focused pictures. One should have the experience to predict the exciting moments of the sport being photographed and move up close - ideally with focal lengths over 300mm - then the program may reduce shooting techniques to pressing the release. The program process should not imply lack of experience; the high shutter speed has priority. Movements are to be frozen and reproduced in sharp focus. This is not accomplished with the largest lens aperture but with a working aperture which is automatically reduced by a factor of 0.75 to allow even fast lenses to benefit from the best possible depth of field. If there is more light, first and foremost the shutter speed is increased. Up to a maximum of three speeds are available. The shutter speed which defines the blur limit, i.e. 1/focal length, is increased by up to three more stages. As a result a high-speed 200mm f/1.8 lens with an adjustment range between 1/200 sec. and 1/600 sec. is obtained. The aperture will close faster as the speed is increased only when the maximum value has been reached due to sufficient illumination of the subject. Speed and aperture selections then reduce the amount of light in a ratio of 40 to 60.

This type of exposure control is particularly useful in practical applications in the telephoto range over 200mm. Should the photographer start a series prematurely, the autofocus is not only able to recognize the approaching movement on time, but early on, and may compute with extreme precision the location of the subject at the time the picture and the next measurement are taken. The first to last shots of even the fastest moving subjects will be in focus. However, first the photographer has to master his camera and be certain that his subject does not leave the viewfinder. All fixed focal lengths beginning with 135mm plus zoom lenses with a minimum focal length above 70mm are suitable to be used with the sports/action program.

Automatic Exposure Control Features

The upper side of the Command Dial is intended for advanced photographers who are familiar with the parameters required for a successful shot. The REBEL series cameras' operating modes are identified by the initial(s) of these automatic exposure features:

P stands for automatic program which (unlike the Green Zone) may be modified by the photographer.

Tv stands for Time value priority (shutter speed is selected by the photographer). Tv is also called shutter priority mode.

Av stands for Aperture value priority. This function is generally referred to as aperture priority mode.

A-DEP stands for auto depth of field. This program uses all three metering points of the REBEL X/XS's AF system. In this mode the camera automatically sets the proper lens aperture to produce a depth of field encompassing the subject points selected by the photographer. If the built-in flash unit has been folded down or if the camera doesn't feature a built-in flash, long exposures may be selected by the camera when great depth of field is desired, despite the risk of camera shake. A tripod is recommended for such situations. (Earlier REBEL cameras feature a similar **DEP** mode).

M stands for manual adjustment. In this mode both shutter speed and aperture are set by the photographer.

Technical information for the selected mode appears on the LCD display panel. Exposure time and aperture information, possibly in conjunction with a plus or minus symbol, is also displayed in the viewfinder.

In all programs, with the exception of M mode, multi-zone metering is used to determine exposure. Simply pressing the Partial Metering Button switches the camera to partial metering at any time. This is indicated by a star symbol in the viewfinder.

Each metering result is stored (regardless of the metering technique) as long as the shutter release is pressed lightly. All program modes warn of overexposure or underexposure; exposure time, aperture or both will blink. In manual mode the + symbol will prompt an increase and the - symbol a decrease of the aperture; or, if the Av key has been pressed, an increase or decrease of the shutter speed.

Automatic Program Mode

In automatic program mode (P), aperture and shutter speed are selected by the camera. To achieve this, the camera's exposure control considers the focal length of the lens. The inverse value of the focal length is the basis for the control curve for exposure time. Depending on focal length and varying light intensity, the curve may be adjusted up to five times the current value of the focal length.

Sometimes it is disconcerting when exposure time and aperture values are displayed in unfamiliar numbers. For example, the combination of shutter speed and aperture of 1/750 and f/13 suddenly appears in green at the bottom of the viewfinder. These combinations do not create problems and are extremely precise thanks to the EOS lens's electromagnetically controlled apertures. Unusual, stepless shutter speeds such as 1/900 have been successfully used for a long time.

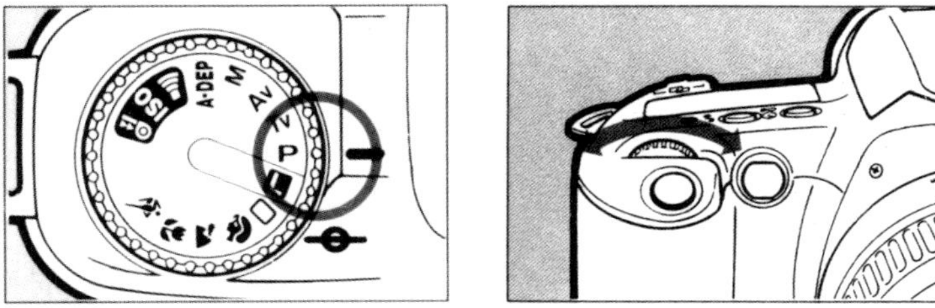

In the program mode, both shutter speed and aperture are automatically selected by the camera. These settings may be adjusted by using the Electronic Input Dial (see text for details).

Due to the comprehensive shutter speed control in addition to normal combinations of exposure time and aperture, erroneous exposures are almost impossible. However, should the risk of such an exposure exist, exposure time and aperture data in the viewfinder will blink. If there is too much light (for example, when using super-high-speed films in sunshine), a neutral-density (ND) filter is helpful. If there is not enough, flash may be used.

In P mode the REBEL series cameras do not warn of camera shake because Canon engineers assume that anyone using creative programs is aware of this problem. The same is true of the elective use of the flash unit. Once the photographer presses the flash activation button, the shortest possible exposure time for flash, a shutter speed of 1/90, is automatically set.

In normal lighting situations automatic P mode is a convenient alternative even for creative photographers. They may simply adapt the automatic program as desired or required (for one shot at a time). By turning the convenient Electronic Input Dial, exposure time and aperture may be changed simultaneously without losing sight of the subject. Because the information is displayed in the viewfinder, the input dial adjustments are visible immediately; this change in exposure time and aperture is called Program Shifting.

By simply turning the input dial, all available aperture values and corresponding shutter speeds may be adjusted based on measured light conditions. For example, when the brightness corresponds to an exposure value of 13 and the attached lens is a standard 50mm, the following combinations (without intermediate values) of apertures and exposure times will result: f/2 and 1/2000 sec.; f/2.8 and 1/1000 sec.; f/4 and 1/500 sec.; f/5.6 and 1/250 sec.; f/8 and 1/125 sec.; etc. up to f/22 and 1/15 sec. With the touch of a finger the automatic program may be adjusted specifically to high shutter speeds for moving objects or, conversely, to a particularly large depth of field, without requiring a deactivation of the automatic features and without taking the camera off the eye. Once a value has been set, it is stored for exactly 6 seconds. With the use of zoom lenses, program shifting should occur only after the focal length has been adjusted because the aperture values will change when the focal length is adjusted. Don't be surprised if the smallest aperture of f/22 and then an aperture of f/27 is indicated for the same lens. This range reflects that a zoom lens is in use which has a variable maximum aperture, which also translates into a variable minimum aperture.

Shifting the combination of shutter speed and aperture and additional partial metering are possible only in P mode. In the fully automatic mode (the green rectangle), these adjustment options are not available.

Shutter Priority Mode

By setting the Command Dial to Tv (shutter priority) the camera is switched to automatic aperture adjustment. In this case the photographer selects a shutter speed between 30 and 1/2000 in increments. After selection the camera automatically sets an aperture appropriate for the lighting conditions and shutter speed. The basic setting suggested by the camera is always 125 (1/125 second). If the LCD aperture indicator shows the aperture value constantly, the aperture defined by multi-zone metering has been set. If, however, the largest aperture value blinks, this means underexposure. By turning the electronic input dial, the shutter speed may be set to slower speeds until the blinking stops.

If the smallest aperture value is blinking, this indicates overexposure. To correct the exposure, the shutter speed must be increased by turning the dial until the aperture value no longer blinks. This automatic setting does not warn of camera shake.

The shutter priority mode is used mainly when the photographer requires a specific shutter speed for artistic reasons. In this

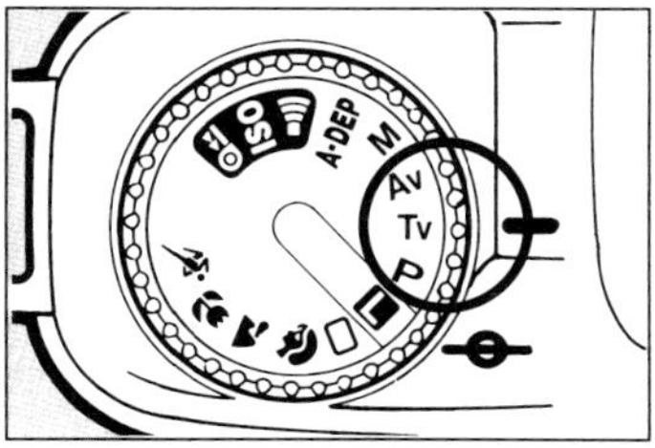

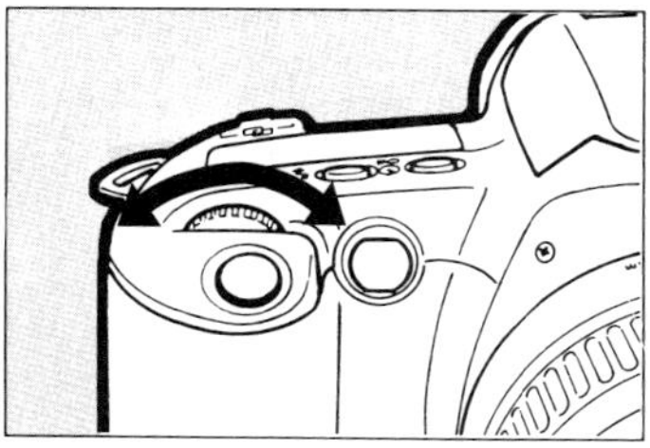

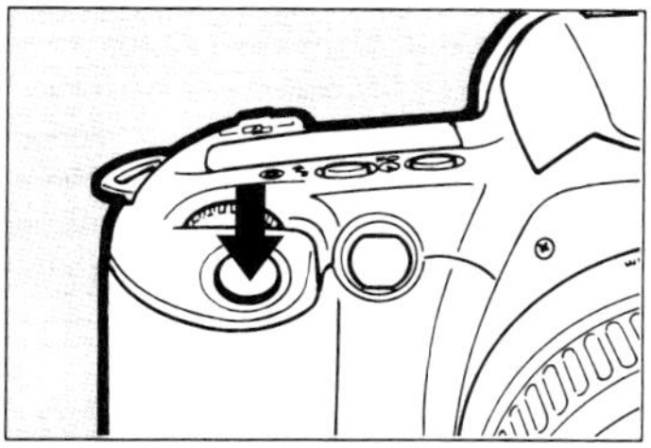

In shutter priority mode (Tv), the shutter speed is selected with the Electronic Input Dial, the camera automatically sets the lens aperture for correct exposure.

program the aperture acts exclusively to control the amount of light and its creative effectiveness is neglected in favor of the required shutter speed. Partial metering may be used and short exposure times (1/200 and faster) should be selected when pictures are taken from a moving vehicle, when a large print is the intended final product or when sports or action shots of fast-moving subjects are taken. Generally, fast shutter speeds are used to stop motion. But also the reverse is possible, slow shutter speeds (about 1/30 and slower) used in conjunction with the shutter priority mode produce creative motion blur effects.

The Tv program, with a preliminary selection of extended exposure times from one to several seconds, is suitable even for shots of buildings. In this case, anything that is moving during exposure (vehicles or people), will be blurred. Extremely long exposure times make objects moving through the picture completely invisible. This is a favorite trick to make high-traffic areas appear desolate.

Aperture Priority Mode

In aperture priority mode (Av) the aperture is selected by the photographer with the Electronic Input Dial. In this mode the ex-

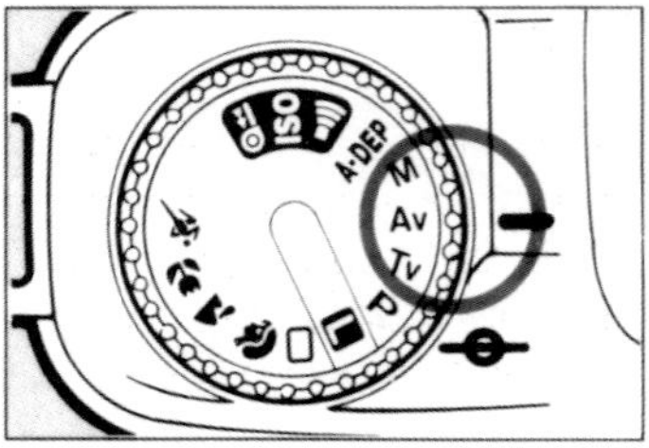

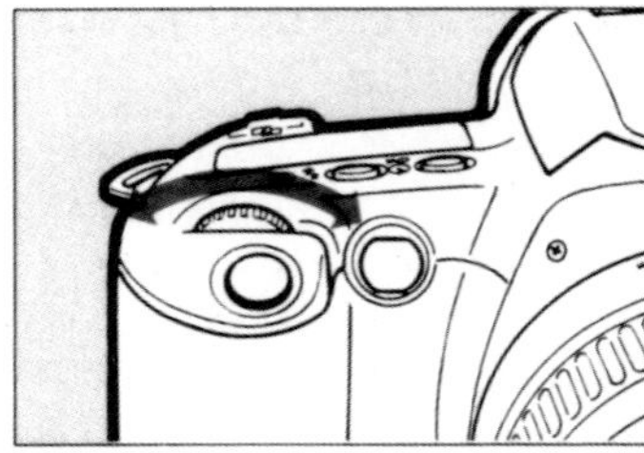

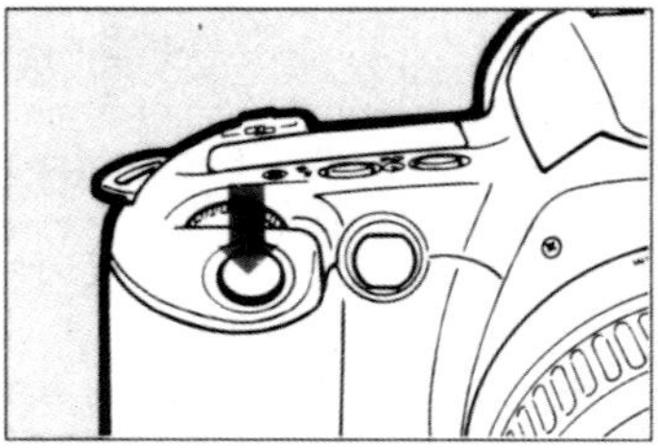

In aperture priority mode (Av), the aperture is selected with the Electronic Input Dial and the camera automatically picks the shutter speed for correct exposure.

posure may be determined by multi-zone or by partial metering. The initial value always suggested by the camera is an aperture of f/5.6. To achieve proper exposure, the exposure control system automatically selects the required shutter speed as a function of the existing amount of light.

Av is the exposure mode best used when depth defines the image - or whenever depth of field is important. It may be the case that only a slight expansion of the spatial depth is desired (for example, sacrificing the sharpness of background in a portrait shot.) On the other hand, it is sometimes desirable to create an image which is sharp from front to back to produce particularly effective shots of landscapes or buildings. The REBEL series is capable of capturing these types of scenes better, more easily and even more clearly with its DEP or A-DEP depth of field feature.

In Av mode erroneous exposures may occur - though less frequently than when the shutter priority mode is used - and are indicated by a blinking aperture value. Underexposure occurs only when a shutter speed of 30 seconds is not long enough; overexposure occurs when 1/2000 is too long. to cut back excessive light. In both cases the aperture selection may be adjusted by turning the input dial.

Automatic Depth of Field Program

Photographic subjects are usually three-dimensional but are recorded on the film in two dimensions. A similar flat plane of sharpest focus exists at the subject. It is only on this plane that a sharp image is formed. Objects in front of or behind the plane do not come to sharp focus and are rendered more or less out-of-focus.

When viewing a print or projected image, our eye will see some of the area in front of and behind the plane of sharp focus and also apparently in focus. The depth of this area of apparent sharpness is referred to as depth of field. Depth of field varies with lens aperture, and is smaller with large apertures and greater with small apertures.

The depth of field may be computed and is listed in depth of field tables available for each lens focal length. The Canon REBEL X/XS's A-DEP setting eliminates the need to study tables for shooting situations. This program allows the photographer to simply define the space which is to be reproduced in sharp focus. To accomplish this the two external AF metering fields should be directed at the beginning and the end of a space in which a sharp image is desired. The camera then automatically computes the required aperture.

Should the aperture selected not be adequate to produce a sharp image of the desired space, the smallest aperture number of the lens used will blink on the display. If the shutter release is still pressed, a correct exposure based on the multi-zone metering information is taken (with the smallest possible aperture).

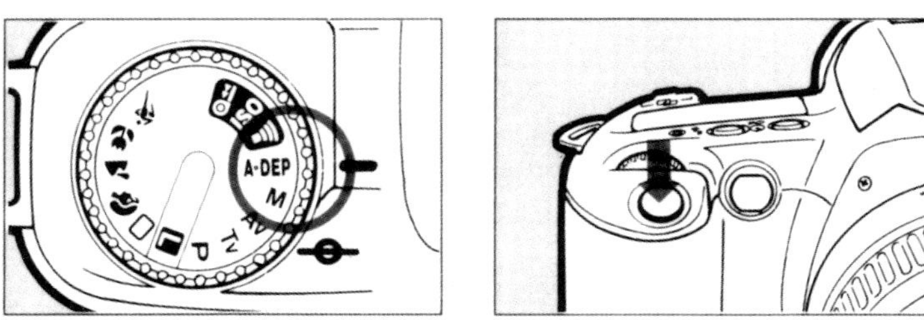

With the REBEL X/XS's automatic depth of field mode (A-DEP), the photographer can select the desired depth of field.

However, should there be enough time for additional attempts, the required focal range or imaging scale should be reduced. To achieve this it is possible to move farther back or to stay in the same place and use a shorter focal length and start over.

When this smallest aperture display blinks, at least one correctly exposed picture is possible; when both displays in the viewfinder blink, an erroneous exposure will occur. If there is inadequate light, flash may be added but then the camera switches out of the A-DEP mode and works in normal automatic P mode.

When using zoom lenses with the A-DEP mode, you must adjust the lens focal length first and then operate the two depth settings. If you forget this and change the focal length after setting one depth, the A-DEP operation will be cancelled and you must start over.

The DEP program in the earlier REBEL models works in a somewhat similar fashion. First, the focus mark is pointed to the closest point of desired focus and the shutter button pressed halfway. The focus symbol and "dEP-1" will appear in the viewfinder. This step is repeated for the farthest point or "dEP-2." When the shutter button is depressed halfway a third time the appropriate aperture selection appears in the viewfinder. If this is not a permissible setting, the readout will flash, however, when the final is exposure is made the camera will select the best combination of shutter speed and aperture for the desired depth of field. For more detail, see the chapter *Earlier Rebel Models.*

Manual Exposure Control

When the camera is switched to manual its default aperture setting is f/5.6. The electronic input dial and the Av adjustment key are used for manual exposure compensation to set the required combination of shutter speed and aperture.

If the same procedure is followed at all times, manual adjustments are smooth and surprisingly fast. To achieve this, the electronic input dial is turned until the desired shutter speed appears. The viewfinder then indicates the shutter speed and aperture. The metering system indicates in the viewfinder and on the display monitor any deviation (in EV values in 1/3 increments) from the correct exposure determined by the camera meter.

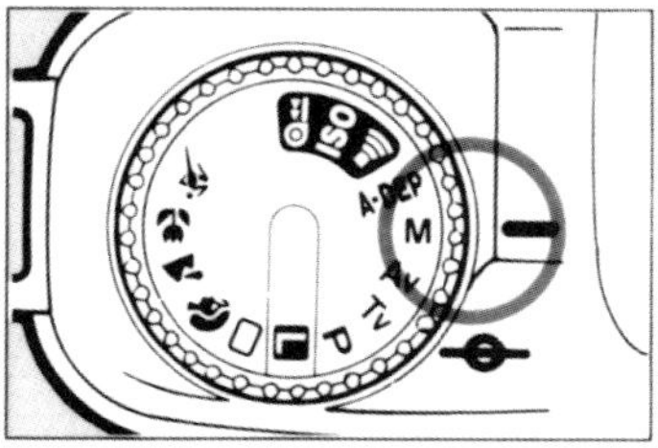

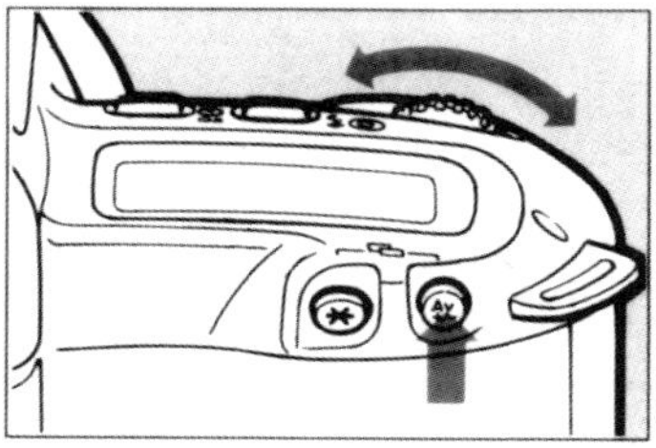

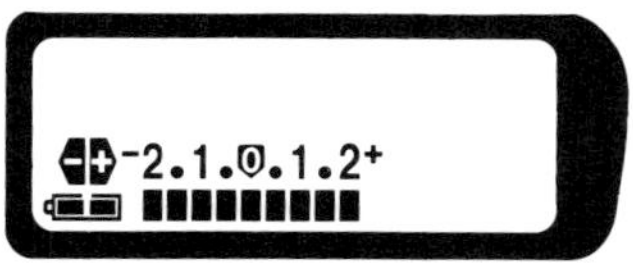

Manual metering is done by observing the + and - indicators either inside the viewfinder or on the top-mounted LCD panel, and adjusting shutter speed or lens aperture (or both) until both the + and - symbols are lit.

The shutter speed can always be set manually, however, there is no warning of potential camera shake. Manual metering is a center-weighted integral process. In particular, when series are shot or when pictures are to be shown later in presentations using lap dissolve techniques, it is preferable to avoid brightness differences in shots having identical illumination. When a subject requiring shooting with different focal lengths is to be used, partial metering is recommended. Experienced photographers use this technique even with telephoto lenses in order to get point-accurate results. Selective metering, however, is precise only when the correct points are measured. Otherwise the risk of erroneous exposures is considerably greater than with multi-zone metering. In critical cases it is best to use a Kodak Gray Card as the optimal metering subject. Generally, all exposure meters, including those in the Canon REBEL series are calibrated to this card's reflectance of 18%.

In televised sports broadcasts, distinct image brightness changes are always noticeable when a switch from a wide-angle setting to a super-telephoto setting takes place. The image becomes lighter when the details are in the shadows or it becomes darker with full illumination. The same may happen in still photography because normally greater brightness differences must be dealt with in the wide-angle range than when details are shot with a telephoto lens. This will become obvious when the focal length of a zoom lens is changed. (In multi-zone metering this risk exists only in critical ranges.) Partial metering will determine metering differences at the shortest and longest focal lengths, even when the exposure is correct for both situations. Such differences may be prevented by a single metering operation and subsequent manual adjustment.

Partial metering is suitable in all problematic lighting situations which might strain even multi-zone metering - especially if artistic effects under critical lighting conditions are desired. After all, only the photographer knows what detail should be emphasized by special lighting and not even the most sophisticated automatic exposure program can make these decisions. In particular, this principle applies to lighting situations with excessive brightness differences between the main subject and the background such as stage settings or backlit subjects. In these instances the photographer must decide the most appropriate illumination. As described, the portrait of a girl at sunset or a backlit windmill (with direct, incident light) may be realized by using at least six different levels of exposures, whereby all results are usable. The technical choice is based on the desired mood of the final photograph.

Time Exposure

As mentioned before, the REBEL series cameras offer a large range of automatically and manually controlled shutter speed settings. With all REBEL cameras, this range may be expanded in manual exposure control mode. To achieve this, the electronic input dial is used to select bulb in M mode. On the LCD monitor, bulb will appear as the next display following 30. In this setting the shutter will remain open as long as the shutter release is pressed. These shots require a tripod and, with the REBEL X/XS a remote cable shutter

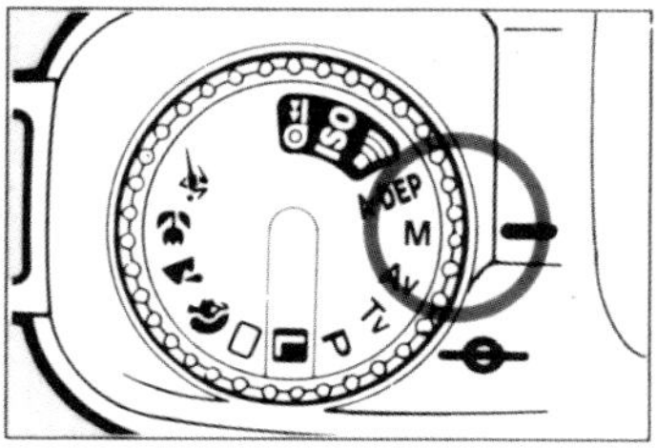

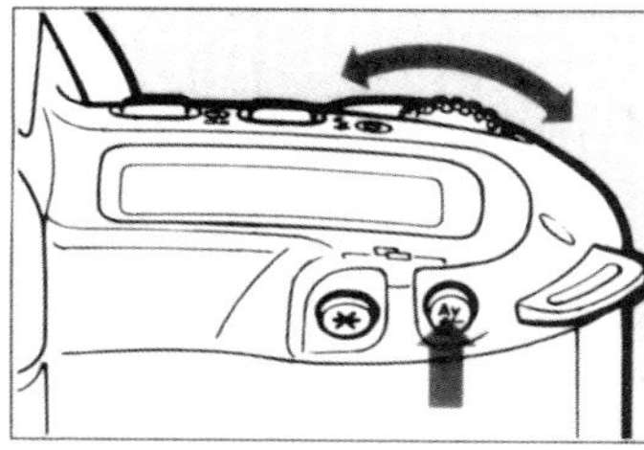

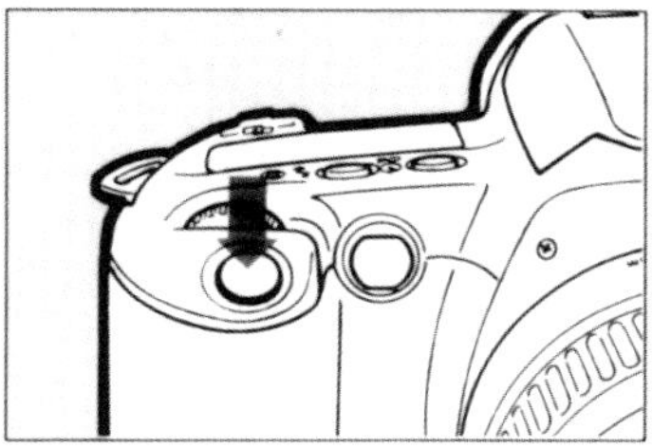

In manual mode, the aperture is set using the Av button and the Electronic Input Dial.

release RS-603E (available for these models only as an accessory) is suggested. With the camera setting on bulb the remote control shutter release should be pressed twice, once to open and once to close the shutter. See also, Accessories Chapter.

In this manual setting, which is outside the metered range, the Canon REBEL series cameras will not warn of erroneous exposures.

Multiple Exposure

After pressing the Partial Metering Button and the Exposure Compensation Buttons at the same time, the Function Symbol (two overlapping rectangles) will appear on the LCD panel. Now it is possible to select the number of exposures to appear on the same frame by turning the Electronic Input Dial. Although numbers from one to nine may be selected, it is possible to take any number of exposures by resetting the number before taking the last photo in the sequence. This is easy because the numbers count down as each exposure is made.

The most basic type of multiple exposure shot involves exposing two images on one frame. If the background is dark or even black, many image details may be exposed next to each other on one frame without requiring any camera adjustment except for

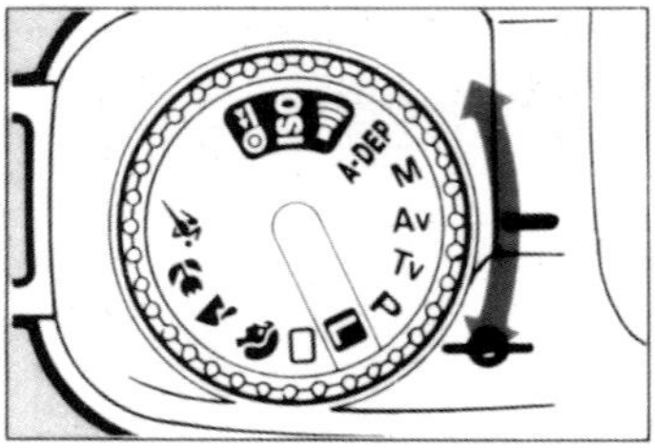

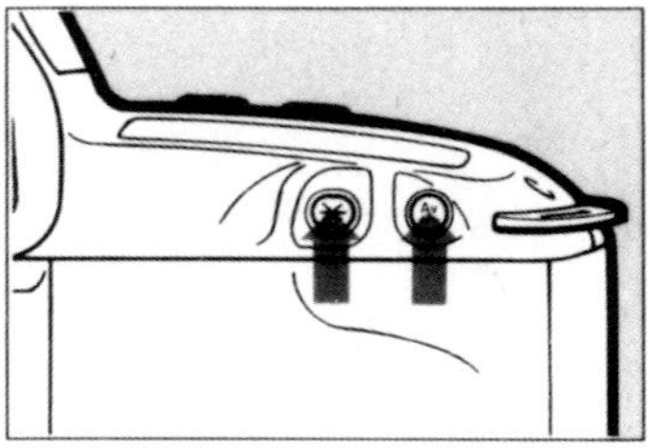

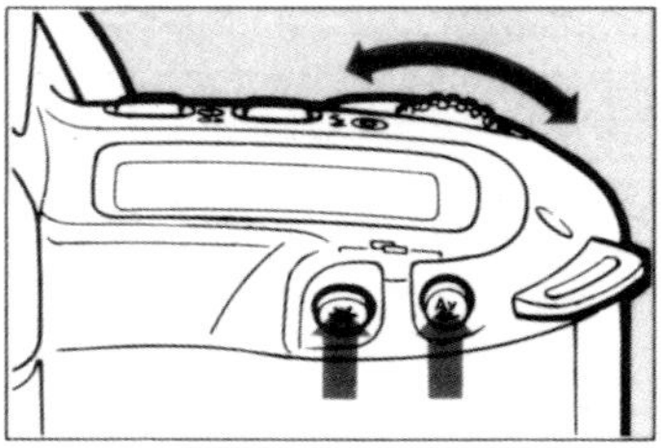

In the creative modes, you may make use of the * button to activate partial metering. The Av button, in combination with the Electronic Input Dial, allows you to set exposure compensation for over- or underexposure.

the intended number of individual exposures. Each subject detail is exposed normally. Normal in this context means "detail-specific," (by using partial metering to prevent the background from affecting the measured result). Only an overlap of picture elements must be given consideration when the exposure is adjusted. The film can handle only one quantity of light - which is clearly defined by the film speed - for recording a precise image of the subject. Because this factor relates to only one exposure, superimposed details are exposed with double the light when a double exposure is taken. Each individual shutter speed must be reduced so that the sum of light of all shots at the overlapping points corresponds to the value for an ideal single exposure.

In this situation, the correction values are input as light values. One light value less means that the exposure must be reduced by one aperture setting or the shutter speed reduced by one value setting.

The most important aspect of taking multiple exposures is not the frequency of the exposure, but rather the frequency of overlapping picture elements. Correction information (for example, recommending a reduction by an exposure value of -1) for double exposures refers only to situations in which the first and the second exposure are superimposed completely or partially. Each shot must be underexposed by one aperture or shutter speed value. A triple exposure requires an exposure value correction of

Program	Auto-flash	Manual Flash	+/– Compen-sation	Multiple Exposure	AE Lock
P		X	X	X	X
Tv		X	X	X	X
Av		X	X	X	X
A-DEP		X	X	X	X
Green Zone	X				
Portrait	X				
Landscape					
Close-up	X				
Sport					
Manual		X	X	X	

Program Features

-1.5 (1/3 of what would be a normal exposure setting). A quadruple exposure is corrected by a factor of -2. However, if images overlap only twice, the correction must be only that used for a double exposure.

Appropriate corrections can be manually input in the REBEL series. To do so, the Exposure Compensation Button is pressed and the correction factor set by turning the Electronic Input Dial.

Once the function icon appears on the LCD panel, the number of multiple exposures is entered by turning the dial. The correction factor itself is displayed in the viewfinder. After shooting the number of programmed exposures, the ME function will be automatically deactivated; the normal number of frames appears again and the photographer must manually reset the +/- correction to zero. This program may be aborted at any time by designating the number of multiple exposures as 1. However, should a multiple exposure in progress be aborted, the next exposure must be manual and the lens must be closed so that the film may be transported to the next frame.

Don't forget to alert your film processing lab when dropping off a multiple exposure roll so that the multiple exposure frames will be printed and not presumed faulty. The easiest way to do this is to make sure that "print all" is indicated on the special instructions portion of the film envelope.

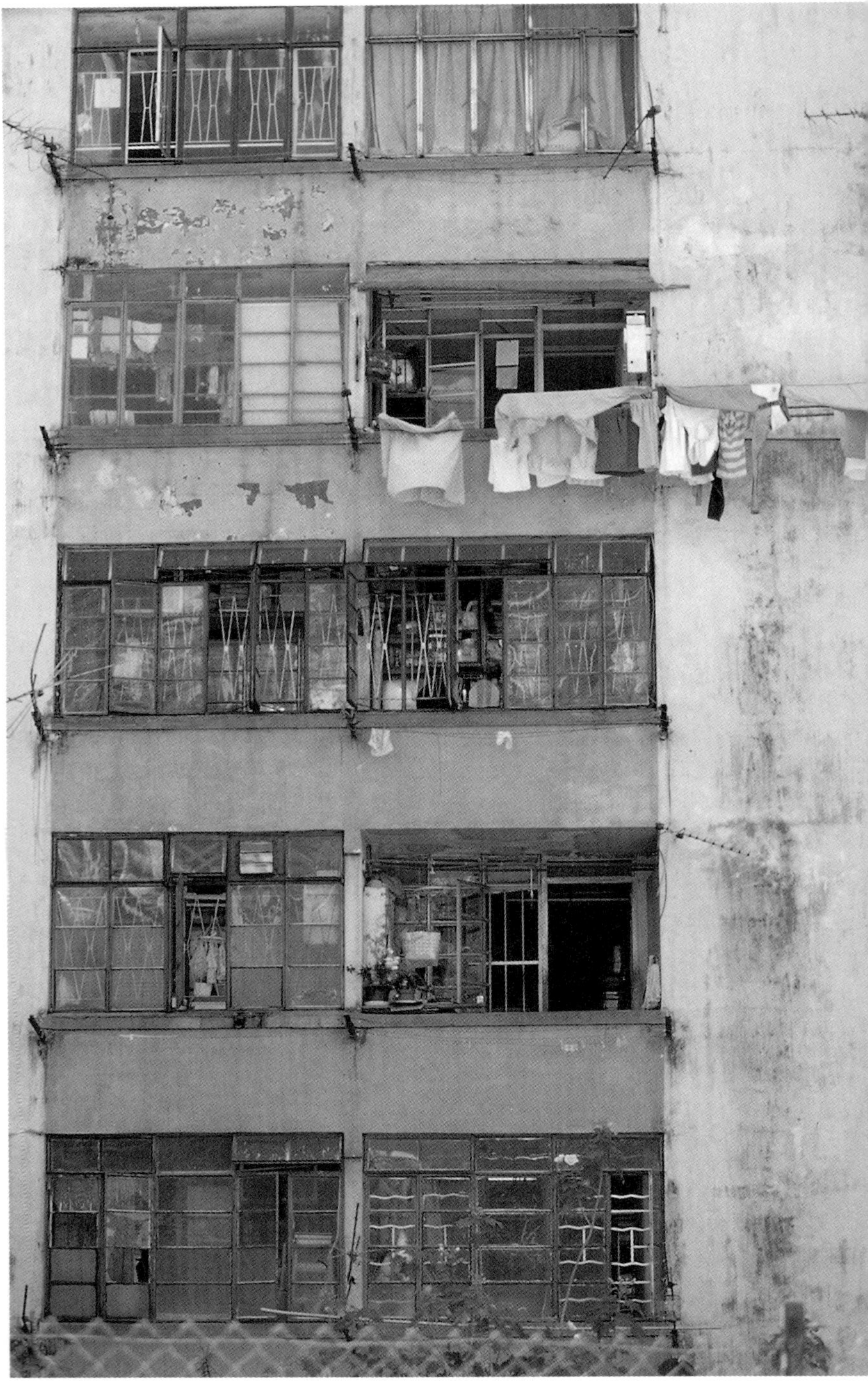

Creative Photography

Image Composition

The REBEL cameras will provide perfect exposures. However, the photographer must still select and frame a subject. First, however, one must learn to "see" or visualize an image to select the most interesting part of a subject in its perceived environment. The human eye is at its most effective seeing objects at a viewing angle of 46 degrees but is capable of focusing at only a much smaller angle. Because sharpness is also concentrated in the range of greatest interest, one may talk of "selective" perception. The framed part of any image should show only what is important. This effect is most easily achieved by omitting extraneous image information. Approaching the subject sufficiently closely or adjusting the lens to put only the subject in the picture are ways of doing this. A zoom lens should be set for the greatest focal length to allow immediate viewing of the largest possible image when the camera is held against the eye. Therefore, the image content seen by the lens, first is a function of the adjusted image frame.

A 50mm lens (or a zoom lens set at 50mm) "sees" like the human eye (with the same viewing angle). Pictures shot at this focal length are always perceived as "normal." With a focal length of less than 50mm, each lost millimeter increases the image content. The lens viewing angle is increased in proportion to the reduced focal length. An even greater image angle due to an additional reduction of the focal length will result in a super-wide-angle range (from 28 to 20mm with EOS lenses). If the camera is held properly, there will be no problems with perspective except the feeling that the image narrows dramatically toward the horizon.

Without a shift lens, an image like this would have a problem with converging vertical lines and exaggerated perspective. This effect can also be reduced by taking the photo from a greater distance with a telephoto lens.

Page 61

[UPPER] A telephoto zoom is ideal for photos of ships. The lens can be zoomed to get just the right cropping as the ships move to different locations.

[LOWER] The fully automatic mode of REBEL series cameras is able to cope well with images such as this, without being overly influenced by the light buildings or the dark sea.

Page 62

[UPPER] This photo taken with a wide-angle zoom emphasizes the perspective of the train.

[LOWER] Photos with both light and shadow like this are best taken with the Rebel's Green Zone or P, program mode. The metering system will automatically assess the scene and select the exposure.

Page 63

[UPPER] Photos taken from such angles show converging verticals, but the eye is more accustomed to accepting this perspective so long as it is not over-exaggerated by the use of too short a lens.

[LOWER] Night photographs can be taken easily with the REBEL cameras by using the Av, aperture priority mode and simply letting the camera select the shutter speed. Exposure times are usually long, so a good tripod is a necessity.

Page 64

[UPPER & LOWER] The built-in flash on the REBEL XS camera operates automatically. It adds sparkle to the highlights in images like these, and keeps detail in the shadows from being lost.

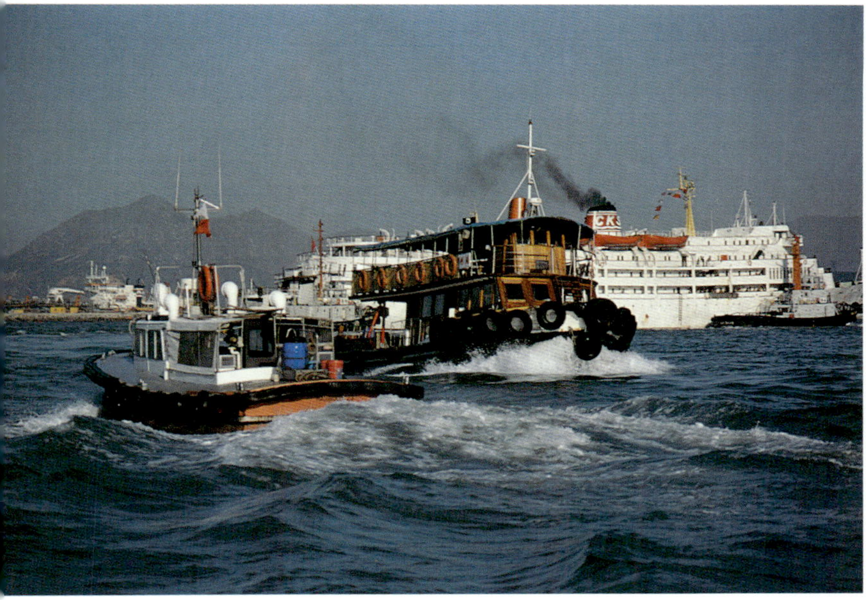

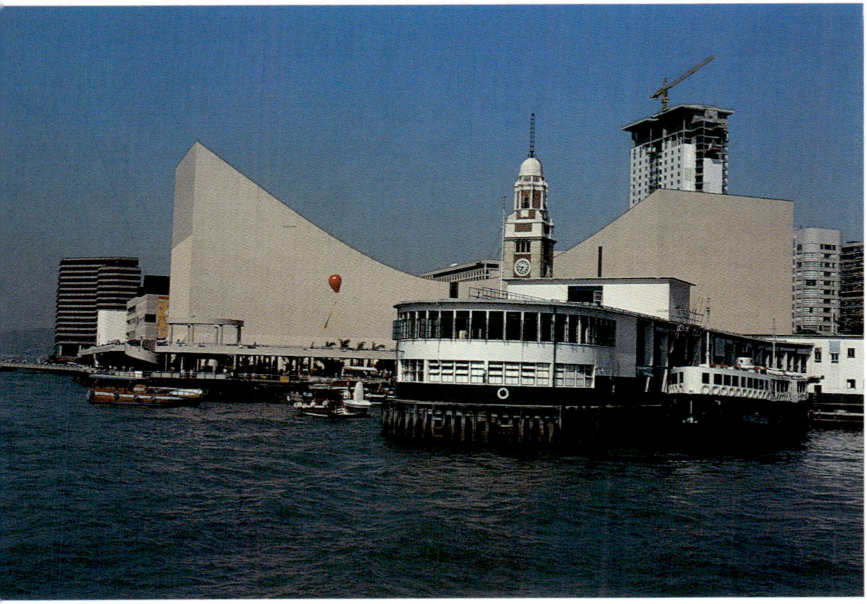

– A –

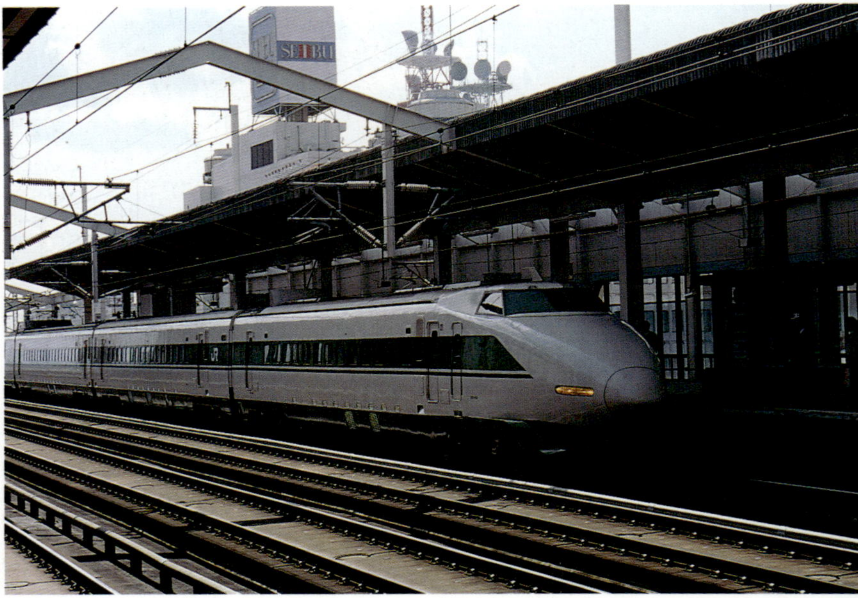

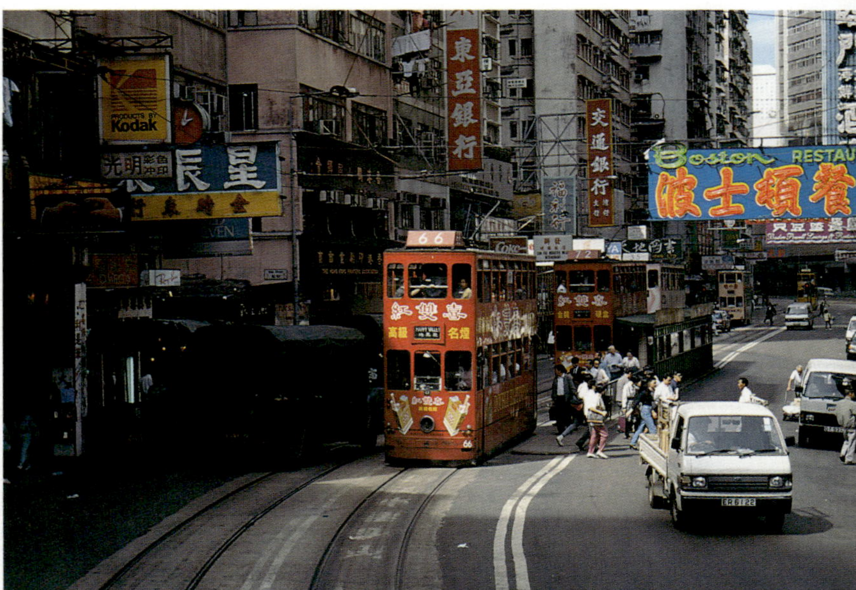
PRODUCTS BY
Kodak
光明彩色沖印
東亞銀行
交通銀行
Boston RESTAUR
波士頓餐
66
紅雙喜
高級
名煙
72
ER 6122

– B –

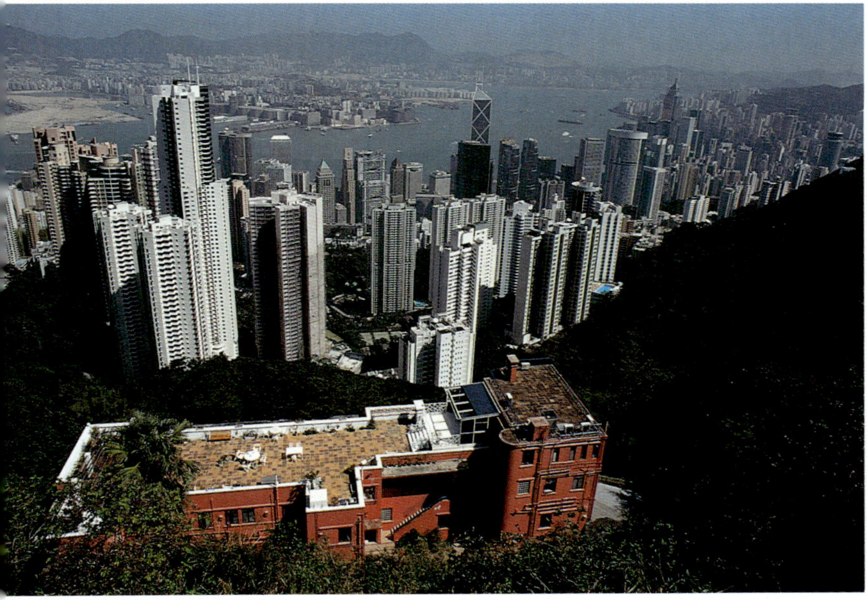

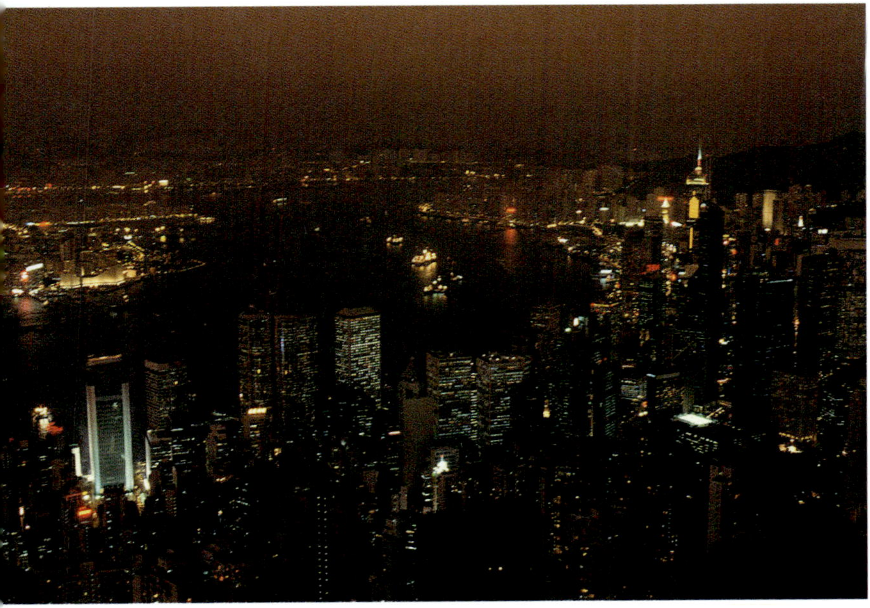

– C –

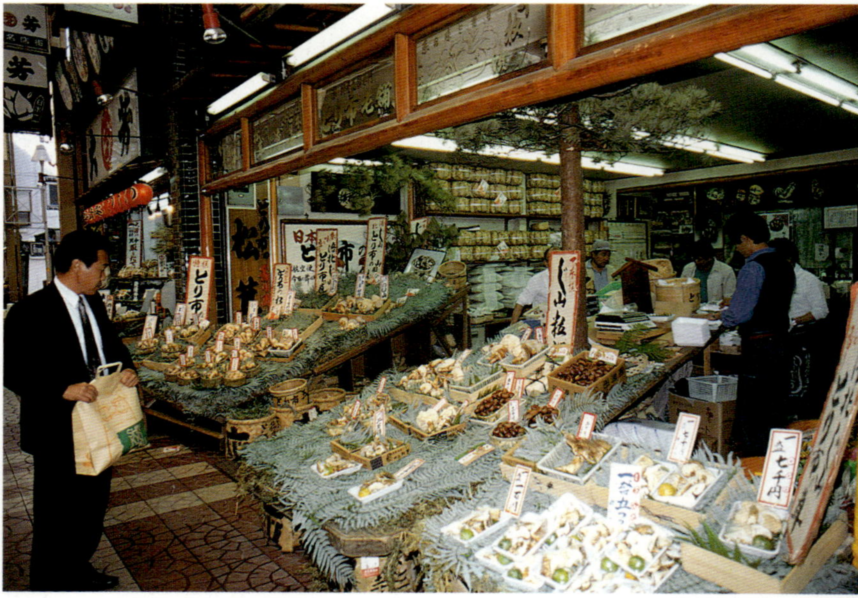

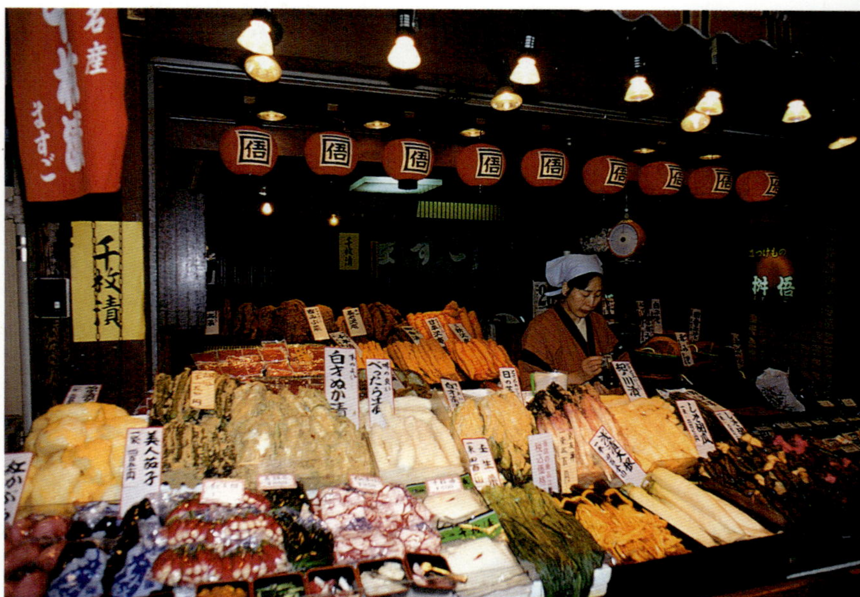

– D –

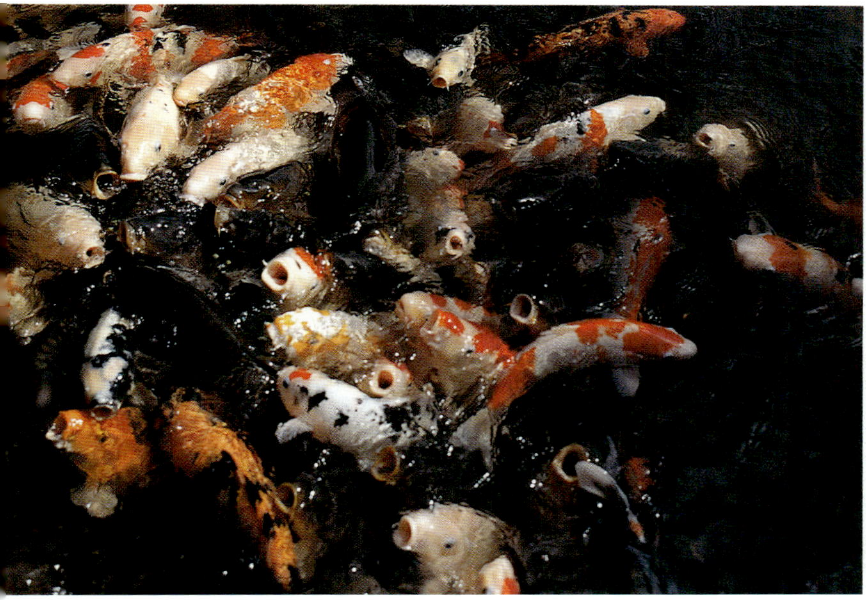

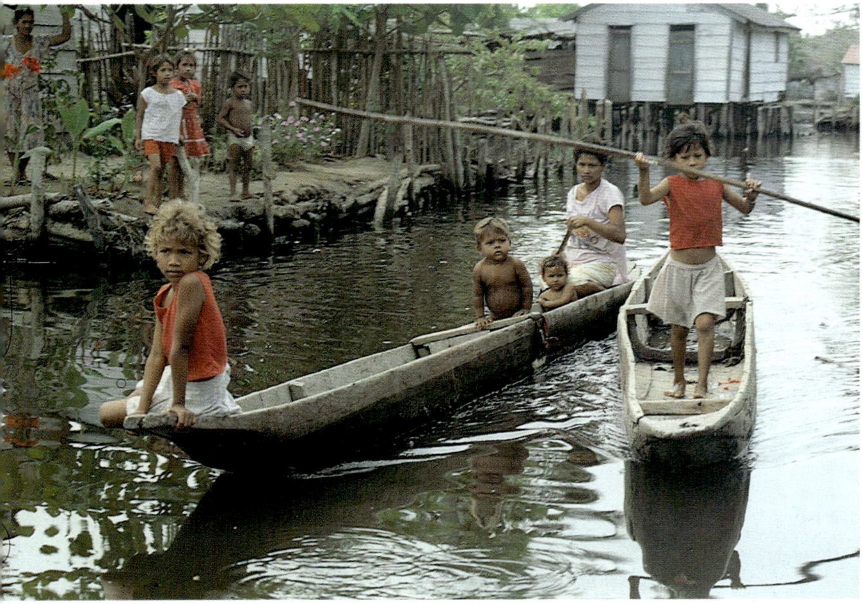

– E –

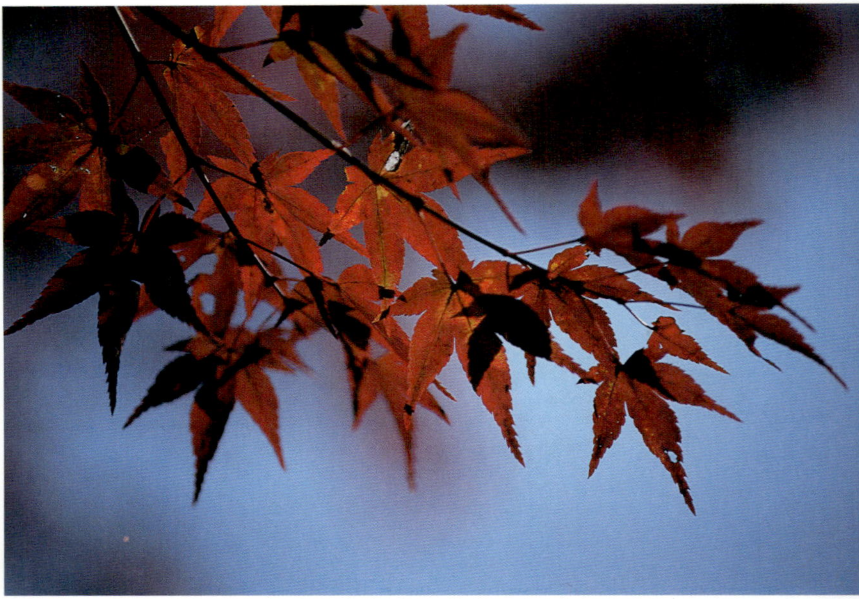

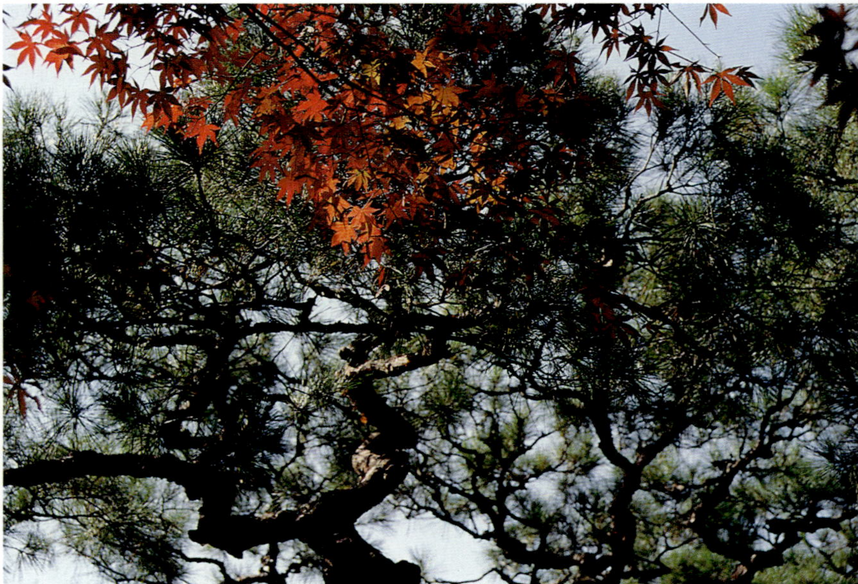

– F –

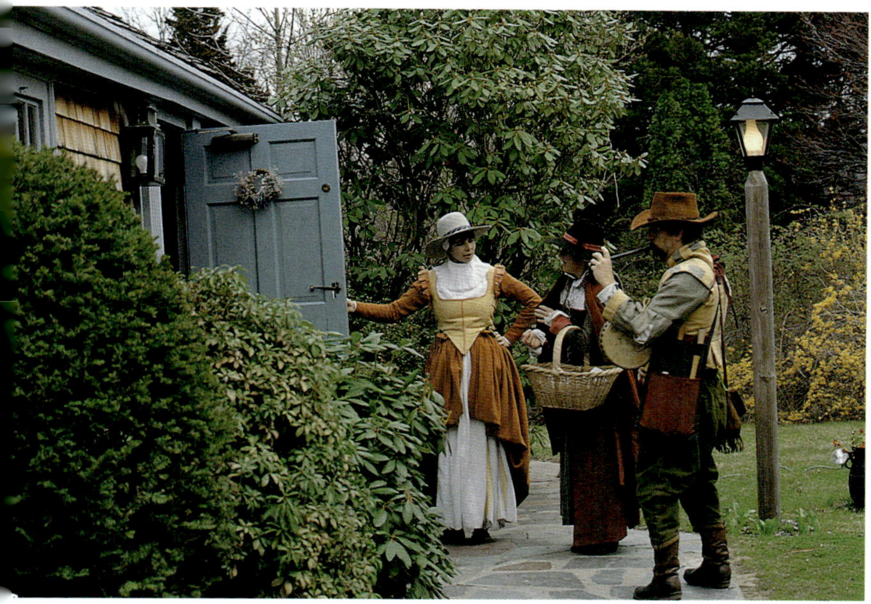

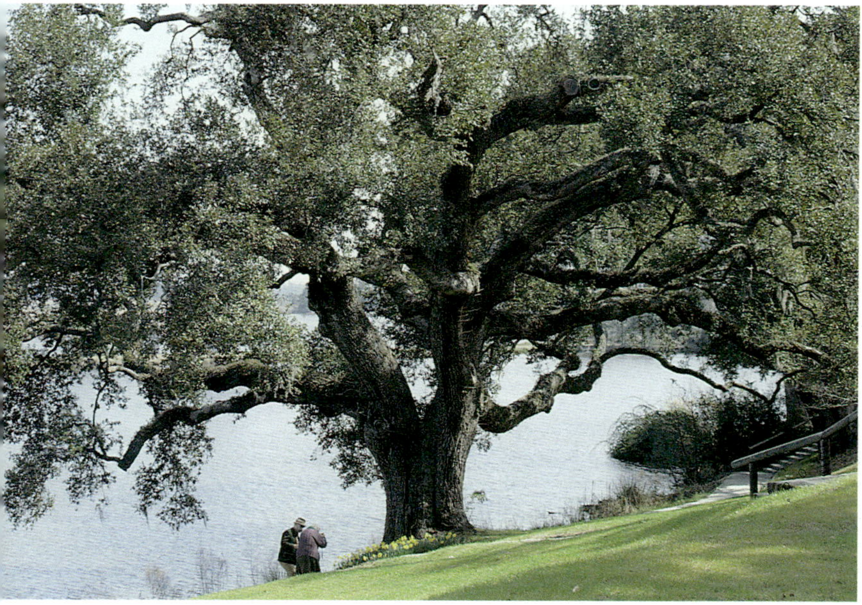

– G –

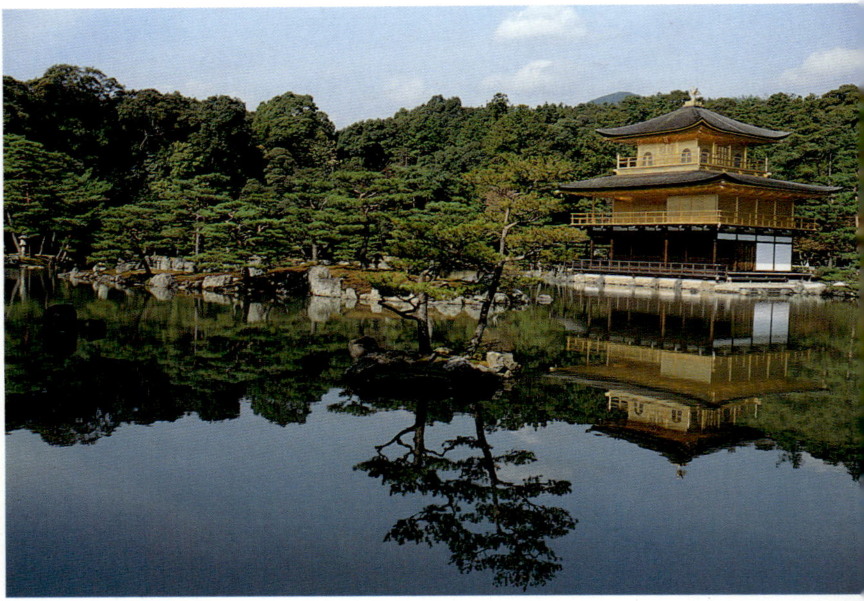

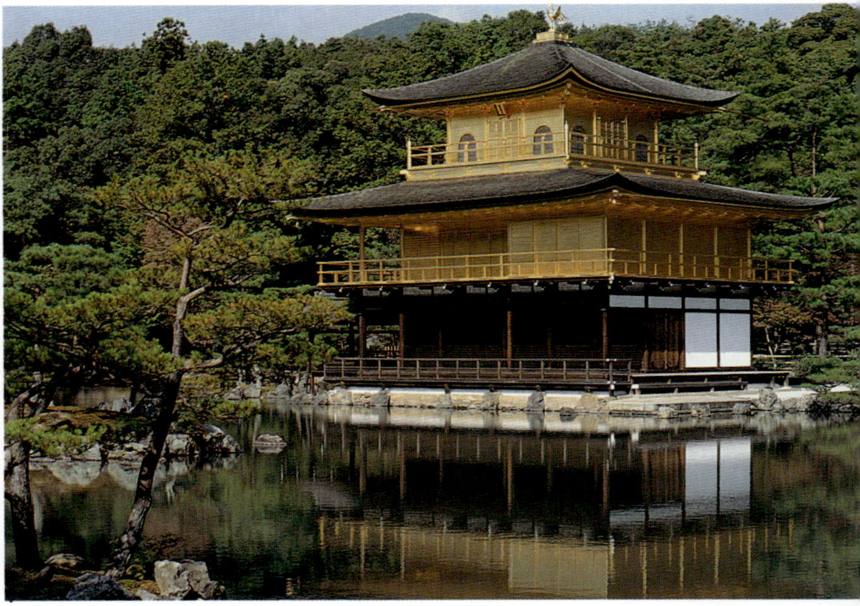

– H –

Page 65

[UPPER & LOWER] For travel photographs, the very fast EF 28-70mm f/2.8 L lens may be the ideal choice. It allows use of a fast shutter speed due to its large maximum aperture, and is extremely sharp.

Page 66

[UPPER] By using a relatively large aperture it is possible to bring the main subject into sharp focus and blur the background so it will not be distracting.

[LOWER] A smaller aperture has been used to bring the background into focus, and the photographer has relied on the difference in color to separate the foreground from the background.

Page 67

[UPPER & LOWER] The Canon EF 20-35mm lens may be the ideal lens to capture a scene. Its 35mm range is ideal for photos like the upper one, while at 20mm it can capture a wider view as in the lower photo.

Page 68

[UPPER & LOWER] Often a subject will benefit from several different compositions. In such a situation, a telephoto zoom lens can be ideal.

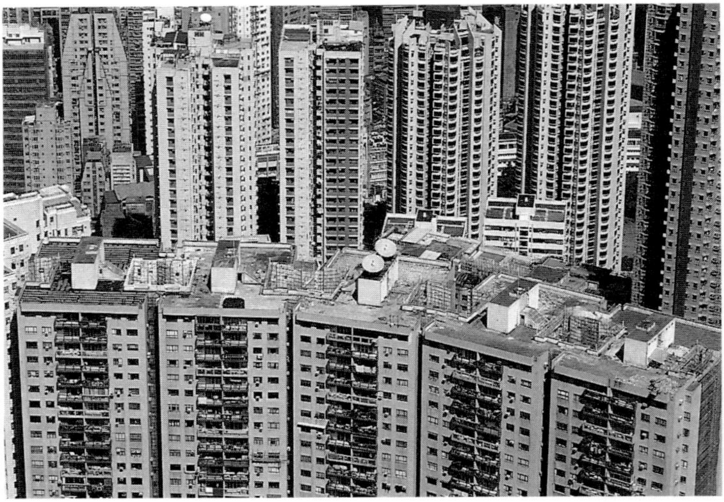

Telephoto lenses work well for shooting architectural images with normal perspective and minimum convergence of vertical lines.

The reverse approach is taken when the lens focal length is longer than 50mm. The viewing angle becomes smaller and the framed subject in the picture becomes noticeably larger. As a result, pictures taken in a focal length range of 50 to 100mm will still be perceived as normal because they offer the viewer a very reduced, framed image. The normal telephoto range from 100 to 200mm already produces somewhat of a "telescope" effect. Lenses with focal lengths of more than 300mm are usually considered to be super-telephoto.

Principally, the main subject can be emphasized by framing; a few aesthetic basics should be observed. The simplest method is to have the subject fill the frame. This is may be done with almost any subject.

Should full-size subject framing not be attainable or desired, lighting may give the picture appealing qualities. Emphasizing the main subject by illumination is the simplest method. A single spotlight directed at a subject forces the viewer to look at the resultant light spot. The same effect as created by a single spotlight may also be provided by nature: a light beam breaking through a cloud lighting up an alleyway or a forest path. Larger-area

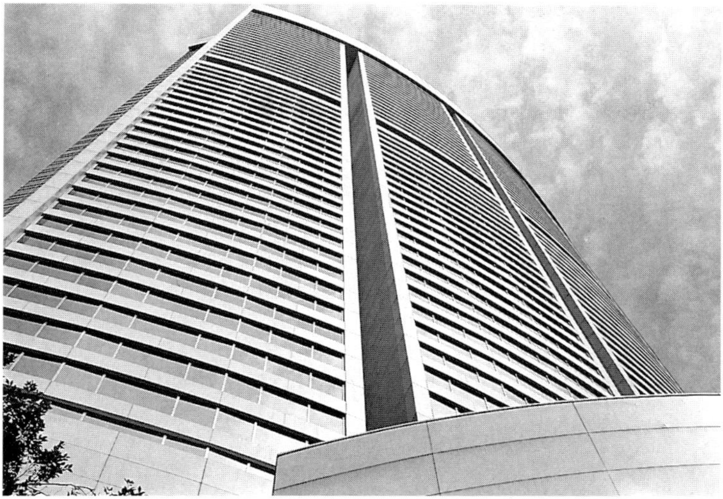

With the use of a super wide-angle lens, architectural photos can be given a unique interpretation with strong and dynamic lines.

contrasts of light and dark, such as a view through a window or a passage through a gate, may bring comparable results.

Colors, too, will influence image composition. Contrasting colors create visible differences, a person dressed in red on a green meadow will certainly stand out. Certain colors such as yellow are perceived by the human eye as particularly brilliant while darker tones such as dark-blue or violet are noticed less. In general, warm colors will move toward the foreground of a picture while cold colors will recede. This is particularly true for blue, a cool color. Often this fact is not given enough consideration when small subjects or still lifes are photographed. Light areas are more conspicuous than dark areas; therefore, light-colored spots in the background will draw the viewer's eyes. In the same way a sharp image is noticed more readily than one which is out of focus. Consequently, a photographic play with selective focus is particularly impressive. A sharp detail in the foreground with a blurred background is always appealing. A portrait in front of an out-of-focus background allows the eye to linger on the model. Selective focus is one of the secrets of good photography.

Graphic Form

A composition understood by the viewer will produce an interesting picture. A graphic image composition will enhance such an interpretation. Those who have an opportunity to view thousands of pictures in a high-volume photographic laboratory frequently get a strange impression when looking at pictures. Most appear as if the photographer had just discovered the subject and shot it in that exact situation. This is not the best possible shot. The interesting features of the scene have been presented in a photographically ineffective form because the photographer neglected a number of considerations. First, there is the difference in the way the camera and the eye view a subject. The human eye's perception is selective. Even if the eye is interested in a subject. triggered by optical form or color stimuli, it will only register one or the other. The surrounding area (to the right and left, to the front and back) of the selected subject will not be acknowledged voluntarily. Selective perception is how trees end up growing out of people's heads and too many uninteresting small subjects end up next to the main subject in photographs. The camera is just a recording tool which indiscriminately picks up everything it sees. Without a critical eye behind it, it records anything within its viewing angle.

A photographer's selective viewing will not be aided by the bright viewfinder image because the focusing system will only display that part of the subject plane which is in focus. The actual effect of the surroundings will normally not be visible. The viewing screen will only show the image as it would appear with the largest aperture and not with the actual later distribution of light and dark, or depth of field of the final image. Thus, image composition errors will be noticeable only when it is too late. The differences between perception and photographic reproduction are even greater. Let's take an example.

A viewer discovers a subject with a clear geometric form such as a door or a store window display. The door and the window have vertical and horizontal lines which form a 90 degree angle at the point of intersection. Nine out of ten times a reproduced image of the door will not have a measurable angle of 90 degree. The vertical lines or the horizontal lines are not parallel to the image edges. The geometric graphic image of the door has not been

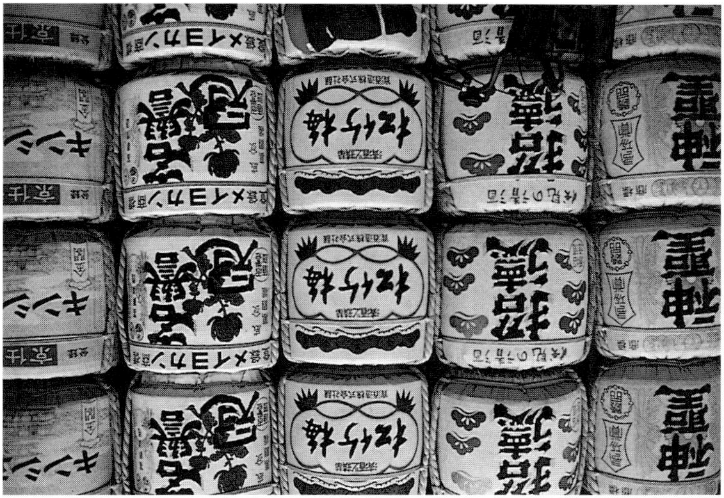

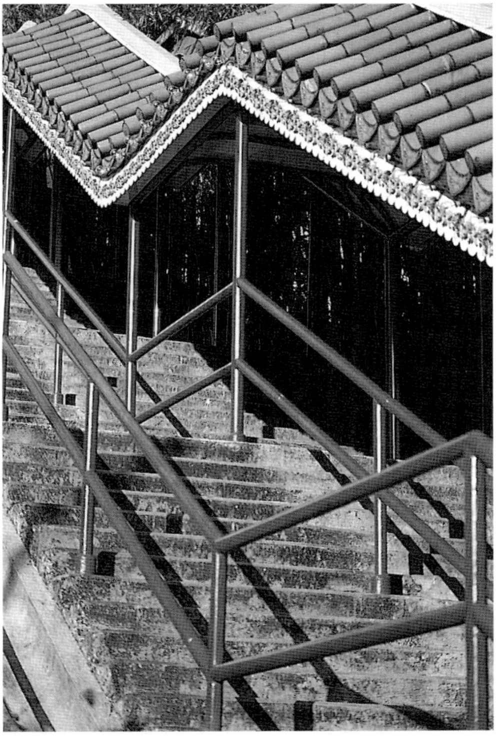

[UPPER] Repetition can be used to great effect. Even if the subject is unrecognizable, the graphic pattern in a photograph is attention-getting.

[LOWER] The dynamic, diagonal lines of an otherwise boring subject really give the image a feeling of rhythm and motion.

transferred correctly. This is not the camera's fault. It registers only optical impressions. Therefore, it is usually wrong to attempt to take pictures of the subject as seen by the human eye. The reverse approach is guaranteed to be more successful. View the subject as seen by the lens. This has a few significant advantages if one is capable of acting accordingly. It is better to simplify composition as much as possible. Wherever there is more detail in color or form, the image will be clearer and more extensive.

When composing potential photographs it is helpful to ask why an image is appealing in the first place. Some scenes are better left unphotographed. When an interesting subject is found, compositional elements can be considered. Assuming the subject is a door, an upright format may be chosen where the door frame is parallel to the image edge. In this case the camera is best located directly in front of the subject so that the subject plane and the film plane are parallel.

Location is Important

Interchangeable lenses make the REBEL cameras a versatile picture-taking tool which will turn a photographer's ideas into great pictures. Fortunately, the photographer is still needed; he or she must choose the subject and the location, as well the composition of the picture. The REBEL X/XS allows a photographer to decide whether to determine his or her own technical parameters (creative programs) or employ subject-specific programs. There are many well-known photographers who have never learned to take full advantage of their cameras' technical features. They don't need to because their creativity has been defined by the selection of their subjects, the location of the camera, framing and timing.

In this context interchangeable lenses offer important options. From a selected camera location, they produce the desired image segment at a desired scale of reproduction. For example, when the focal length is changed without changing location by zooming or changing the lens, the scale of reproduction will change relative to the new focal length. If the new focal length is shorter, the subject will be reproduced smaller and the imaging field will be larger. More information will be in the picture in exactly the ratio of the focal lengths to each other. Therefore, a focal length of 35mm will reproduce everything half as large as a 70mm setting; at 140mm the scale of reproduction is doubled. An object at a height of 2 mm at a focal length of 35mm will be four times taller at 140mm. If the location is not changed, an increasing focal value results in an increasing scale of reproduction while an increasingly smaller segment is taken out of the original subject. There are no "telephoto" or "wide-angle" lenses, only a change of the scale of reproduction. This concept is important if a given subject is to fill the frame. An understanding of these scale changes may also help prevent poor investments when lenses are purchased and, furthermore, allows the less experienced photographer to better evaluate the efficacy of a zoom lens. A 35-70mm zoom lens doubles the scale of reproduction; at 35 to 135mm the scale-change factor is almost four-fold.

Depth of Field

A change of the scale of reproduction without a change of the distance does not affect perspective but it does affect the depth of field. This is the subject space (in front of and behind the plane of focus) which is still perceived as being in focus. The greatest depth of field is offered by pinhole cameras which form the image by using a tiny opening and no lens at all. Also, the greater the scale of reproduction, the smaller the depth of field. Because a telephoto lens will produce a larger subject image, the subject space appearing in focus is reduced. Telephoto shots have less apparent depth of field. Conversely, a wide-angle lens will reduce the scale of reproduction and the depth of field will appear greater.

Since one cannot change the laws of optics, it is best to utilize them. There is, for example, a creative opportunity in selective focus. The photographer assures that only a small part of a picture is sharp and the remaining image area is dissolved into a blur. A wide-open telephoto lens aperture and a subject in the close-up range produce a most effective result. However, by taking advantage of the depth of field, it is also possible to create pictures leading the viewer to believe that everything in the foreground and background is in focus.

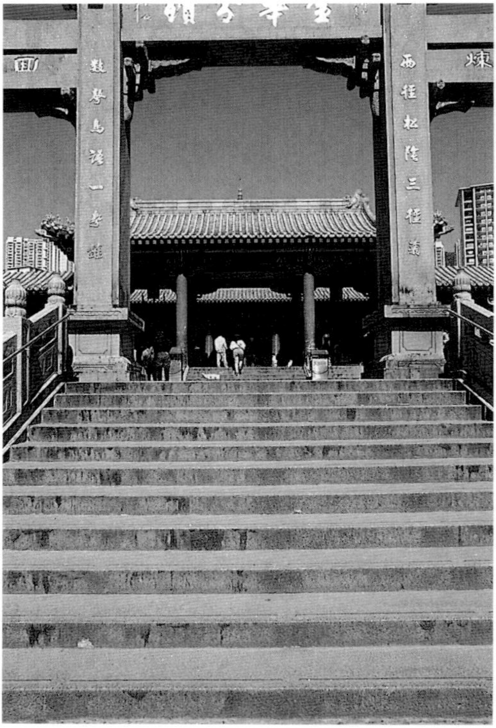

The small people in the background give scale to this photograph and help to exaggerate the height of the steps.

Photographers using a REBEL camera will experience the depth of field phenomenon only upon viewing the finished picture but may determine the spatial range to be in focus by utilizing the A-DEP program. The required aperture and resultant shutter speed values are computed and adjusted by the camera. Once the A-DEP setting is selected, the image frame is selected so that the starting and end points of the selected depth of field are within the wide AF metering field. The camera indicates in the viewfinder and on the display monitor the shutter speed and aperture required to realize the desired depth of field range. If these values are considered acceptable the shutter may be released. This is how easy picture-taking is made by the automatic depth of field feature.

If the smallest aperture value blinks in the viewfinder, the depth of field criteria desired by the photographer cannot be real-

By using a wide angle lens it is possible to include a large object in the foreground without eliminating the main subject in the background.

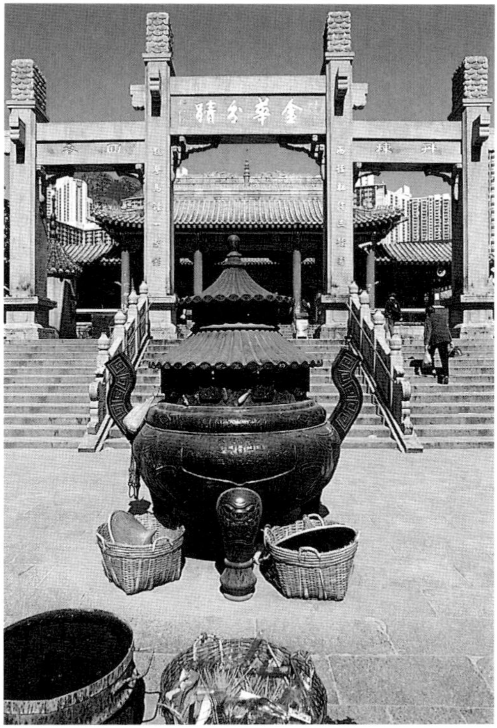

ized. Frequently, it is better to reduce the focal range in the foreground than to aim at a point located farther in the background. Depth of field is always distributed with 1/3 in front of the plane of focus and 2/3 behind the plane of focus.

Focal Length History

In its infancy, photography offered no distinctions among wide-angle, standard and telephoto lenses. In 1890 the first photographic Galilean telescope capable of magnifying a subject four times was introduced. However, only after Oskar Barnack invented small format, 35mm photography did it suddenly make sense to manufacture lenses with greatly varying focal lengths, as well as fast apertures, for photographic purposes.

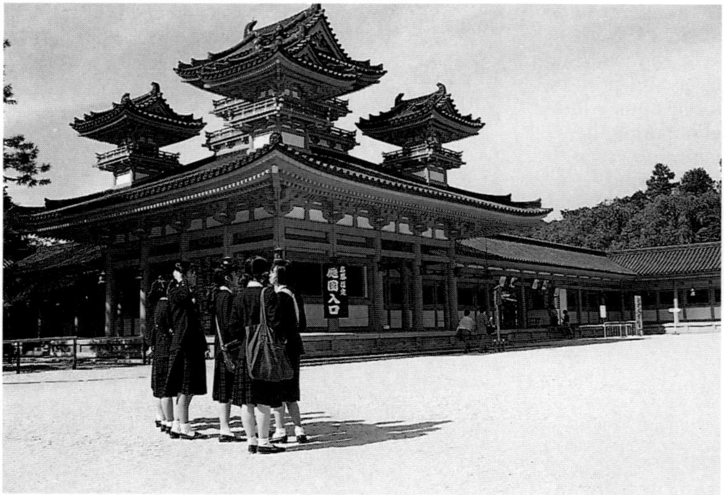

This photo has powerful converging vertical lines due to the low angle from which it was taken. The people in the foreground add life and scale to the image.

Along with the change from romantic photography to the new realism and the first successes of photojournalism came an increased demand for interchangeable lenses. In the 1960s, interchangeable lenses became a standard feature of 35mm SLR cameras.

Perspective

Regardless of whether lenses or focal length settings are changed, the perspective of a subject is the same for all shots provided the same camera position is used for taking pictures. Perspective changes only when the photographer changes location – the relationship between subject and background is altered. However, because questions inevitably arise regarding dynamic wide angle and space-constricting tele-perspective, here are a few comments concerning the concepts of perspective and distortion.

The vertical lines of a skyscraper photographed with the camera held at an oblique angle are viewed as falling lines and distorted. The lines of railroad tracks converging in the distance,

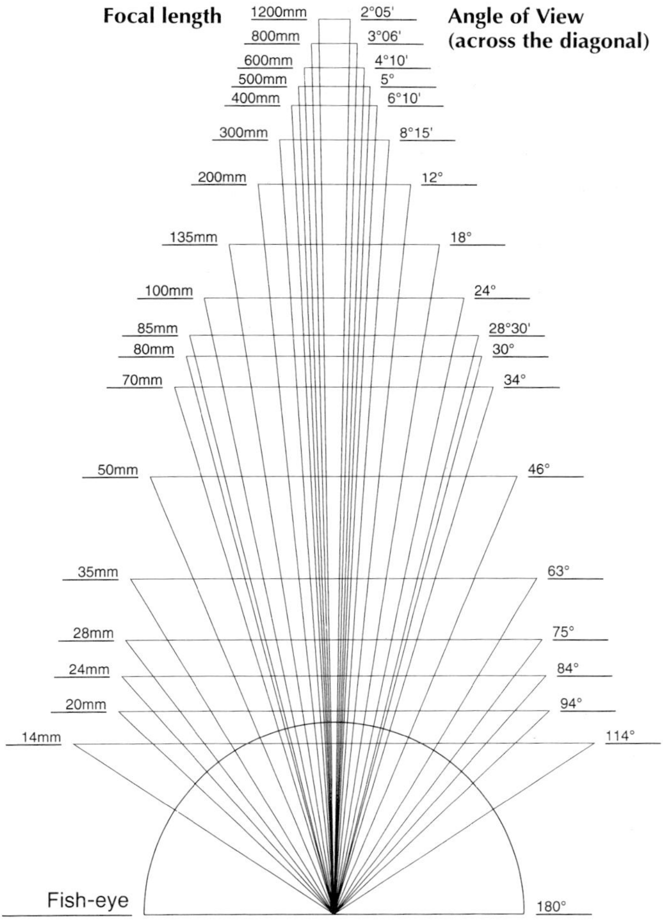

The chart shows the relationship between focal length and angle of view. The angle of view in all cases is measured on the diagonal of the image.

however, are accepted as normal even though both phenomena follow the same laws of linear perspective. In order to obtain true-to-life images following the law of linear perspective, artists used the precursor of the photographic apparatus, the camera obscura.

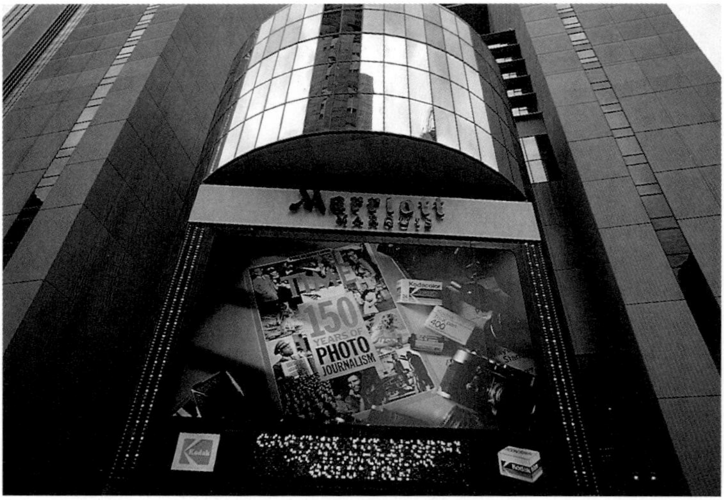

This view from below increases the effect of converging vertical lines and exaggerated perspective.

A truly distortion-free image can be achieved only when photographing a two-dimensional object. Three-dimensional subjects require a plane which is parallel to the camera. In both cases the surface to be reproduced must be exactly parallel to the film plane; otherwise trapezoidal or rhomboidal distortions occur. Of course, this also applies to a circle. In perspective reproduction it appears as an ellipse. The circle retains its circular form only when it is parallel to the film plane. Unless this parallel arrangement exists, the subject is distorted. Any miniaturization, reduction in length or convergence of parallel lines constitutes a perspective distortion. Only the photographer's or viewer's perception will differentiate what is considered natural (correct perspective) or abnormal (distorted).

By selecting the focal length and the camera-to-subject distance carefully, the photographer can modify the degree of distortion. The degree of distortion may be controlled and, therefore, this image composition technique is employed deliberately by creative photographers to compress image information and to increase the emotional content of their photographs.

When as many pictures as possible exhibiting different characteristics are to be taken of a subject it is easiest to just change the focal length and the shooting distance. Cutting the shooting distance as well as the focal length in half makes subjects appear in a steep perspective. The size in the foreground is emphasized and the vanishing lines appear to converge much sooner in the background. The effect is the opposite when both shooting distance and focal length are doubled. The foreground and background appear compressed. This effect may be achieved rather easily with a zoom lens; however, the shooting distance must be changed at the same time.

One effective utilization of perspective (provided the camera is held vertically) hinges on the realization that not only parallel lines are reproduced based on the laws of linear perspective. For example, many photographers will reach for a wide-angle lens when the busy life in a narrow alleyway is the subject. In most cases the result is boring because the wide-angle lens changes the relationship between the foreground and the background so that the close-up range is reproduced relatively large and the background extremely small. In this situation the photographer who wants to convey the mood and atmosphere of an over-crowded alleyway will step back farther and use a telephoto setting. The "space-constricting effect" (the recognizable linear perspective) suddenly fills the same alleyway with lots of people milling around. Each lens takes advantage of typical viewing habits which are affected greatly by the relationship between the shooting distance and between the subject and the background.

Subject Recommendations

Techniques and Equipment

This alphabetical list of subjects is an overview discussing the most favorable operating modes, required accessories and possible problems encountered in carrying out special photographic tasks. This list is meant to offer ideas and facilitate entry into fields previously unexplored. Of course, none of the tips and hints offered are obligatory because anything that applies to other creative activities applies here too. Only those who dare to be different produce the exceptional.

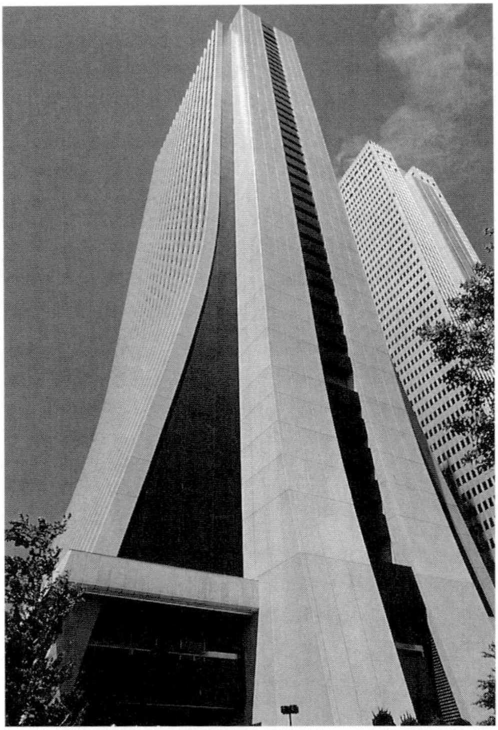

Left: Pointing the camera up at a subject will cause converging lines and distorted perspective which exaggerates its size.

Below: A wide angle lens has been used to exaggerate the perspective in this photo of a tuna auction.

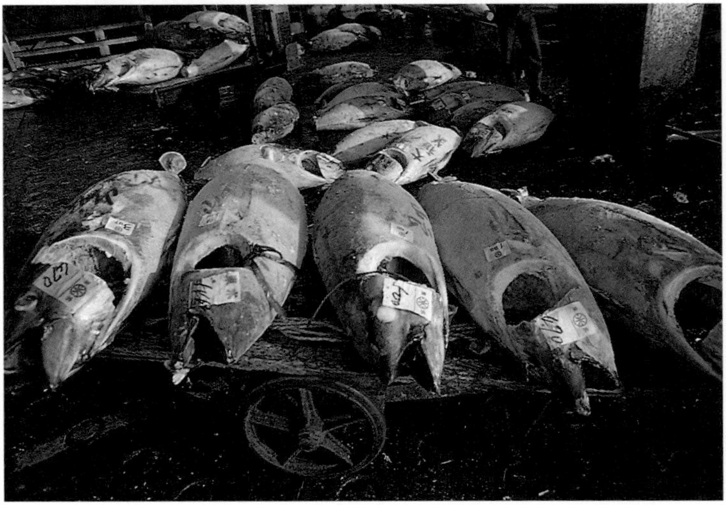

Architecture
This comprehensive field utilizes almost all picture-taking techniques and may be undertaken in almost any one of the REBEL's programs.

Tall buildings: Using a telephoto lens and positioning the camera farther from the subject will greatly decrease the convergence of the vertical lines in the picture. The optimal operating mode is the A-DEP program to ensure the entire building is in focus. See pages 51-52 for details on using the A-DEP program. The use of a small aperture for sufficient depth of field and a long lens may result in a shutter speed that is too slow to handhold the camera. Bring along a tripod or fast film.
Hallways, alleyways and streets: Use fully automatic mode with a telephoto lens. If the length of a hallway is to be emphasized, wide-angle lenses and A-DEP automatic mode are advised.
Stairs: Try to describe up and down movements with your finger in the air and consider this idea in your composition. Stairs, like bridges, should be on a diagonal in the picture.
Views through openings: Use the A-DEP mode in combination with multi-zone metering or, should pure outlines be desired, selective metering of the illuminated area of the subject.

Astronomical Photography
Exposure times of up to 4 hours with an aperture of f/8 and ISO 100 film are required when the sky is to follow the circular motion tracks of the stars in the picture. To define the approximate dimensions of the picture, a strong pocket flashlight is pointed at the dark sky and the image viewed through the camera viewfinder aligned with the emitted light beam. Of course a tripod is required, along with the accessory Remote Release (RS 60E3).

Babies
Certainly it is a matter of personal taste whether high-speed film and fast lenses are used to arrive at mood-enhanced pictures or whether flash pictures are to capture every detail. Fill flash techniques are compatible with both. The portrait program or the Green Zone setting are ideal. In both programs the REBEL's built-in flash unit will be activated automatically. A blinking aperture display signals an erroneous background exposure.

Boats

Boats should be shot at a slight angle from the top so that they are surrounded only by water in the picture or from the bottom to set them off against the sky. By using an underwater housing, pictures may even be taken from the water surface up. To do so, the REBEL X/XS may be set on fully automatic mode (green rectangle) or landscape program for shooting with a wide-angle lens. To create impressive images, the diagonal should be emphasized in action shots of sail and motor boats.

Coins and Jewelry

From the viewpoint of picture-taking technology, coins and jewelry are included under the topic Copy Work. However, an optimal gold-tone may be achieved only by mounting a polarizing filter to the camera and to the source of illumination. Circular polarizing filters must be used on REBEL series cameras. Linear polarizing film screens for light sources (lamps or flash units) are inexpensive and available from professional photo dealers.

Copy Work (Reproductions)

Copy work requires precise alignment of the original and the camera. The film plane and the original should be parallel. In addition, uniform illumination is required. Artificial light may be used because unwanted reflections occur frequently. Low-sensitivity, fine-grained films (ISO 25 to ISO 50) should be used for black-and-white photographs. Only line drawings require special copy film.

Automatic metering produces a correct exposure when the metered zone of the original is approximately 18% reflective. Therefore, a gray card should be used to determine the exposure values. The camera must be used in the manual mode. The Canon EF 50mm f/2.5 Macro lens is ideal for this purpose.

Families and Family Occasions

If available, a Speedlite should be used for bounce flash exposures. To avoid photographer stress, the camera should be set on the Green Zone and the rest should be left to automatic operation control. The camera ensures optimal exposure balance of flash and ambient light in bright rooms. If mood and atmosphere are to be dominant, special effects may be achieved with flash and time exposures in aperture priority (Av) mode. Small zoom lenses or focal lengths between 28 and 135mm are ideal. The higher the telephoto setting, the softer and better the depth of flash exposures. When wide-angle direct-flash shots are taken, only the adjusted shooting distance is illuminated optimally. The brightness loss in the depth is significant. Bounce flash and a large shooting distance should be used for subjects covering extended depth ranges such as people at a dining-room table.

Festivals

Subjects at carnivals or ethnic festivals are best captured with a snapshot setting (sports program) and zoom lenses with a focal length of up to 200mm. Backlit subjects should be photographed with fill flash. In the sports program mode the flash constitutes the main light and the background of the picture will remain dark.

Fireworks

A tripod, focal lengths between 100 and approximately 200mm, a "bulb" time exposure and a standard aperture of f/5.6 are a good start. Wait for about 3 to 5 bursts of fireworks before closing the shutter again. Pictures become most effective with clear and generous silhouettes of houses, trees or people.

Fog

Landscapes with a clear foreground are suitable for the ambiance of fog. In aperture priority (Av) mode the aperture is preselected and a plus correction made. The landscape program prefers small apertures and should therefore be used only in the wide-angle range.

Flowers

Here the close-up program is used, preferably with a telephoto or zoom lens with a focal length over 100mm, or one of the two Canon macro lenses.

Note: When the scale of reproduction is the same, the depth of field range remains the same, regardless of the focal length.

Close-ups are best taken with the Canon EF Macro 50mm f/2.5 lens in close-up program mode. More exciting from a creative viewpoint is the telephoto range which becomes a macro range in all EF zoom lenses. In programmed autoexposure mode (subject-specific automatic mode) shadow or backlit areas are filled in automatically. The flash should remain energized in Av, Tv and M modes.

Important: A tripod and patience are recommended, also the Remote Release RS-60E3 for the REBEL X/XS.

Groups

Use the A-DEP snapshot program when people, as well as the background, are to be in focus. Fill flash is not possible in this mode. If fill flash must be used, it is better to switch to Green Zone mode because then fill flash will be added automatically.

Landscapes

REBEL cameras have a separate program for landscapes. It is adapted mainly to wide-angle lens shots. When telephoto lenses are used, it is best to use the Green Zone mode.

When choosing subjects in a landscape, special attention must be paid to the foreground and to appropriate staggering of image areas with respect to the center and the background. Multi-zone metering produces best results.

Lightning

Proceed as described in the section discussing fireworks, however, do not select exposure times exceeding 30 seconds. Sometimes lighting flashes last longer than 1/10 seconds, therefore, the use of a tripod makes sense. A minus correction to 1 or even 2 is recommended, as well as the smallest possible apertures in order to achieve an automatic time exposure (Av). Recommended image composition: landscape in the lower third and sky in the remainder of the picture.

Macro Exposures

All close-up shots are easiest when the REBEL's close-up program is activated and EF 50mm f/2.5 Macro, EF 100mm f/2.8 Macro, as well as all other EF zoom lenses are used. Photographers who want to get closer to the subject than 1:1, will want to use bellows (not yet available from Canon). Aperture Priority easily permits shots with a reproduction ratio of 2:1.

Night Exposures

Night exposures always require a minus correction (at least when slide films are used) when they are supposed to appear to be taken at night. The best "night exposures" are made at dusk.

Portraits

The Canon REBELs have their own portrait program. For impressive pictures the subject is approached by using the telephoto feature of a zoom lens, close enough that either only the head or the head and the torso fill the picture. The focus is set on the eyes and held by light pressure on the release button.

Sports

The high art of snapshot photography may be practiced particularly well at smaller events. Almost any type of sport has an ideal observation point. At automobile, motorcycle or bicycle races it is the curves. These may be mastered particularly impressively by using A-DEP mode and continuous film advance. Field games are best observed near the goal: The sports program or Tv mode are used here. When using the latter, a shutter speed of at least 1/1000 should be preselected. For shots at the start and finish lines in track and field events the sports program mode will produce the best results when competitors run toward the camera.

Television

Pictures taken of the television screen require a tripod. The screen should fill the picture as much as possible. The shutter speed must not be faster than 1/30 second. Switch off room light to avoid interfering reflections.

Water

This relatively difficult subject often requires long exposure times because motion blurs accentuating the water's flow are desirable when pictures are taken of brooks, rapids or waterfalls. This requires a tripod and a series of shots beginning with the smallest aperture and aperture priority (Av) to test the effect.

On calm days lakes, ponds and canals frequently provide brilliant reflections which produce the most intense colors with the sun at the photographer's back and polarizing filters (to intensify the effect). Wider-angle lenses allow photographing closer to the water, in landscape mode.

Weddings
Here everything may be photographed in Green Zone automatic mode and with flash (Canon Speedlite is recommended for soft illumination). Groups may also be photographed using this automatic mode. A separate program is available for portraits. Fill flash should be used for exposures in the shade.

When taking telephoto exposures a photographer should remember that telephoto shots are always better illuminated. In any event, it is advisable to wait a few extra moments, after the flash-ready indicator has lit up. The aperture should be opened and set to f/5.6. Selecting a smaller aperture restricts the shooting range of the flash too much.

Winter
Grazing light gives snow-covered fields more depth. Backlighting is the most effective but also most difficult type of lighting. In high altitudes a polarizing filter will produce an almost black sky. Therefore, a skylight filter should be used to prevent excessive blue coloration in the shadow areas. Manual selective metering using a substitute gray surface or Kodak Gray Card is recommended.

Photographs taken while snow is falling require extremely slow shutter speeds. A large foreground and a relatively dark background are desirable. Exposures of snow-covered fields taken at dusk or night are particularly effective. With aperture priority (Av) they are easy to photograph. Another option is a series of exposures with minus corrections only.

10 Tips for Better Travel Pictures

1. Make plans and check equipment, especially batteries, in advance.
2. Try to shoot evocative rather than just illustrative pictures. Do not confine yourself to strict documentation. Try to capture moods.
3. Learn to observe. Often patience is more important than any staging. Hold a slide frame in front of your eye to learn to see photographically.
4. Move as close as possible to the subject.

5. Instead of capturing extensive exposure series using the same framing, lift the subject out by taking shots from different perspectives.
6. Do not just change the focal length. Change the distance and hence the perspective. Try to take photographs from the perspective of a frog or bird.
7. Force yourself to see image compositions and graphic relationships consciously. Only those who master the rules of classic image composition will be able to break them.
8. Always aspire for the best optical and technical quality in your pictures. To achieve this, examine the viewfinder image carefully. Use a tripod or monopod, polarization filters and fill flash.
9. Take pictures in extreme lighting and weather situations and at unconventional times of the day such as early in the morning or at dusk.
10. Always ask permission before taking pictures of people.

Canon EF Lenses

Canon is one of the few camera manufacturers who have always considered their own complete line of lenses crucial to high-quality photography. It is not surprising that pioneer efforts in this field are frequently connected with the Canon name. This includes technical equipment features which have become quality concepts in lens construction. For example, Canon has pioneered such ideas as internal focusing, lenses of calcium fluorite and aspherical lens surfaces, both ground and polished and glass molded aspherics.

Although still technically not discontinued, the era of the Canon FD lenses ended with the introduction of the first EOS 650 in 1987. There were things that the Canon lens designers wanted to do which simply could not be done within the constraints imposed by the FD mount, primarily due to the relatively narrow diameter of the FD mount itself. Certain high speed lenses would require rear glass elements which were too large in diameter to fit into FD mounts. Also, Canon realized that mechanical lens linkages were simply not accurate or durable enough for the lenses of the future.

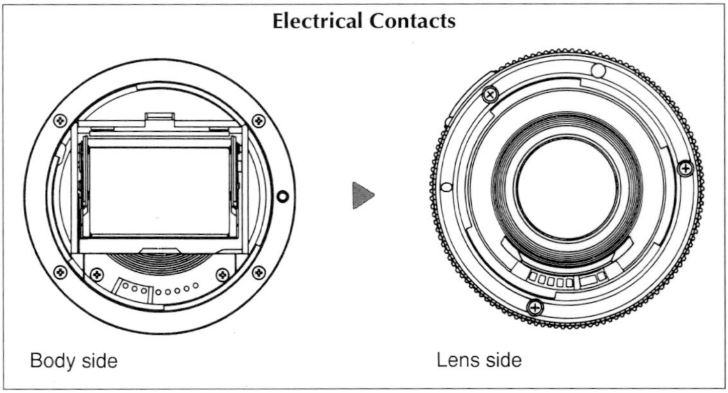

This drawing shows the lens bayonet mount of the camera (left) and the rear of the lens (right). Note the electrical contacts on both which mate when the lens is mounted.

The Canon EF Mount

The result of all of this was that Canon's engineers decided to make a complete break with FD mount tradition and introduce a totally new lens mount. The Canon EF mount, which is much larger in diameter, features a simple bayonet design and utilizes no mechanical linkages between the camera and the lens. Not only do these gold-plated contacts convey information between the camera and the lens, they also carry the electrical power for the autofocus motor and the diaphragm motor, eliminating the need for a separate battery compartment in the lens. Canon concluded early in their research that the autofocus motors belonged in the lenses, where the motors could be placed as closely as possible to what they actually moved, and each lens could be fitted with a motor best suited to its needs and specifications. This has resulted in several different types of motors used in EF lenses.

The first type of motor Canon designed for EOS lenses was the Arc Form Drive (AFD). This is a very traditional small electrical motor but with its components arranged in an arc shape so that it will easily fit into lens barrels. While the AFD worked very well, it wasn't quite fast enough and has been replaced now with a new generation of motor.

Because of special design considerations, one Canon EF lens uses a traditional small electrical motor with a long drive shaft. This was the only sort of motor Canon could fit to the 100mm f/2.8 macro lens which has an exceptionally long extension. This is the only EF lens which does not use AFD or one of the two types of USM technology.

Ultrasonic Motors

The most advanced motor now being used is hardly a motor at all in the normal sense of the word. It is simply two metal rings with special surfaces on their mating sides. These rings are held in contact by springs and one is fixed to the lens barrel while the other is free to turn. An electrically excited piezoelectric crystal acts as an oscillator at ultrasonic frequencies to vibrate the rings. Because of the nature of their surfaces, the standing wave generated in the rings causes them to rotate against one another. Since one ring is fixed in place, the other one turns and its direction of rotation and speed are controlled by the frequency and intensity of the wave generated. This unusual device is referred to by Canon as an Ultrasonic Motor (USM).

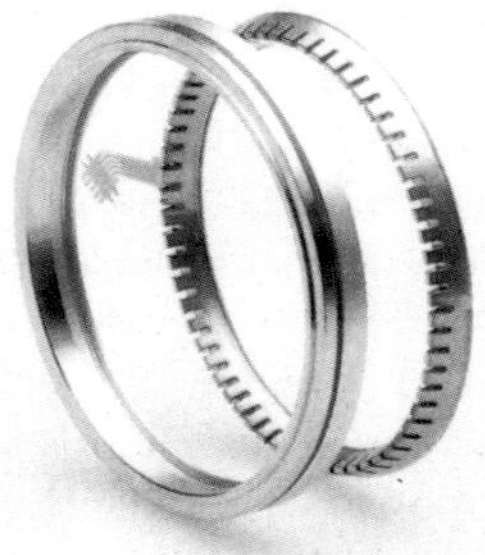

Ring-type USM motor. This motor is the fastest and quietest, but is expensive to manufacture. This technology uses a high-frequency vibration to drive the lens.

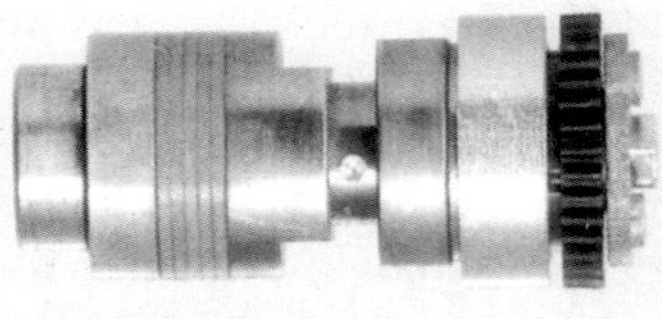

The newer Micro-USM operates on the same principles, but is suited to mass production and is much less expensive. It is being used in place of AFD motors on all newer Canon EF lenses.

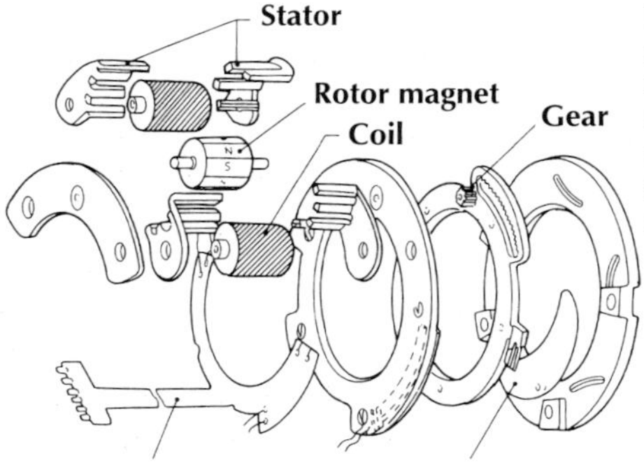

This diagram shows the construction of Canon's unique electrically-driven diaphragm mechanism, which uses stepper motors for precision and repeatability of aperture setting.

Initially the manufacture of USM motors was extremely cost-intensive and quite complex, therefore, relatively small numbers were built, and these motors were first used only in professional lenses. Continued research on USM technology has resulted in a second generation of USM which is much less expensive to make and much smaller in diameter. These are now replacing the original AFD motors as new lenses are designed and old lenses redesigned. Ultimately Canon intends to have all EOS lenses powered by USM drives.

The advantages of these special ultrasonic motors are that they permit automatic focusing in almost all fields of professional photography. These motors do not have a clutch to prevent an immediate start and thus, are capable of a rapid response to even the most difficult automatic focusing problems. Because an inaudible frequency of 20,000 Hertz is responsible for the lens' non-coupled direct drive, there is no virtually noise. This is a big plus for photographers who do not want to call attention to themselves. Also, USM technology does not require the photographer to change settings on the lens for manual focusing mode.

EF Lens Performance

At the time the first EOS models appeared in 1987 thirteen EF lenses were announced. In the interim 30, more EF lenses have been introduced. The total number is not surprising, and the high proportion of zoom lenses covering focal lengths from 20 to 300mm is impressive. Almost half of the zoom lenses and numerous fixed focal lengths in extreme performance ranges are of professional caliber (marked L). Canon's optical systems in general and the EF lenses in particular are so amazing that possible image aberrations and their causes need be given relatively little attention.

The considerable challenge to optics engineers requires that they reduce aberrations appropriate to the problem to be solved by the lens, thus preventing residual aberrations occurring with proper use from being conspicuous. Technical and scientific use and many professional applications require not only good quality but best quality. In these cases, it is important that maximum performance quality of lens and camera are noted, hence the L designation.

Care of Lenses

Although the electrical contacts on the back of EF lenses are much less delicate than pins and levers, they still should be protected from environmental dust and dirt and particularly from fingerprints when the lenses are not on the cameras. That is the purpose of rear lens caps. Always put one on each lens the minute it is taken off the camera, and keep it there until just before that lens is again mounted onto the camera. The same goes for the rear glass of the lens, which is easily scratched. Similarly, front caps should be left on all lenses when they are not actually in use.

If you do get dirt or dust onto the front or rear glass of your lens you can easily and safely remove it. First simply see if it will blow off. Camera dealers sell small squeeze bulb blowers for this purpose or you can buy an ear syringe from a drugstore. Gentle puffs of air will usually get rid of most dust and grit. If you encounter stubborn material, then you may resort to the brush, which should always be a soft "camel's hair" (actually made from squirrel's tail hair) brush. Use this in a sweeping circular pattern starting at the center and working to the edges. Hold the lens either sideways or with the glass surface to be cleaned pointing down so that gravity will carry away the offending matter. Then try the blower again. This should work.

If you still don't have success, resort to lens cleaning tissue or a special lens chamois and wipe gently, again in a circular motion from the center. If even this does not work, moisten the tissue with a drop or two of lens cleaning fluid and try again, exerting only very gentle pressure. If none of these work, carry the lens to a professional.

Don't be a fanatic about dust, however. A few specks of dust on the front of your lens, a few on the rear, or even a few on the inside glass elements will not have a noticeable effect on your photos. Reasonable cleanliness is important, not rigidly clinging to the idea that a single dust speck is ruination.

Lens Characteristics

Lenses are characterized by two parameters: maximum aperture (or lens speed) and focal length. Maximum aperture indicates the largest opening available on the lens. The aperture opening controls the amount of light that passes through the lens. In effect, a lens aperture works similar to the eye's iris. Aperture openings are expressed as f/stops which are actually fractions. For example, f/16 is a smaller aperture opening than f/11. Therefore f/2.8 is a relatively large aperture. An aperture of f/2 is even larger yet. By opening the lens one full f/stop, twice the amount of light passes to the film. The amount of light is cut in half whenever the aperture is closed down to the next higher f/stop number (ie. from f/11 to f/16).

The second lens parameter, always indicated in milimeters these days, expresses focal length. This is usually considered the most important lens reference value and it is independent of any film format. Inside each lens assembly light rays coming from infinity are bent so that they meet in a point of focus. The distance from the rear-nodal point (optical center of the lens) to the film plane is defined as focal length. The image angle covered by a lens is a function of focal length. A larger image angle becomes a wide angle, a small image angle becomes a telephoto, and a variable image angle is characteristic of a zoom lens.

The Canon term EF stands for electronic focus. It characterizes every interchangeable lens that is compatible with Canon EOS-system cameras. Some of these lenses may also be used on Canon camcorders and digital still cameras. L identifies ultra-professional lenses and USM indicates that a lens is focused by an ultrasonic motor. The abbreviation TS-E identifies Tilt-and-Shift lenses with Electrical diaphragm operation, and Macro indicates that a lens is specifically designed for the close-up range allowing significant magnification.

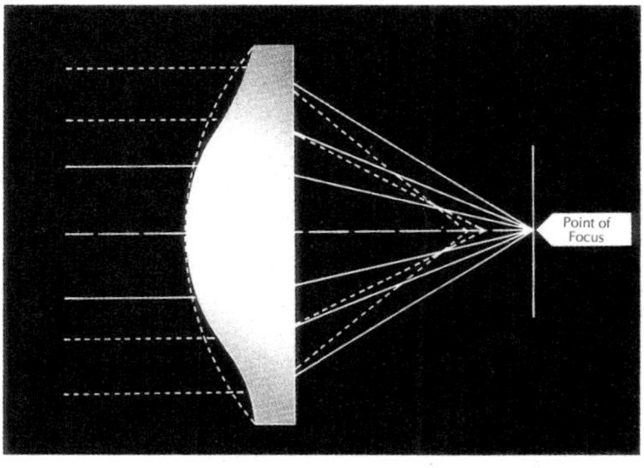

Aspherical lens elements have a non-spherical curvature which allows them to focus light rays striking all parts of the lens surface at a common plane.

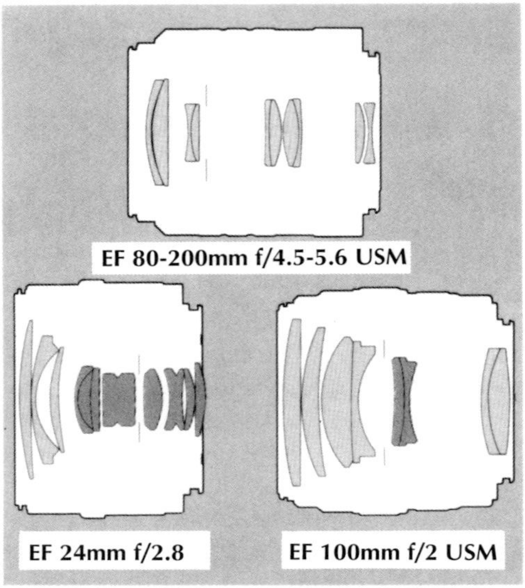

Cross-section views of some typical Canon EF lenses.

The Impressive List of Canon EF Lenses

Fixed Lenses

Canon EF 14mm f/2.8 L USM
Canon EF 15mm f/2.8 Fisheye
Canon EF 20mm f/2.8 USM
Canon EF 24mm f/2.8
Canon TS-E 24mm f/3.5 L
Canon EF 28mm f/2.8
Canon EF 35mm f/2.0
Canon TS-E 45mm f/2.8
Canon EF 50mm f/1.0 L USM
Canon EF 50mm f/1.4 USM
Canon EF 50mm f/1.8 II
Canon EF 50mm f/2.5 Macro
Canon EF 85mm f/1.2 L USM
Canon EF 85mm f/1.8 USM
Canon TS-E 90mm f/2.8

Canon EF 100mm f/2.0 USM
Canon EF 100mm f/2.8 Macro
Canon EF 135mm f/2.8 Soft Focus
Canon EF 200mm f/1.8 L USM
Canon EF 200mm f/2.8 L USM
Canon EF 300mm f/2.8 L USM
Canon EF 300mm f/4.0 L USM
Canon EF 400mm f/5.6 USM
Canon EF 400mm f/2.8 L USM
Canon EF 500mm f/4.5 L USM
Canon EF 600mm f/4.0 L USM
Canon EF 1200mm f/5.6 L USM

Zoom Lenses
Canon EF 20-35mm f/2.8 L
Canon EF 20-35mm f/3.5 - 4.5 USM
Canon EF 28-70mm f/3.5 - 4.5 II
Canon EF 28-80mm f/2.8 - 4.0 L USM
Canon EF 28-80mm f/3.5-5.6 USM
Canon EF 35-70mm f/3.5
Canon EF 35-105mm f/4.5 - 5.6
Canon EF 35-105mm f/4.5 - 5.6 USM
Canon EF 35-135mm f/4.0 - 5.6 USM
Canon Superzoom EF 35-350mm f/3.5 - 5.6 L USM
Canon EF 50-200mm f/3.4 - 4.5
Canon EF 50-200mm f/3.4 - 4.5 L
Canon EF 70-210mm f/3.5 - 4.5 USM
Canon EF 75-300mm f/4.0 - 5.6
Canon EF 75-300mm f/4.0 - 5.6 USM
Canon EF 80-200mm f/2.8 L
Canon EF 80-200mm f/4.5 - 5.6
Canon EF 80-200mm f/4.5 - 5.6 USM
Canon EF 100-200mm f/4.5 A
Canon EF 100-300mm f/4.5 - 5.6 USM
Canon EF 100-300mm f/5.6 L

Three Lenses for the Beginner

The beginner is faced with a very difficult choice. With so many lenses to pick from, so many of them seemingly similar, how do you decide which lenses to buy? As a first point, I will recommend taking care to shop with a reputable photo dealer. Beware of bargain-priced camera outfits which are advertised something like, *"Canon EOS Rebel XS with three lenses....only..."* and at a ridiculously low price. The old rule applies, know what you are buying and whom you are buying it from.

It used to be that most 35mm cameras were sold with a 50mm lens as a standard package. This was so much the case that the 50mm came to be known as the "normal lens" and is still often referred to that way. Canon does indeed offer three different "normal" lenses for the EOS cameras, 50mm f/1.0, 50mm f/1.4 and 50mm f/1.8, and for some photographers they are the right choice. More often today photographers are finding that they are happier with a "normal zoom". My personal "normal" lens is the 28-80mm f/2.8-4.0 L USM, which I have used for several years. It

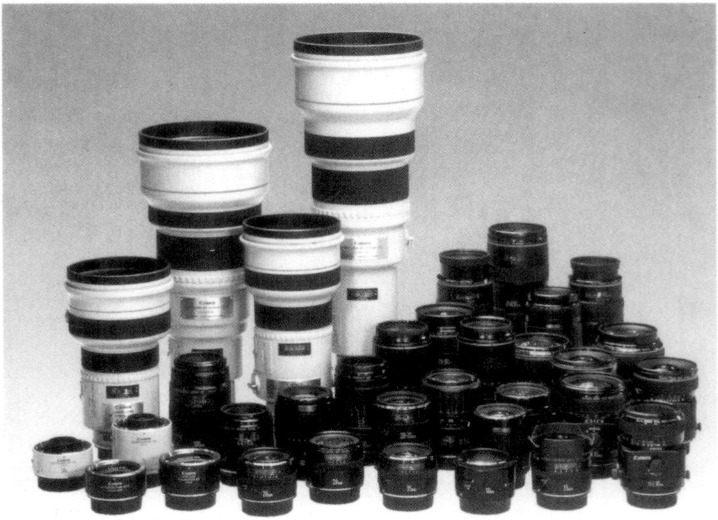

From extreme wide-angle to extreme telephoto, Canon makes more than forty different EF lenses.

is an expensive lens, admittedly, but it is incredibly sharp and replaces three fixed lenses at minimum: 28mm, 50mm, 80mm.

My three lens location kit would ideally consist of 20-35mm f/2.8 L, 28-80mm f/2.8-4.0 L USM, and 100-300mm f/5.6

L series lenses. What is this L? Canon makes two separate series of EF lenses which might be thought of as standard and super. The L series, which stands for Luxury, are their absolute top of the line professional lenses. All of them have superlative performance characteristics, and all of them are expensive. But if your goal is to buy absolutely the best possible optics, nothing else can touch them.

A more realistic three lens kit would consist of the lower priced 20-35mm f/3.5-4.5 USM, the 35-105mm f/4.5-5.6 USM, and the standard 100-300mm f/4.5-5.6 USM. These lenses are all very good, and many professionals do use them. In the case of the first two, the economy of price is achieved by making them slower, but this also makes them smaller and lighter which is an advantage. In the case of the 100-300mm, the difference is that the L uses very exotic glass types and has a higher degree of color correction. Whether you would notice a difference or not depends on your own critical standards and what your photos are used for.

Whether the slower and less expensive wide angle and normal zooms will meet your needs depends entirely on the type of photography you do. If you habitually work outdoors in bright light, they would certainly be adequate. If your forte is low light photos by available light, then you would want the faster lenses and might bypass zooms altogether in favor of the very fast fixed focal length lenses. If you do a lot of close-up work, one of the two macro lenses may make more sense to you. The important thing is to know in advance what it is that you want to do photographically and then to match the lenses you buy to the tasks. It makes no sense to buy a particular lens just because it will impress people if you have no earthly use for such a lens!

Normal Lenses

Normal lenses have a focal length corresponding approximately to the size of the film diagonal which, in the 35mm format, is about 43mm. Consequently, all the lenses within this class feature focal lengths between 40 and approximately 60mm. A standard of 50mm has been preferred since the beginning of the 35mm era due to manufacturing and optical considerations.

Four lenses having a focal length of 50mm are available for the EOS Rebel cameras and other EOS models, but only three are so-called normal lenses. The fourth is a macro lens for a particularly large close-up range.

All four lenses have an angle of view of 46 degrees across the diagonal. Image effects achieved with these lenses correspond more or less to what the eye perceives. Even though zoom lenses within the normal lens range are used more and more frequently in place of fixed focal length lenses, the latter still continue to be important. The most obvious advantages to standard lenses are low weight and lens speed (maximum aperture).

Canon EF 50mm f/1.8 II: The maximum aperture difference between a small zoom lens and this fixed lens is almost two stops - a significant difference between the EF 50mm f/1.8 and a zoom lenses with this focal length! The normal lens focuses as close as 18 inches (45 cm) and therefore covers a reproduction scale of 1:15.

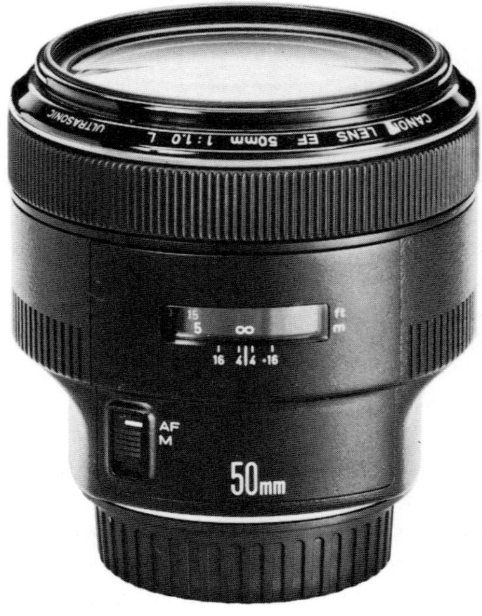

The EF 50mm f/1.0 L is an unusually fast specialty lens designed for low-light photography.

A 50mm comparison: The EF 50mm f/1.8 left, versus the EF 50mm f/2.5 Compact Macro.

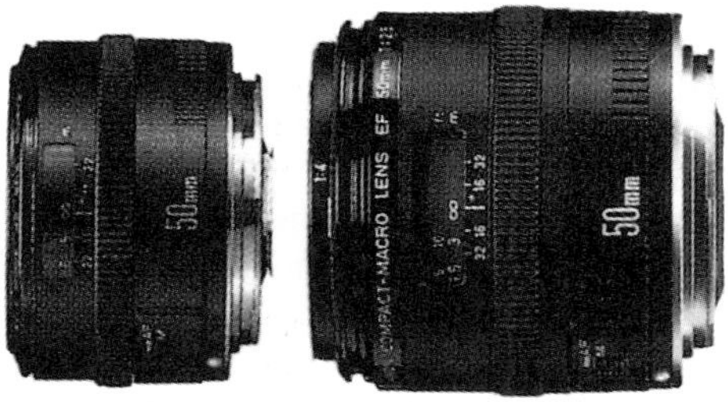

The optical system consists of 6 elements in 5 groups. The lens has has an AFD motor for automatic focus but may be manually focused as well. The focusing speed from infinity to the shortest distance setting is 0.44 seconds. The lens may be closed to an aperture of f/22. The filter diameter is 52mm. The front ring does not rotate during focusing which is important when using polarizing and effect filters. The standard lens has a length of only 1.7 inches (42.5 cm) and weighs under 7 ounces (190 g).

Canon EF 50mm f/1.4 USM: This lens has a maximum aperture of f/1.4, half a stop faster than f/1.8. It is convenient for taking pictures at the theater or circus, as well as in museums, churches or other places with low-light conditions. With high-speed film, there may not even be a need for flash. This lens provides a very bright viewfinder image, high resolution, high contrast and excellent color balance; it has capabilities not even remotely met by many standard zoom lenses, and its performance is exceptional even at full aperture.

Comprised of 7 elements in 6 groups, with a close-up limit of 18 inches (45 cm), the lens has a length of 2 inches (5 cm) and weighs only 10 ounces (290 g). Thanks to the ultrasonic micromotor this lens can focus extremely quickly, making practically no sound. It also allows manual adjustment without deactivation of the AF function.

Canon EF 50mm f/1.0 L USM: Currently, this is the only autofocus standard 50mm focal length lens with a photographer's dream aperture of f/1.0. The lens system consists of 11 elements in 9 groups having a total weight of just over 35 ounces (1000 g). Its optical system includes two aspherical elements and special elements made of ultra-low dispersion glass with a high index of refraction. The main advantage of this optical system is high quality with a very large aperture. The lens is one stop faster than the 50mm f/1.4 lens.

The lens focuses down to 24 inches (60 cm). When shooting objects at a distance, i.e. a street scene, the lens' focusing range can be limited. This allows the system to focus more rapidly in a shorter, usable range. Focusing the long distance from infinity to 24 inches (60 cm) takes exactly one second.

A maximum aperture of f/1.0 certainly is not a requirement for everybody; however, those shooting subjects in difficult lighting conditions will be aided by this lens. The depth of field with an aperture of 1.0 and a shooting distance of exactly 24 inches (60 cm) begins at 23.8 inches (59.5 cm.) and ends at 24.1 inches (60.3 cm).

The lens has a length of 3.2 inches (81.5 mm), a maximum diameter of 3.6 inches (91.5 mm) and a filter thread of 72mm. Its weight is just over 34 ounces (985 g). The smallest subject area (reproduction ratio 1:11) is 9.1 x 13 inches (22.8 x 34.2 cm).

Fisheye and Super Wide-Angle Lenses

The days when an image taken with a fisheye lens brought gasps of astonishment to an audience are long gone. Everyone has seen the fisheye effect, in fact far too much in my opinion. This is not to say that we should renounce all use of fisheye lenses, just that we should use them judiciously. Canon's 15mm f/2.8 fisheye for EOS is one of the best of these special lenses. Fisheye lenses are examples of barrel distortion gone mad, and totally uncorrected. The only straight lines which will be rendered straight are those passing through the exact center of the image.

Canon has chosen to give us a full-frame fisheye, not one of the sort which produces a small circular image in the center of the film. This one fills up the frame and provides approximately a 180 degree view diagonally from corner to corner. This can be used to produce very exaggerated perspectives in views of interiors, and can also be used for sweeping panoramas of landscapes in which the distortion will not be obvious unless the lens is tilted up or down. My friend George Lepp, the well known nature photographer, tells me he uses the fisheye for very close flower photos, sometimes getting all the way down on the ground and looking up at the flower from below. Don't be afraid to try unusual things like this, the photos may be spectacular and certainly will get you to thinking about ways to use unusual perspectives.

Perhaps not as spectacular as photos taken with fisheye lenses, photos taken with ultra wide-angle lenses can still be remarkably striking. These lenses lend themselves to providing unusual perspectives and opening up spaces indoors as well as outdoors. In the area of ultra wide-angle lenses Canon has two lenses of fixed focal length and two zoom lenses. These are the EF 14mm f/2.8 L, EF 20mm f/2.8, EF 20-35mm f/2.8 L and EF 20-35mm f/3.5-4.5.

You may well wonder what distinguishes the 14mm from the fisheye, but the answer is quite simple. While the fisheye design allows barrel distortion to go uncorrected, distorting straight lines into arcs as they become farther from the image center, the 14mm is a rectilinear design with maximum correction for distortion. In other words, if aligned carefully this lens will provide images without barrel distortion. Any wide-angle lens will produce distortion if tilted up or down, but rectilinear ones will have no distortion if aligned carefully. For this purpose, an accessory bubble level with attaches to the camera hot shoe is a useful accessory, and readily available from better photo shops.

One of the most important advantages of ultra wide-angle lenses is that with them you can take in large areas from very short distances, and this is particularly an advantage indoors in cramped surroundings. These lenses open up such surroundings, making them appear more spacious. Advertising photos of auto interiors are generally taken with wide angle lenses for this reason; viewed through a 20mm, the cramped cockpit of a Lambourghini Diablo looks like the spacious interior of a Mercedes limousine! Don't think that these lenses are just for indoors, however, they are also very useful out and about in the city. Just don't tip the lens up to get the tops of the buildings in, the exaggerated perspective of an ultra wide-angle lens makes the buildings look as if they are falling down!

Canon EF 15mm f/2.8 Fisheye: The Canon EF Fisheye focuses down to 8 inches (20 cm). This value does not represent the distance to the front of the lens but the distance to the film plane. Due to this extreme perspective and the small scale of reproduction this focal length features extreme depth of field so that not even the

The Canon EF 15mm f/2.8, a fisheye with a 180° angle of view.

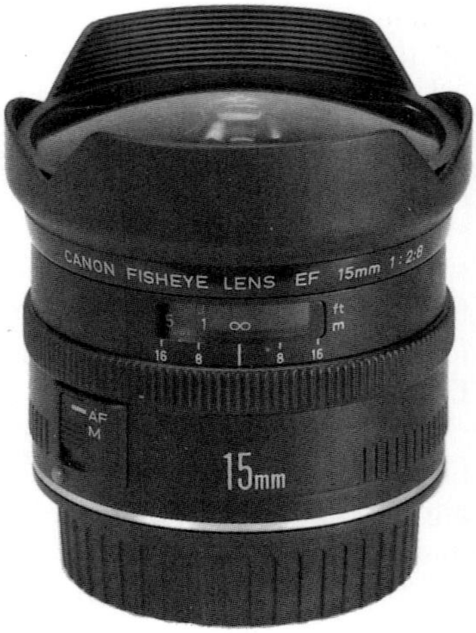

smallest aperture of f/22 need be set when everything - from a few inches to the horizon - in the picture is to appear sharp.

The built-in lens shade does not accommodate a standard screw-in filter. Therefore, the lens has a special snap-in filter mount. Filter gels, such as Kodak Wratten® filters, must be cut to a size of 31 x 31 mm and inserted in the filter mount. From an optical viewpoint, it is of no consequence whether a filter is mounted in front of the lens or within the lens.

The optical system is comprised of 8 elements in 7 groups. The AFD focusing from infinity to 8 inches (20 cm) is exactly 0.36 seconds. The smallest subject area is 6.9 x 10.3 inches (17.1 x 25.7 cm). The lens length is 2.4 inches (6.2 cm) and the weight is 12 ounces (339 g).

Canon EF 14mm f/2.8 L USM: This super wide-angle lens continues the old FD lens tradition and expands the current maximum 20mm super wide-angle range down to a fabulous 14mm. The most amazing feature of the new EF 14mm lens is the USM motor. Until now Canon has preferred the AFD motor for the wide-angle range because the distance transfer could work with different shooting ranges with different effects; this allowed fine-tuning in the close-up range. If, however, the 20-35mm zoom is described as having fast AF adjustment, extremely fast must be used to describe this lens.

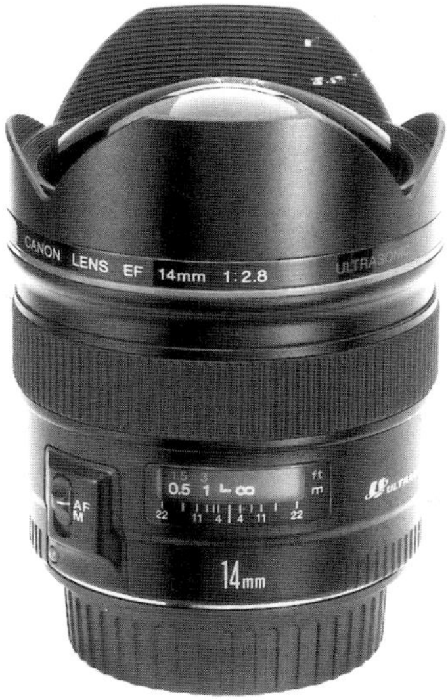

Canon's EF 14mm f/2.8, a very sharp, high-speed, super wide-angle lens.

The super wide angle exhibits surprisingly little vignetting (although some is still evident in this focal length range). Also, typical distortion is very minor thanks to the exceptional configuration of the optical system. Even though this system is principally based on the Canon FD 14mm lens, it has been redesigned completely from an optical viewpoint. The second of the 13 elements in 10 groups is aspherical, which compensates for distortions along the edges. Astigmatism which is particularly annoying at very short shooting distances is neutralized by internal focusing. In so doing the distance between the front lens and the focusing element changes as the distance is changed. Instead of a genuine lens hood these lenses have an abbreviated lens hood, which also acts as a front lens protector to prevent scratching of the domed front lens. The lens' construction allows the insertion of the gel filter in the optical path; there is no conventional filter mount. The Canon 14mm super wide-angle lens may be used in an exceptionally effective manner, especially with a reproduction scale of 1:10 and a shooting distance of 10 inches (25 cm). When the close-up setting and depth of field are used optimally a sharp image over the entire range is obtained.

The lens has a front lens diameter of 3.3 inches (7.7 cm) and a length of 3.5 inches (8.9 cm). Its smallest aperture is f/22. The

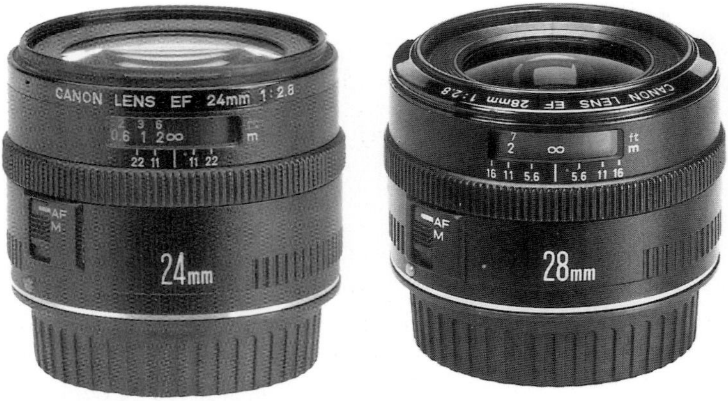

The EF 24mm f/2.8 and EF 28mm f/2.8, two wide angle lenses which are ideal for landscape photography, photojournalism, architecture and interior photography.

lens which weighs less than 20 ounces (560 g) no longer has an AF on/off switch for manual focusing, a change which applies to all lenses with an ultrasonic motor. Instead, these lenses feature a new mechanical system for automatic focusing so that manual focus is possible even in AF mode.

Canon EF 20mm f/2.8 USM: This lens is another that Canon has chosen to update from the old FD series. It has a 94 degree angle of view making it an excellent choice for showing more of a scene or for photographing in close quarters. The lens has a front lens diameter of 3.1 inches (7.75 cm) and a length of 2.75 inches (7.0 cm). Its smallest aperture is f/22, and the lens weighs less than 15 ounces (405 g). The minimum focusing distance is .8 feet.

Canon EF 24mm f/2.8 and Canon EF 28mm f/2.8: Both lens configurations have proved themselves in FD systems and were updated for EOS use. Whether the 24mm or the 28mm lens is the more sensible solution is mostly a question of preference. The 24mm lens exhibits optimal correction at only 12 feet (4 m) because its engineers assumed that the sharpness in the infinity range is mostly a function of depth of field and rarely of direct adjustment. Because of floating elements the close-up range offers high-quality image reproduction; for the 24mm lens down to 10 inches and for the 28mm lens down to 12 inches.

The lens has an image angle of 84 degrees. At the shortest shooting distance, this results in an image size of 7.5 x 11.1 inches (18.5 x 27.7 cm). The focusing speed is 0.44 seconds. The super wide-angle lens has a length of about 2 inches (48.5 mm) and weighs only 8.5 ounces (270 g).

Short Telephoto Lenses

Short telephoto lenses, those in the general range from 70mm up to about 150mm, are often called portrait lenses. Compartmentalizing them is an injustice though, since they are useful for a large number of subjects other than just for portraits. The EOS line boasts six lenses which fit into this range, and sixteen zoom lenses! You certainly have plenty to choose from here.

Lenses are really well suited to portraits only from the range of about 70mm up to about 150mm, because they force the photographer to think in terms of head and shoulders shots, and they provide a very undistorted and flattering perspective for the portrait subject. Ideal working distance is maintained ranging from about four feet at one extreme to about twelve feet at the other. Typically, lenses are used for portraiture at wide apertures to throw backgrounds and foregrounds out of focus and place all emphasis on the subject. However you should never let this naming of medium telephotos as portrait lenses persuade you not to use other lenses for portraits. I have often taken portrait photos with lenses in the 180-200mm range and I know a professional glamour photographer in New York who normally takes head and shoulders portraits with 300mm and 400mm lenses because he likes the perspective better. Since his photos grace the covers or major magazines around the world, others must agree. I have been in his studio during a session, and he is so far away from the model that he has to shout directions to her!

The point I am really trying to make here is that there are really no rules on which lens to use, only general guidelines. If a particular lens works for you for a particular picture, then it is the correct lens. What really matters behind all of this technical information about cameras and lenses is the final image, ultimately that is all that the viewer sees or cares about.

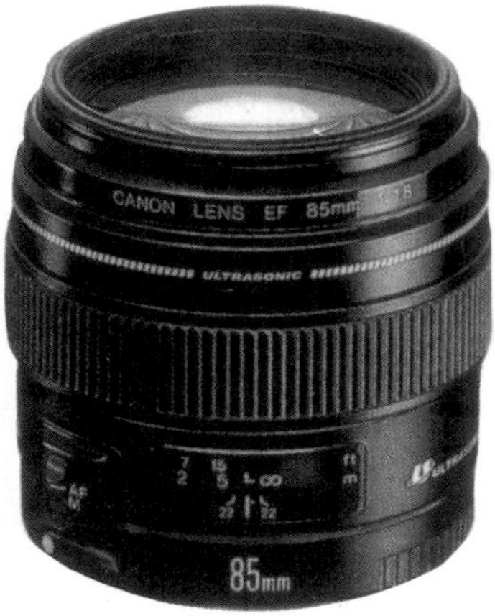

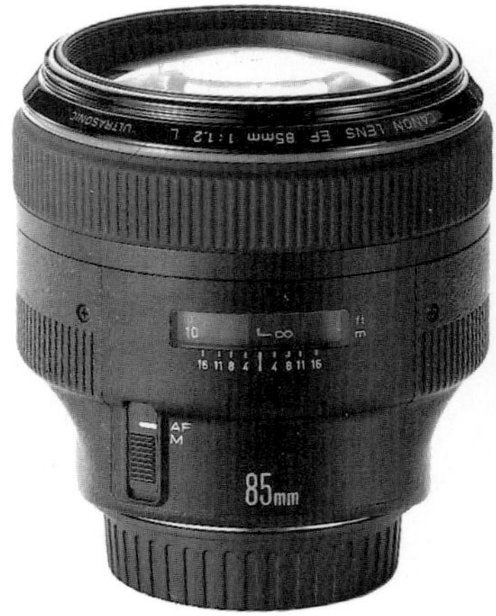

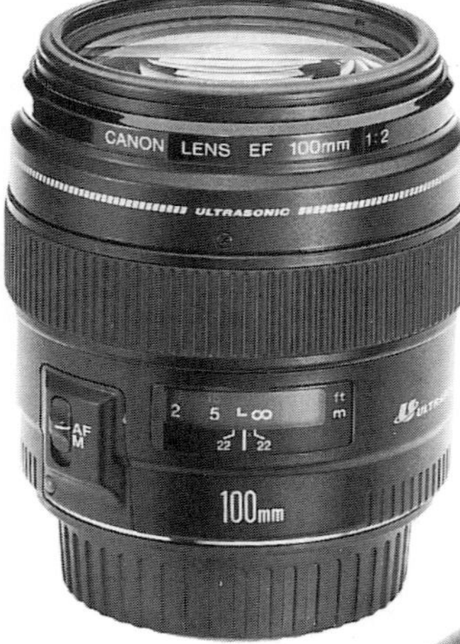

TOP: Two 85mm lens choices, the EF 85mm f/ 1.8 USM (left) and the faster EF 85mm f/ 1.2 L USM (right).

BOTTOM: The EF 100mm f/2.0 USM (left) is an optimal high-speed portrait lens while the EF 200mm f/2.8 (below) is a fast fixed-focal length telephoto.

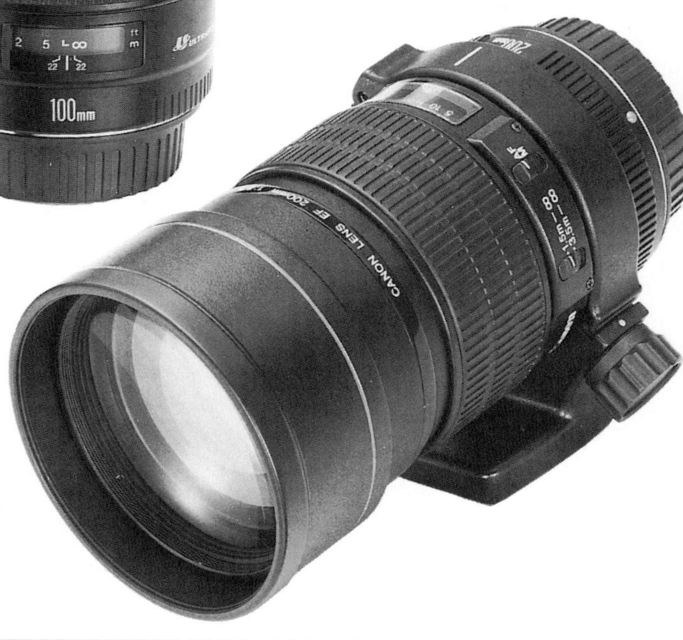

Canon EF 85mm f/1.2 L USM: This ultra-fast telephoto lens has a length of just 4 inches (10 cm) but weighs 35 ounces (1000 g). Together with the Rebel X/XS it fits nicely in the hand, allowing any photojournalist to shoot at 1/30 seconds with open aperture and without a tripod. The ultrasonic motor makes almost no sound. The viewfinder image appears extremely bright due to the lens' high speed of f/1.2. This lens (even though it is much more expensive than the Rebel X/XS camera) will become the personal normal lens for many a quality fanatic.

An aspherical element assures that the aperture of f/1.2 will not be a fad but truly bring expected professional quality. Considering its characteristics, this lens will be cherished by many photographers. It already belongs to the lenses having long focal lengths; however, it does not compress the linear perspective and it does not cause conspicuous spatial restriction. It is most suitable for normal-perspective shots and offers the additional advantage of a slightly smaller imaging field (compared with normal focal length). The scale of reproduction is enlarged by a factor of 1.7. This is a very pleasant ratio for portrait, landscape and action shots. Large apertures allow exact tuning of the depth of focus as may be desirable for portrait and landscape shots.

The super-fast portrait telephoto lens system consists of 9 elements in 7 groups, including an aspherical lens. The design uses additional floating elements in order to ensure high reproduction quality at all shooting distances. The image angle is 28 degrees. The high-speed ultrasonic motor runs the extremely long focusing path from infinity to only 38 inches (0.95 m) in only 1.2 sec. Manual focus is possible at any time. The smallest subject area is 9 x 13.6 inches (22.6 x 33.9 cm). The lens has a length of 3.4 inches (84 mm), a diameter of 3.7 inches (91.5 mm) and weighs 36 ounces (1025 g).

Canon EF 100mm f/2.0 USM: The maximum aperture of f/2 can produce high quality pictures at light levels where photographers with zoom lenses have long since given up. Regardless of the zoom lens used, at the 100mm focal length the fastest aperture will only be f/4.5 to 5.6. This is a difference between 2 and 2-1/2 f/stops. Even after the zoom photographer has reached a shutter speed of 1/30 this lens still allows comfortable hand-held shots at 1/200 to 1/180 for the same subject. Also the viewfinder image is brighter by the same factor. The quality in the close-up range is very high. In addition, this lens offers good image reproduction with a fully open aperture and is ideal for landscapes and portraits. Even normal snap-shots in difficult lighting situations may be handled comfortably. The new USM motor with optional manual adjustment and the internal focusing feature allow lightning-fast focusing over the entire range within 0.4 seconds.

This lens' barrel does not change in length during focusing, providing optimum balance, and the photographer using a polarizing filter will welcome the fact that the front ring does not turn during focusing.. At a length of 3 inches (75 mm) and a weight of 16 ounces (460 g) it fits comfortably in the hand. The filter size is 58mm. The lens hood (ET-65II) should always be attached. The 8 lens elements in 6 groups assure sharpness. The image angle is 24 degrees.

Canon EF 200mm f/2.8 L USM: An ultrasonic motor drives the internal focus of this high-speed telephoto lens. The close-up limit is 4.5 feet (1.5 m). This telephoto lens' advantages are selective sharpness and sharp focus. The lens system consists of 9 elements in 7 groups, with two lenses consisting of UD glass exhibiting anomalous dispersion characteristics. They reduce color errors and ensure high-contrast sharpness.

It would be a pity not to use this lens with the original Canon Extender (1.4x or 2x) to make this lens an AF USM lens featuring values of 280mm f/4 or 400mm f/5.6. In both cases the close-up limit is 4.5 feet (1.5 m). The lens' 12 degree angle offers an impressive perspective in particular in the close-up range. The lens has a length of 8.2 in (280 mm) and a maximum diameter of 5.1 inches (13.0 cm). At a weight of 6.6 pounds (3,000 g) it is certainly no lightweight.

Super Telephoto Lenses

Canon EF 300mm f/4 L USM: In many respects this lens is comparable to the EF 200mm f/2.8. Its exterior is similar to the large gray super lenses and rightfully so because it carries the L in its name and hence may be considered Canon lens nobility. This is truly an inexpensive alternative to the more expensive EF 300mm

Canon EF 300mm f/4.0 L USM

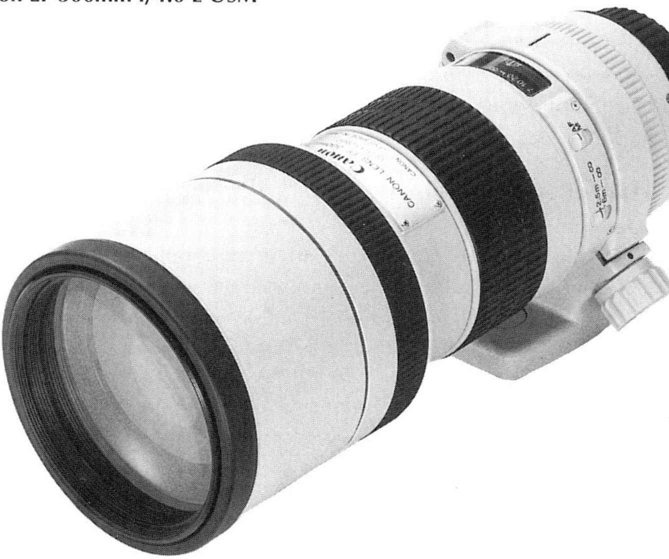

Canon EF 400mm f/5.6 L USM

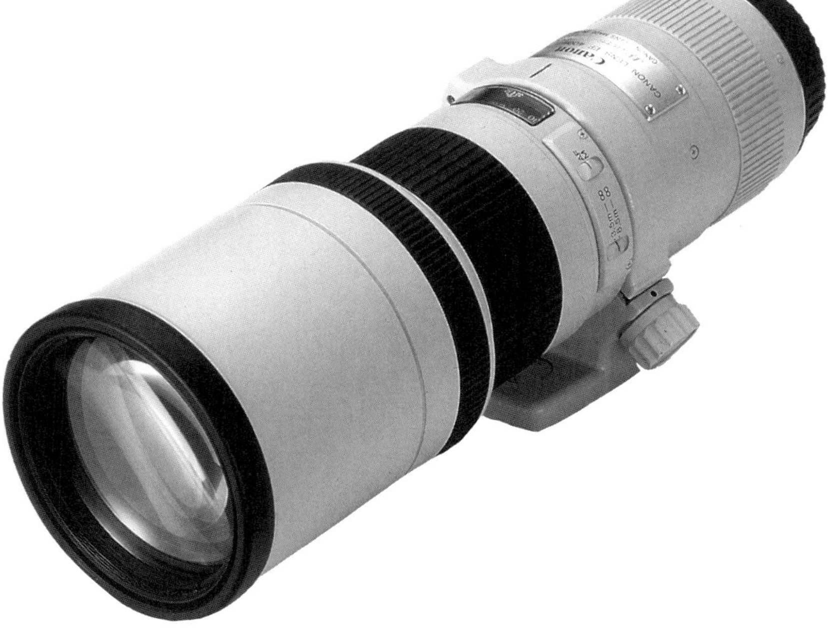

f/2.8 L. This lens has two UD glass elements reduce imaging errors to a minimum. Canon EF Teleconverters may be used, making the lens into 400mm f/5.6 and 600mm f/8 lenses. In this case, however, the lens must be focused manually. The close-up shooting distance is at 7.5 feet (2.5 m), resulting in a scale of reproduction of 1:7.7. Eight elements in seven groups make up the lens having a length of 8.5 inches (21.3 cm) and a diameter of 3.6 inches (90mm) covering a viewing angle of 6 degrees. Its image sharpness and excellent contrast are impressive.

Canon EF 400mm f/5.6 L USM: This super telephoto is the alternative to the 400mm f/2.8 L USM lens which costs considerably more. Two low-dispersion UD elements minimize chromatic aberration. For the first time, a newly developed type of glass was used which exhibits even less light scatter, as well as characteris-

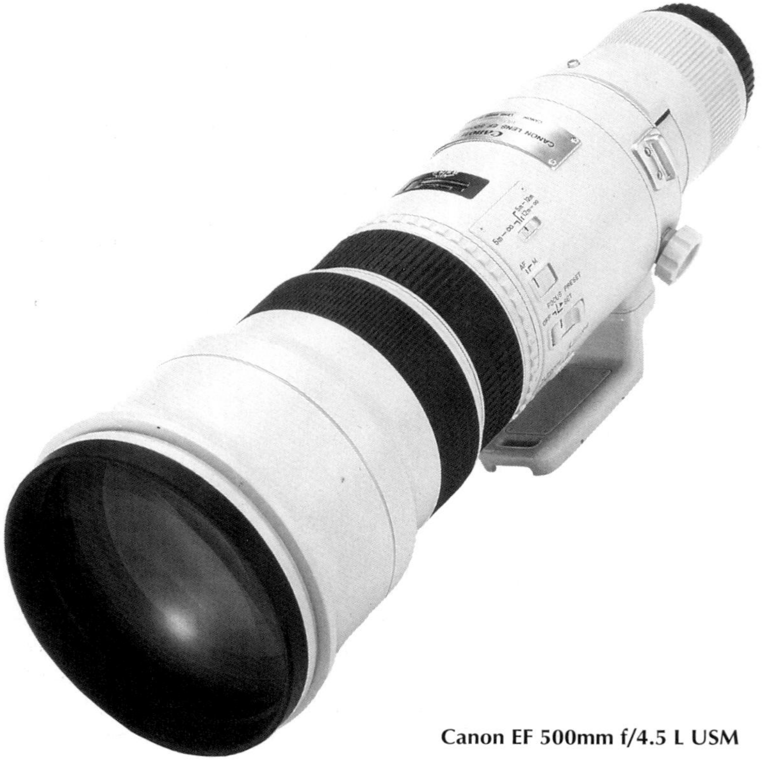

Canon EF 500mm f/4.5 L USM

tics which are normally only achieved by using sensitive fluorite glass lenses.

The micro-USM motor's fastest AF setting covers two focal ranges. For shorter focusing times, the photographer may restrict the distance range from 10.5 feet (3.5 m) to infinity to 25.5 feet (8.5 m) to infinity. An extender may be used but the focus must be set manually due to the rather small maximum aperture.

The lens has a length of 10.4 inches (26 cm), a filter size of 77mm and a weight of 44 ounces (1250 g) making it a lightweight in its class. Even though the tripod mount may be removed for free-hand shots, the use of a tripod (or at least a monopod) is recommended whenever this lens is used.

Canon EF 500mm f/4.5 L USM: This powerful telephoto lens is particularly light-weight and compact. Despite its large initial aperture of 1:4.5, its weight could be maintained at 105.8 ounces (3 kg). Therefore, it weighs only half as much as the EF 400mm f/2.8 L USM. By using lenses of synthetic, crystalline fluorite and glass exhibiting an extremely low index of refraction, residual chromatic aberration errors have almost been eliminated. Sharpness, as well as color reproduction, have been improved significantly. The ultrasonic drive along with the internal focusing system ensure fast focusing. The shortest shooting distance is 15 feet (5 m). A filter drawer holds 48mm filters. Gelatin filters with filter holders may also be used. The lens has a length of 15 inches (39.0 cm) and a maximum diameter of 5.2 inches (13.0 cm). The optical system consists of 7 elements in 6 groups.

Large Aperture Telephoto Giants

Four powerful giants for professional applications are the optical treats of the Canon EF interchangeable lens program. They are immediately noticeable because of their entirely atypical cream color. All of them have a large metal lens hood, a stable foot with a rotating mechanism and tripod thread mount, as well as loops for use with a carrying strap. The two smaller ones weigh approximately 106 ounces (3000 g), the larger ones, 212 ounces (6000 g). Even though all four belong to one family, each lens has its own special features. All in all they are dream lenses for anyone whose job requires work with such long focal lengths and for those who simply want to indulge themselves.

Fluorite and UD lenses ensure top ratings for contrast and resolution. These special lenses are easy to handle and all four lenses feature storage of a preset shooting distance. It does not matter how many times other distances have been measured, a slight turn of the focusing ring and the lens is reset to the stored value. Sports photographers will really appreciate this feature. In fractions of a second, faster than the camera can be redirected at the subject, the photographer may continue to take pictures in the second preset distance range. Storing values is easy. A successful action is confirmed acoustically.

The ultrasonic motor offers electronic support for manual focusing. On rotating the focusing ring electrical pulses are generated, which signal the lens microprocessor that the ultrasonic motor should run. In this way manual focusing causes almost no vibrations. All four lenses can translate 3 different focusing speeds and offer the photographer the option of adapting the manual adjustment to his or her liking. "Step 1" offers half the rate of rotation which is very useful for portraits or subjects in the close-up range and wherever very precise adjustment is important. "Step 2" uses the normal rate of rotation and "Step 3" uses double the rate of rotation,as is frequently required in sports photography.

The telephoto lens focusing paths are normally relatively long; therefore these four Canon lenses have preset focusing ranges in order to shorten the adjustment process whenever possible. A slip-in filter mount permits the use of filters with these lenses. Normal Canon screw-mount filters in 48mm size or even a circular polarizing filter of the same size may be attached. A special gel filter holder accessory is available. Because all lenses are apochromatically corrected they do not require refocusing when used with infrared film.

The use of a tripod is absolutely essential in order to receive the imaging quality. A stable monopod is recommended if more camera mobility is required, such as for sports shots.

Canon EF 300mm f/2.8 L USM: As far as the optics are concerned, this lens is the successor of the FD 300mm f/2.8 L, which has many devotees among sports photographers. The AF model was the world's first lens with the USM drive. Today it is still the

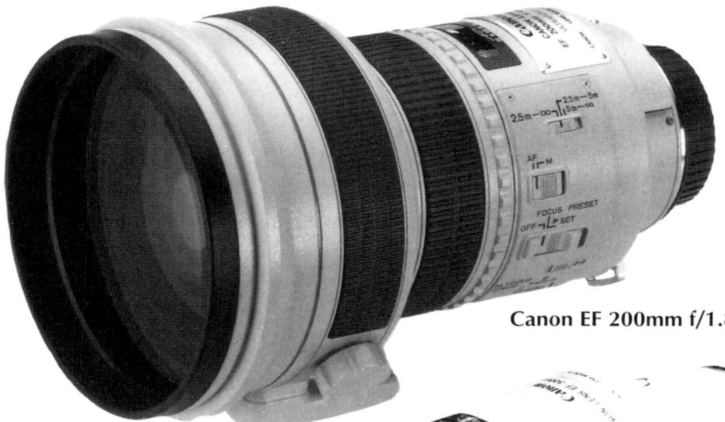

Canon EF 200mm f/1.8 L USM

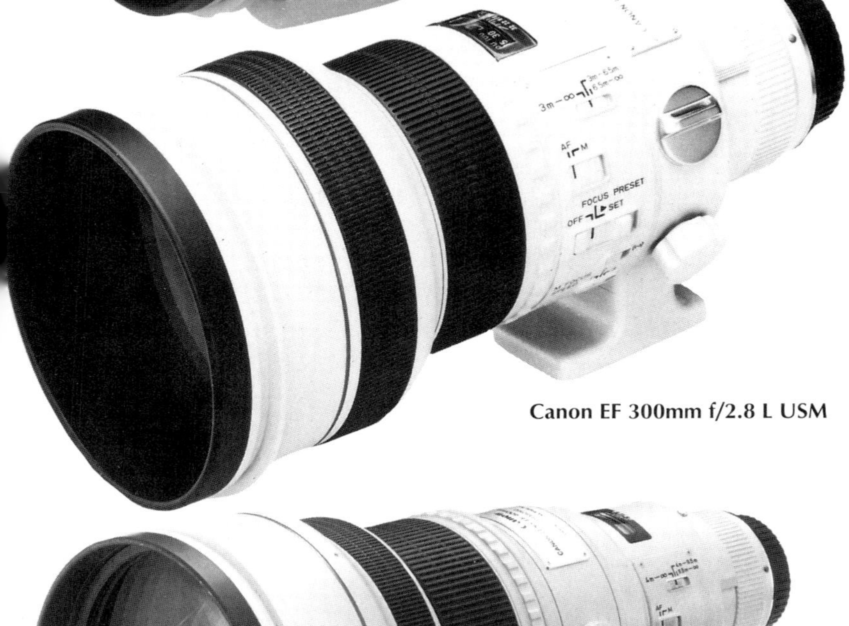

Canon EF 300mm f/2.8 L USM

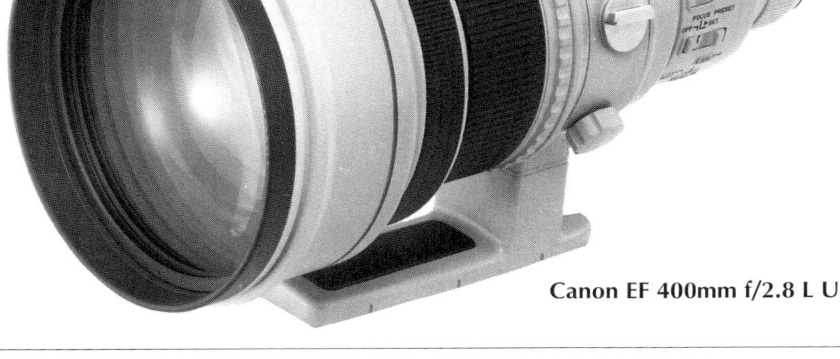

Canon EF 400mm f/2.8 L USM

Canon EF 600mm f/4.0 L USM

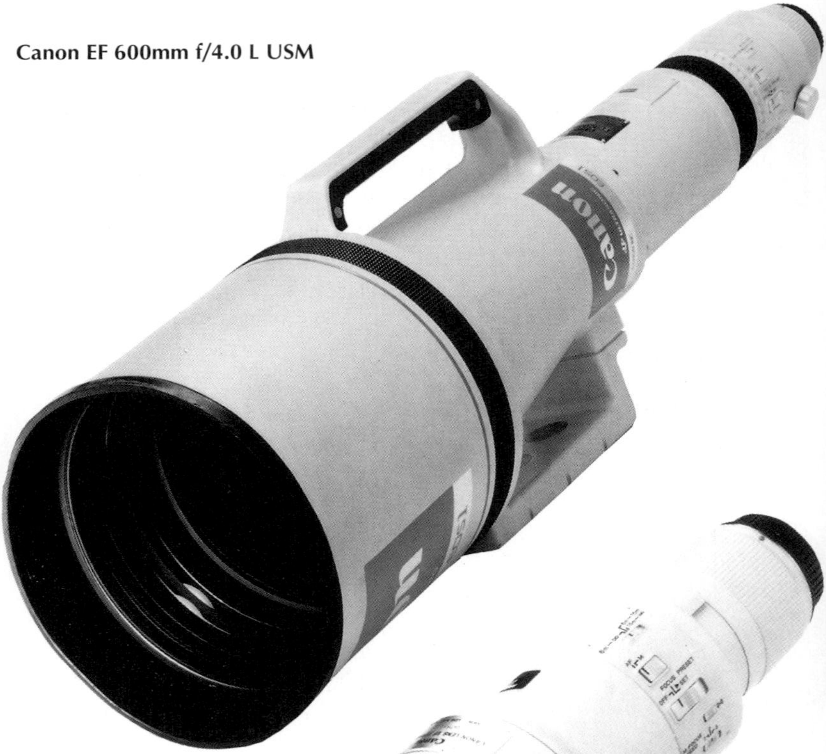

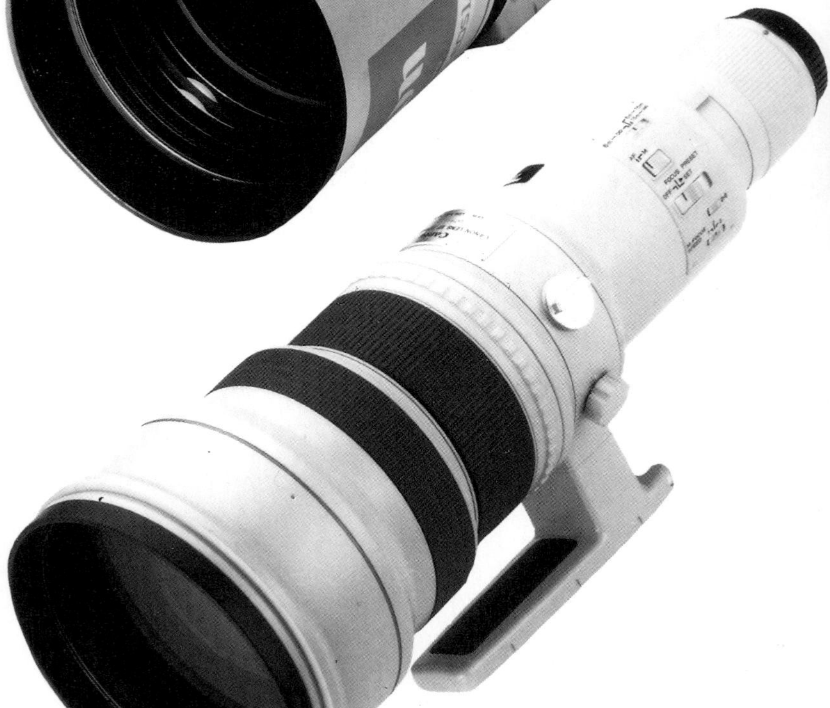

Canon EF 1200mm f/5.6 L USM

star of may football stadiums and playing fields. Many professionals consider this lens the standard from the viewpoints of quality, speed and price. Because the quiet USM drive does the focusing, this lens is equally suitable for stage and theater photographers as it is for animal, landscape, sports and press photographers. It is great for media circuses when photographers are exiled to ditches or behind barriers. With the Canon extenders, focal lengths of 420mm or 600mm at f/4 or f/5.6 are achieved. This lens produces a 6X magnification and, in combination with extenders, an 8.5X or 12X magnification compared to a 50mm normal lens. One calcium fluorite element and one UD glass element provide optical correction for unsurpassed sharpness at great distances along with exceptional color saturation.

Canon EF 400mm f/2.8 L USM: In 1980 when Canon introduced the first FD 2.8/400-mm lens, it became an immediate rage among sports photographers. Now this autofocus 400mm lens shines as the current star. The entire focusing range from infinity to 12 feet (4 m) can be run in only 0.7 seconds. Two UD glass elements ensure professional sharpness, as expected from this L-series lens. Extenders make it into a 560mm f/4 or a 800mm f/5.6. At a length of barely 14 inches (35 cm) it is surprisingly compact and exceptionally suitable for all subjects including landscapes, sports and action, as well as animal photography.

The optical system consists of 11 elements in 9 groups. The diagonal image angle is 6 degrees. Rapid internal focusing is ensured by the USM drive. The lens weighs 215 ounces (6100 g) and has a length of 14 inches (34.8 cm). Its largest diameter is 6.7 inches (16.7 cm).

Canon EF 600mm f/4 L USM: Animal, sports and fashion photographers use this lens regularly. Two UD glass elements with anomalous partial dispersion and a calcium fluorite element with a large diameter were required to eliminate the secondary spectrum to allow this lens to equal other L-series lenses from the viewpoints of quality and performance.

A 1.4x extender makes the Canon EF 600mm f/4 lens into a 800mm f/5.6 lens. By using a 2X extender, it is possible to convert this lens into a 1200mm f/8 super telephoto lens which, however, will have to be focused manually. Other than that, rapid focusing is ensured by the USM drive and the rear component focusing system. A focus-preset function allows a lightning-fast change to a preselected focal setting. The manual focusing ring has a motor-assist. The optical system consists of 9 elements in 6 groups. The image angle is 4 degree and the shortest shooting distance is at 24 feet (6 m). The super telephoto lens weighs 211 ounces (6000 g) and has a length of 18.2 inches (45.6 cm) and a maximum diameter of 6.7 inches (16.7 cm).

Canon EF 1200 f/5.6 USM II: This lens has the greatest focal length of any autofocus lens, and a price to match. It is manufactured only on special order. Only one or two of these are available in the USA and they may be rented by accredited press photographers at large sports events. The data on this lens is quite impressive. Its optical system consists of 12 elements in 9 groups. Two UD lenses eliminate chromatic aberration and ensure a sharp image with maximum aperture.

Three focal ranges may be preselected for the shortest focusing periods aided by the fast and super-quiet ultrasonic motor. Considering an image field of 11 x 16.5 inches (27.5 to 41.3 cm), the first range covers from 42 feet (14 m) to 90 feet (30 m). The second full focal range covers 42 feet (14 m) to infinity and the third from 90 feet (30 m) to infinity. The lens has a length of 33.6 inches (84 cm), a weight of 582 ounces (16.5 kg) and a diameter of 9.2 inches (23 cm). The lens barrel is designed to hold insertable filters having a diameter of 1.92 inches (4.8 cm). A handle allows fast switching between landscape and portrait formats.

It is even possible to use Canon extenders on this monster lens. An EF 1.4x makes this lens into an 1700mm f/8 super telephoto lens, an EF 2x into an 2400mm f/11 lens. This allows shots of details of the moon - of course the maximum aperture is f/11 which requires manual focus.

Zoom Lenses

There are many photographers who simply refuse to use zoom lenses at all because they cling to the old prejudice that zoom lenses are not sharp. Zoom lenses got this reputation in their early days, and the first zoom lenses such as the Voigtlander Zoomar were pretty bad by anyone's standards. But that was many years ago, and much technological progress has been made during those years, and today we have high quality zoom lenses which give very little away to fixed focal length lenses.

Zoom lenses have their advantages and so do non-zooms, and most well equipped photographers will have some of both types for use in different circumstances. For example, even though I usually use the 28-80mm L zoom, I also have the 85mm f/1.8. Why? Because at the 80mm end of its zoom range, the 28-80 becomes f/4, and that is not fast enough for some purposes. Also it does not allow me to set a really shallow depth of field, as I can easily do with the 85mm by simply setting it to f/1.8 or so. For a similar reason I also have a 50mm f/1.8, although I do not use it very much. When I have to use it, nothing else will do.

Early on, Canon has found a relatively simple design principle for zoom lenses. This is why inexpensive zoom lenses exhibiting high quality while retaining small size are now available. The so-called two-group design is responsible for this feature. In this system the front half of the lens is responsible for the adjustment of focal length and distance, while the rear half of the lens acts as compensation for focal shifts due to the focal length changes. The advantages are that front elements remain relatively small. Imaging errors may be corrected much more easily than in the case of zoom lenses having a four-group design. Due to the short focal lengths there is hardly any barrel distortion. The only disadvantage is that only relatively small focal length ranges may be covered.

In practice it has been found useful if the zoom lens is first adjusted to the greatest focal length. As soon as the camera is taken up to the eye and the viewfinder image is in focus, the best possible image has been achieved. Candid situations are best shot right away; then the image angle may be changed to determine whether the image may be framed better. This will happen relatively rarely and, if at all, at the other end of the focal length range. When the focal length is reduced, the distance will be adjusted later only in isolated cases; this situation is more likely to occur in reverse operating mode. In many situations, for example, on a trip or whenever one does not want to carry additional lenses, a focal length range of 35-105mm or even 135mm is ideal. This also means that subjects may be captured in the de-

This variable aperture wide-angle zoom is ideal for interior photography, photojournalism and many other applications.

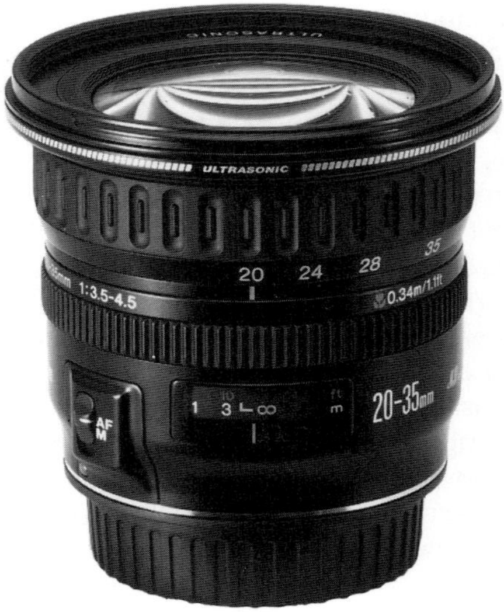

sired image size with a single lens, but there is also the opportunity to be creative with the focal length.

The wide-angle range offers a more comprehensive view of a landscape, allows a large group of people to be in one picture and helps solve restrictive spatial conditions when indoor shots are taken. A focal length range between 80 and 100mm provides twice the subject size from the same camera site. Therefore, this is the ideal focal length range for shots of people and snapshots at parties, sports events, of children and pets. Landscape photography produces pictures exhibiting a rather neutral perspective; however, due to their slight telephoto effect, ensure that the selected image frame does not appear overloaded. All in all, this is a universal focal length range.

Almost all zoom lenses have a so-called macro-setting. This is no substitute for a macro lens. Because it uses the sharpness of the center of the lens a small aperture required. The apparently reduced distance setting represents the actual working range of the lens and should always be set simply for the reason of preventing unnecessary adjustments. The information regarding the close-up setting represents the shortest distance setting for each lens and the normal autofocus ranges from that value to infinity.

Canon EF 20-35mm f/3.5-4.5 USM: Canon has offered a professional-quality lens using this focal length range for more than five years. The 20-35mm super wide-angle zoom lens with a maximum aperture of f/3.5 to 4.5, however, is a surprisingly good-quality lens at an affordable price.

Distortions may become a problem in particular in the super wide-angle zoom range. By consistently using spherical elements Canon has significantly minimized these difficulties and achieved high resolution with only insignificant distortions along the image edges. In addition, a type of diaphragm blocks flare which would ordinarily impair contrast.

The minimum shooting distance is 13.5 inches (0.35 m). The lens system consists of 12 elements in 11 groups and features internal focusing. The front lens does not rotate, filters with a diameter of 77mm, as well as polarizing filters may be used in the super wide-angle range. As is the case with other lenses, a lens hood should be used at all times.

Canon EF 20-35mm f/2.8 L: This top-of-the-line zoom lens has a maximum aperture of f/2.8 over the entire focal length range. Internal focus and the use of an aspherical lens, as well as floating elements ensure sharp images at any shooting distance and focal length. There are 15 lens elements in 12 groups which cover a diagonal image angle of 94 to 63 degrees. Distance settings range from infinity to 20 inches (50 cm). The lens focal length is adjusted by rotating an adjustment ring. This adjustment is translated into a large adjustment in the range of less than half an inch in the otherwise difficult super wide-angle range. This is also one of the technical reasons why an AFD motor was used instead of an ultrasonic motor.

If this lens or the one described earlier is used on the Rebel X/XS, the camera must always be in perfect alignment for vertical lines to remain vertical and for horizontal lines not to appear as diagonals. Falling lines and, likewise, the elliptical reproduction of spherical or circular objects at the image edge in the 20mm range, are not due to a lens error. For the same reason a person should never appear at the image edge when a super wide-angle setting is used. Should a group picture require a super wide-angle lens due to spatial restrictions, care must be taken that persons on the right and left edges of the group are placed approximately 3

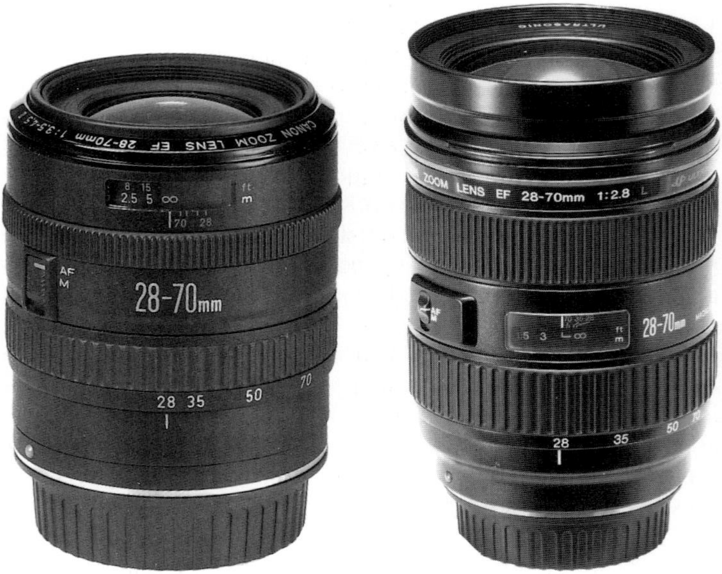

Two popular 28-70mm wide-angle zooms from Canon. Both the f/3.5-3.4 variable aperture zoom (left) and the f/2.8 (right) are fine choices for snapshots and general photography.

feet (1 m) farther back than the persons in the center of the picture. This having more subject in the picture, which is typical of super-wide-angle settings, creates problems for the photographer. It is characteristic of these lenses that they have an extreme spatial effect. An analysis of successful super wide-angle pictures will indicate that the foreground, better yet the close-up range, determines the quality of the picture. The photographer, who pays sufficient attention to all distance planes, as well as their perspective effect, will produce surprising image effects when using this focal length range in all photographic applications.

The 24mm range still produces this strong perspective and spatial effect, however, without distinct widening of the subject at the image edge and the extreme emphasis on the foreground. This focal length range is equally suitable for landscape and indoor shots.

The image angle in the focal length range around 28mm is already considered normal and the image field covered can be illuminated by almost all flash units. With a little thought and practice this focal length range produces a wide-angle effect which can only be noticed by an expert. However, the reverse is also possible. By skillful emphasis of the foreground, attention is drawn to the spatial depth.

This zoom lens covers nearly the entire wide-angle range. Its design includes 15 elements in 12 groups, one of them being aspherical. The image angle ranges from 94 to 63 degrees. The smallest subject area ranges between 29.5 x 19 inches (73.8 x 47.6 cm) and 17 x 11.3 inches (42.6 x 28.3 cm). An infrared index is marked for focal lengths of 20, 24 28 and 35mm. At a length of approximately 3 inches (8 cm) and a diameter of approximately 3.5 inches (89.3 mm) it weighs only 19 ounces (540 g) and is automatically focused by an AFD motor in 0.3 sec. from infinity to 20 inches (50 cm).

Canon EF 28-70mm f/3.5-4.5 II: This versatile wide-angle zoom is one of the least expensive lenses in the EOS program. The optical system includes 10 elements in 9 groups. The image angle varies between 75 degrees and 34 degrees. The AFD motor adjusts the focus from infinity to 20 inches (50 cm) in 0.36 sec. On the macro setting, the lens can be focused down to 15.5 inches (39 cm). The smallest aperture is f/22-29. The lens has a length of approximately 30.2 inches (75.6 cm) and weighs just over 10 ounces (285 g).

Canon EF 28-80mm f/3.5-5.6 USM: This zoom lens, which has become the new standard lens in the zoom range, illustrates Canon's revised basic conception of the EOS system. Improved USM technology and the development of a USM motor for large series integrate the advantages of this AF drive system in less expensive EF lenses. In combination with optical correction by aspherical elements, even these inexpensive lenses are of significantly improved quality. This lens includes one aspherical element. An additional feature of the 28-80mm lens is a built-in lens baffle which moves between the third and the second lens element in order to suppress flare throughout the entire focal length range. All of these features ensure that this zoom lens pro-

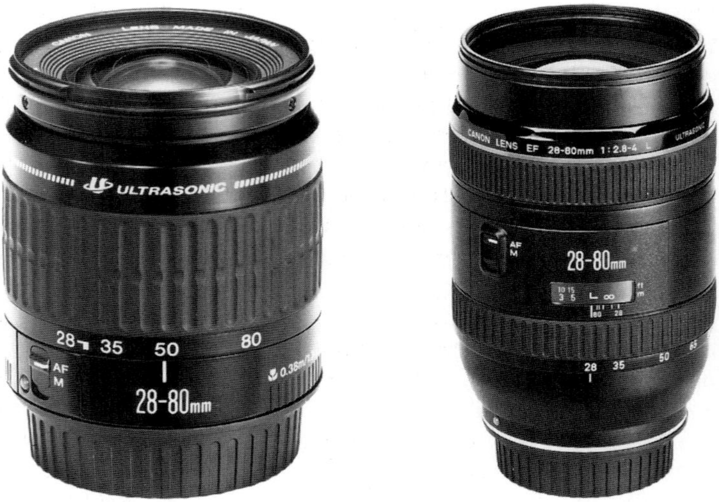

Both the higher priced EF 28-80 f/2.8-4.0 L USM and the EF 28-80 f/3.5-5.6 cover the same zoom range. However, the more expensive lens on the left would be a better choice for professional shooting applications where the ultrasonic motor and higher-quality optics might make the important difference.

vides surprising quality at a favorable price. This lens is installed in such a way that the use of the Rebel X/XS's integrated flash unit does not produce shadows caused by the lens edge. The length of the lens remains constant and full use may be made of the flash unit even at a shooting distance of 3 feet (1 m).

The optical system consists of 10 lenses in 9 elements. It has a length of 3 inches (77.5 mm) and a maximum diameter of 2.9 inches (72mm). Depending on focal length, the smallest aperture is f/22 to f/38. The filter size is 58mm. The entire zoom lens weighs 12 ounces (330 g).

Canon EF 28-80mm f/2.8-4.0 L USM: Another optical treat among the wide-angle zoom lenses is undoubtedly the Canon EF 28-80mm f/2.8-4.0 L USM which has a rotating ring for focal length adjustment. Zoom lenses with sliding rings are still favored by many photographers; however, exceptional lenses such as zoom lenses frequently have a rotating ring for focal length adjustment. If short, critical adjustments must be made, the rotating ring has considerable advantages. Due to variable adjustment translation independent of optical design principles, the path of movement may be extended and adjustment accuracy improved significantly. This is true of the Canon EF 28-80mm f/2.8-4.0 L.

Two aspherical elements ensure very high image quality over the entire focal length range. The optical system consists of 15 elements in 11 groups. The image angle varies between 75 and 30 degrees. The focus is adjusted from infinity to 30 inches (75 cm) in only one second. Depending on the focal length, the smallest subject area is between 21.3 x 32 inches (53.3 x 80 cm) and 8 x 12 inches (20 x 30 cm) and corresponds approximately to the size of a sheet of letter-size paper. In the macro range at a shooting distance of 20 inches (50 cm) the maximum subject size is between 12.8 x 19.2 inches (32 x 48 cm) and 4.8 x 7.2 inches (12 x 18 cm). The entire lens has a length of just over 4 inches (12 cm) and weighs 33 ounces (945 g). At the time of writing this lens has just been replaced with a new EF 28 - 70mm f/2.8 L which, maintains a constant aperture throughout the zoom range.

Canon EF 35-70mm f/3.5: This zoom lens in the standard range of 35-70mm is particularly light-weight and compact. Its optical system consists of 9 elements in 8 groups. The image angle covers 63 to 34 degrees. The AFD motor can run the focus from infinity to 20 inches (50 cm) in 0.41 seconds. In the macro range, the lens can be focused from a distance of 15.6 inches (39 cm). The zoom has a length of approximately 2.5 inches (63 mm) and weighs only 8.6 ounces (245 g). The second version of this lens, with the A suffix, is identical but can only be focused automatically, and weighs about 8 ounces (230 g).

Canon EF 35-105mm f/3.5-4.5: The optical design of the triple zoom consists of 14 elements in 11 groups, including one aspherical element. The image angle may be chosen between 63 and 23 degrees. The AFD motor runs through the entire focusing range in 0.4 sec. With a minimum shooting distance of 3.5 feet (1.2 m) a subject area of between 26.6 x 40 inches (66.6 x 100 cm) and 9.3 x 14 inches (23.3 x 34.9 cm) is attained. In the macro range of 38 inches (95 cm) these values are between 17.4 x 26.2 inches (43.6 x 65.4 cm) and 6 x 9 inches (15 x 22.5 cm). Its weight is 14 ounces (400 g).

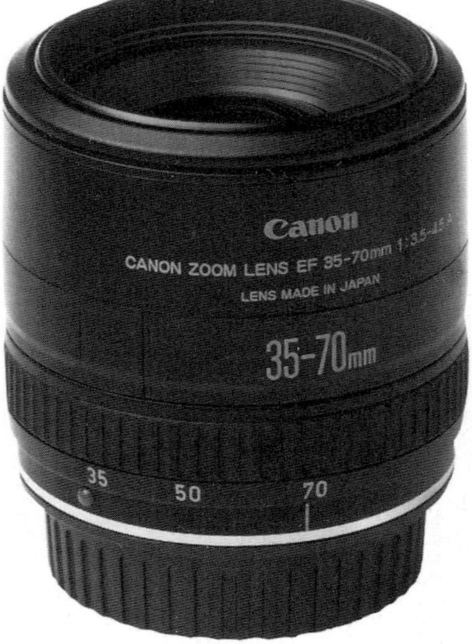

Canon EF 35-70mm f/ 3.5-4.5 A

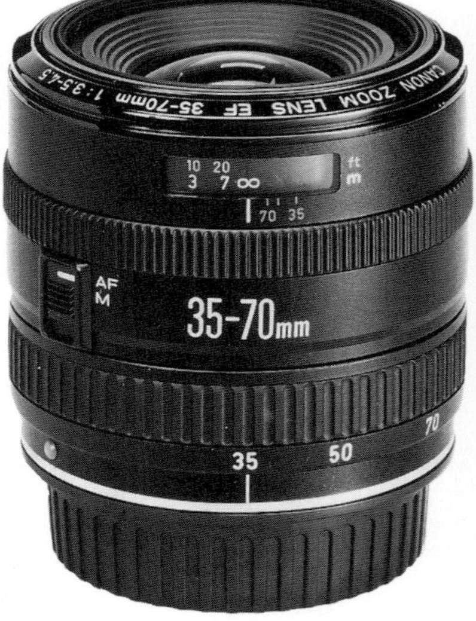

Canon EF 35-70mm f/3.5-4.5

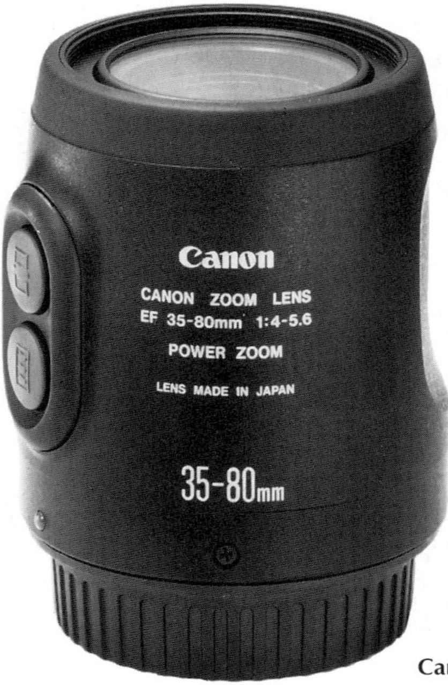

Canon EF 25-80mm f/4.0-5.6 Power Zoom

Canon EF 35-80mm f/4.0-5.6 II

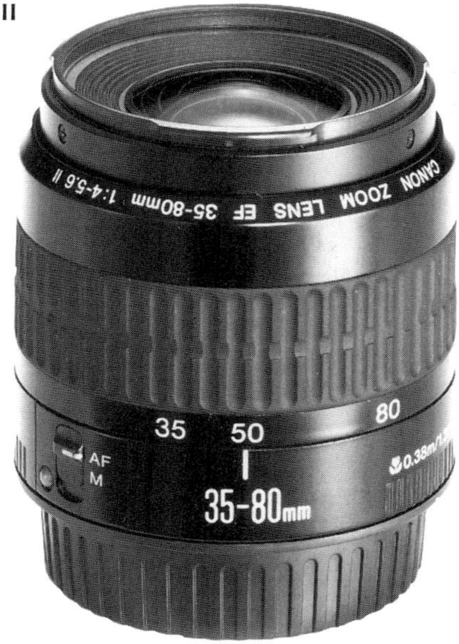

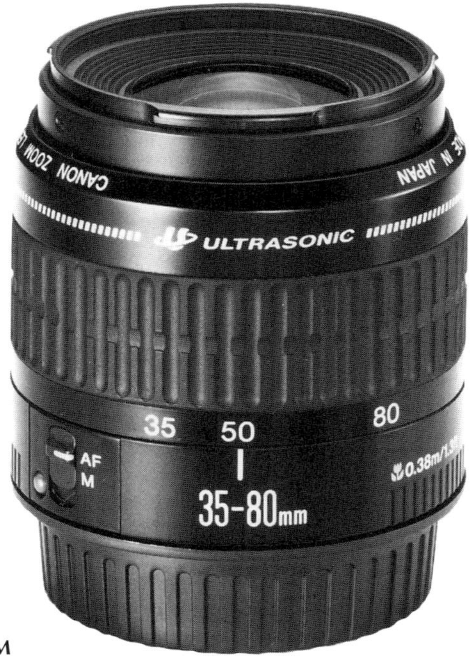

Canon EF 35-80mm f/4.5-5.6 USM

Page 129

A medium telephoto was used here at a wide aperture setting to separate the foreground subject from the background and reduce it to an unobtrusive blur.

Page 130

A range of photos from close portrait to scenic can all be handled with a single wide-angle to telephoto zoom, such as the EF 28-105mm.

Page 131

A telephoto zoom allows both a wider view of the lily pond and a close-up of the blossom, all without changing lenses.

Page 132

A 200mm telephoto lens was used in the upper photo to visually compress the space between the boat and the buildings in the background.

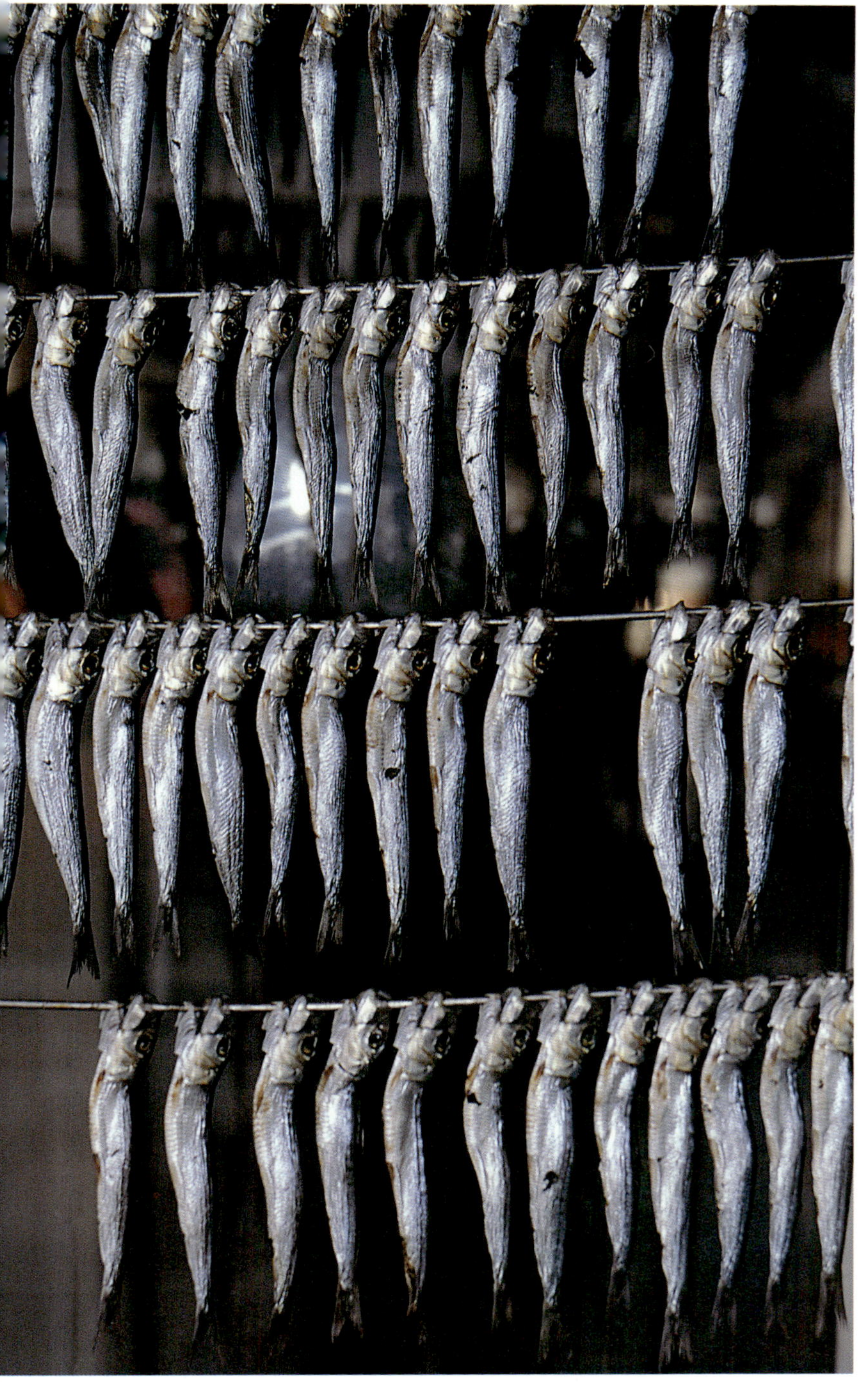

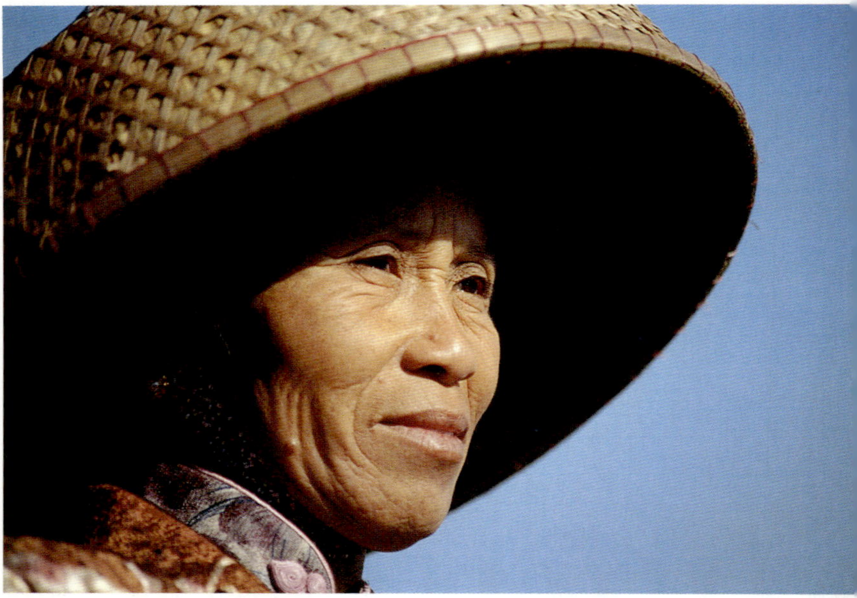

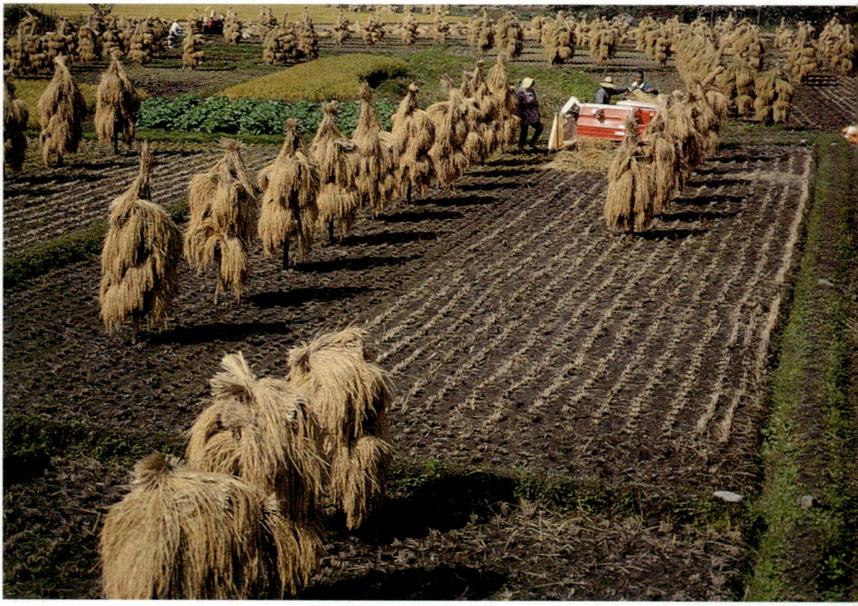

– B –

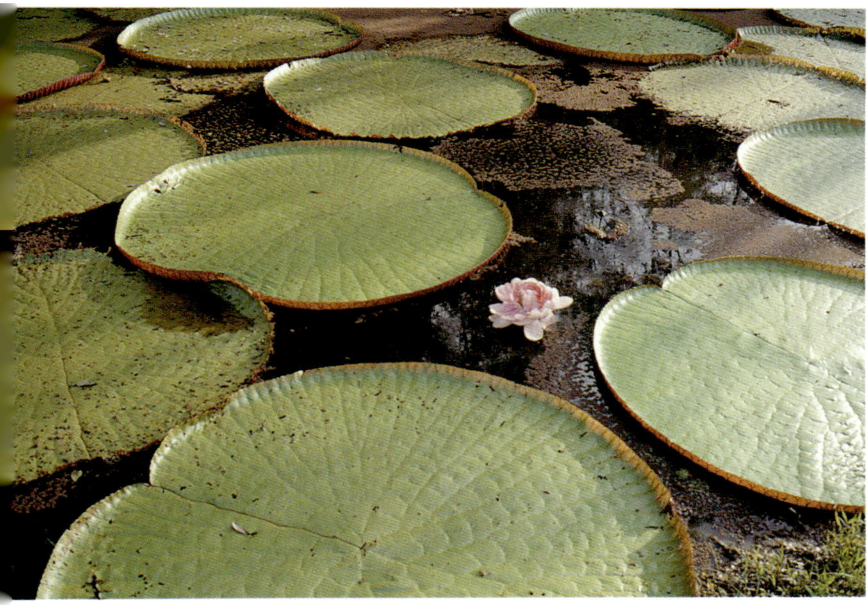

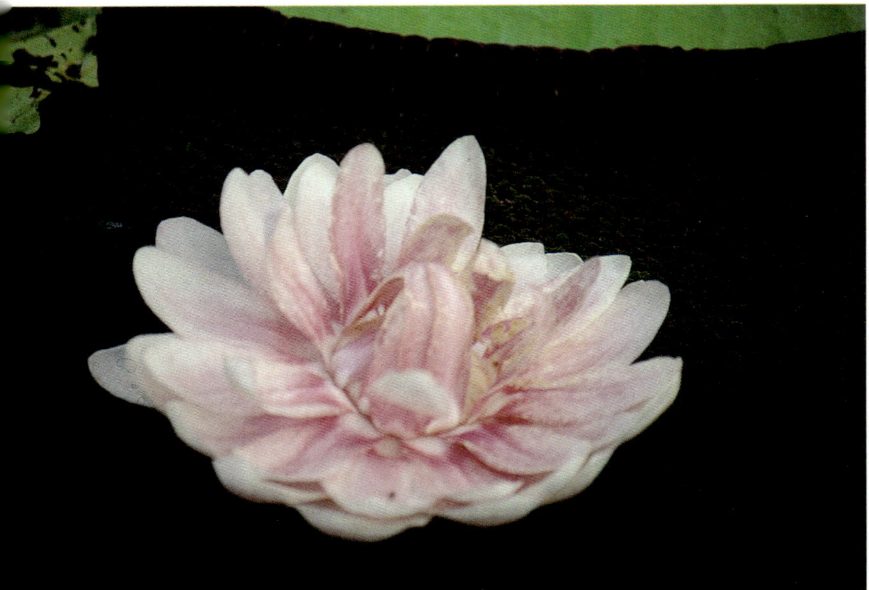

– C –

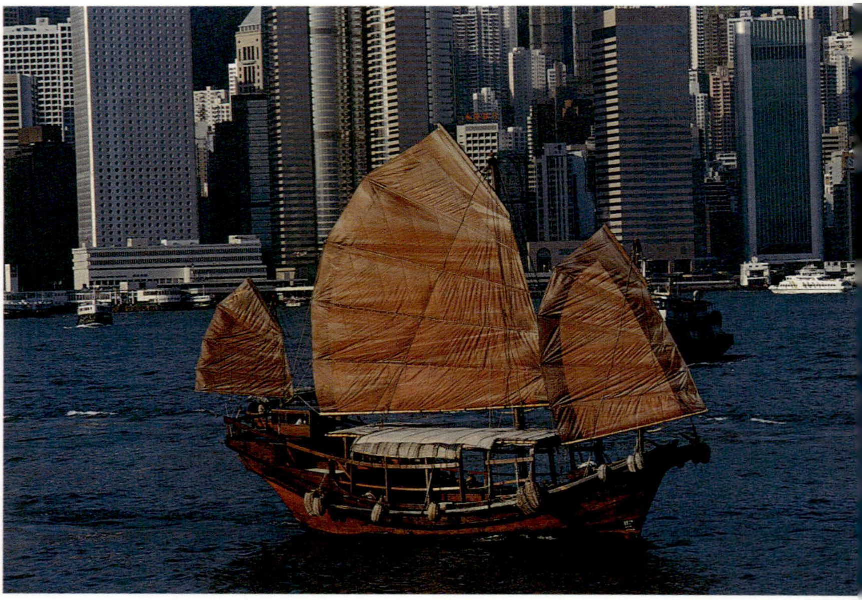

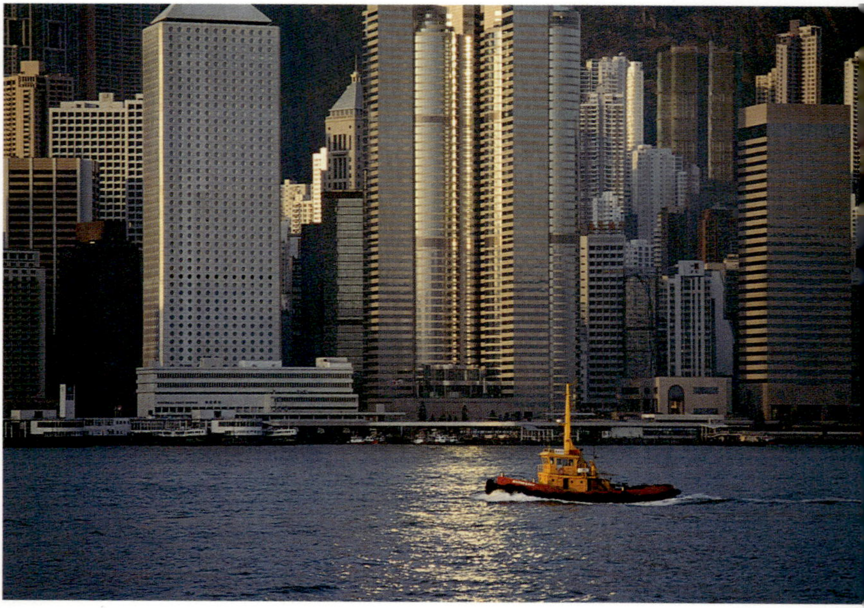

– D –

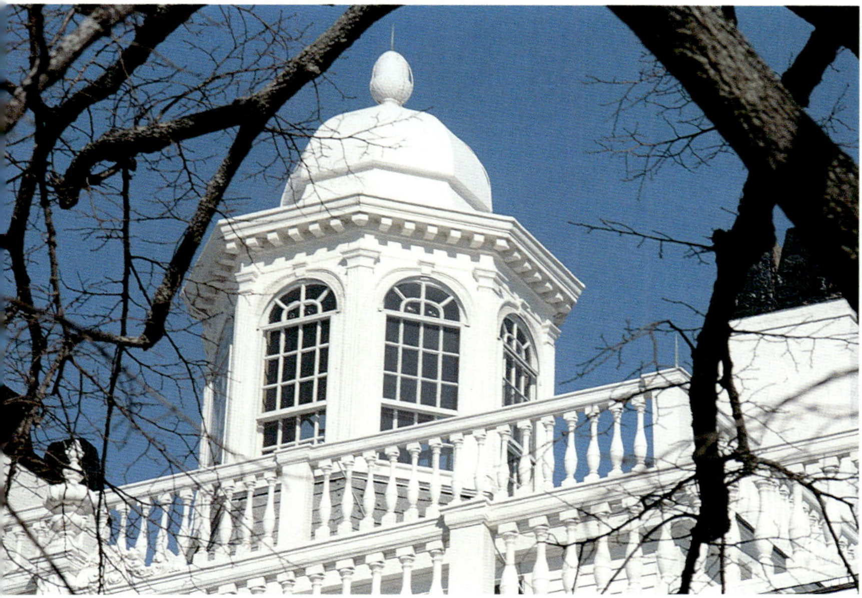

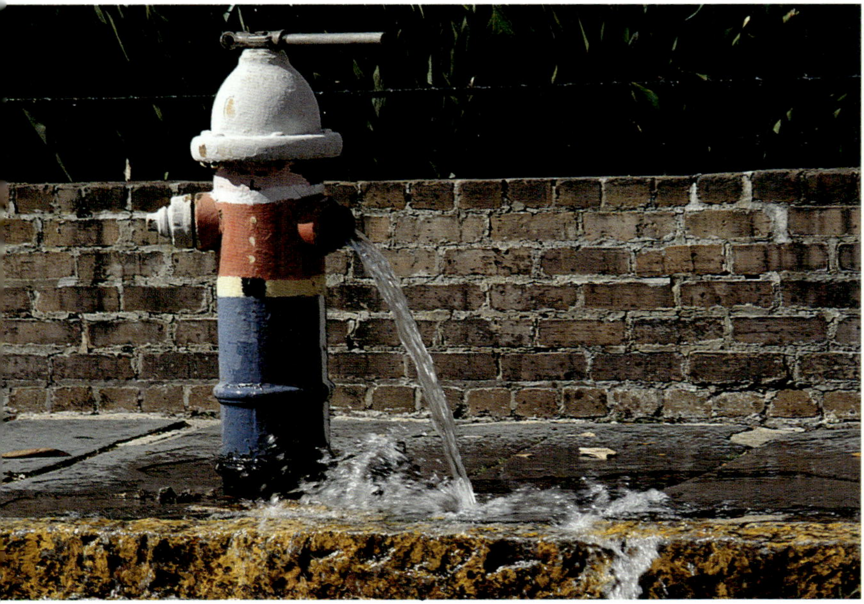

– E –

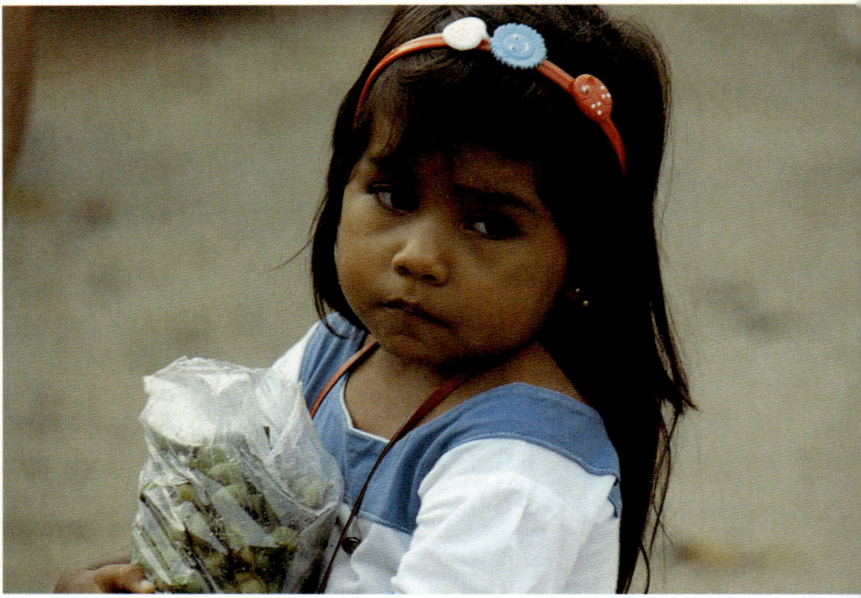

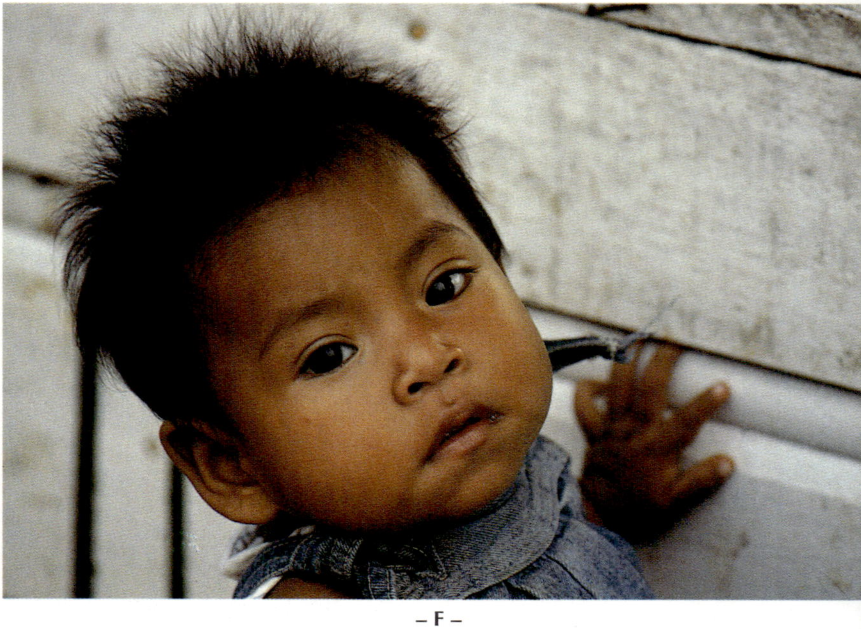

– F –

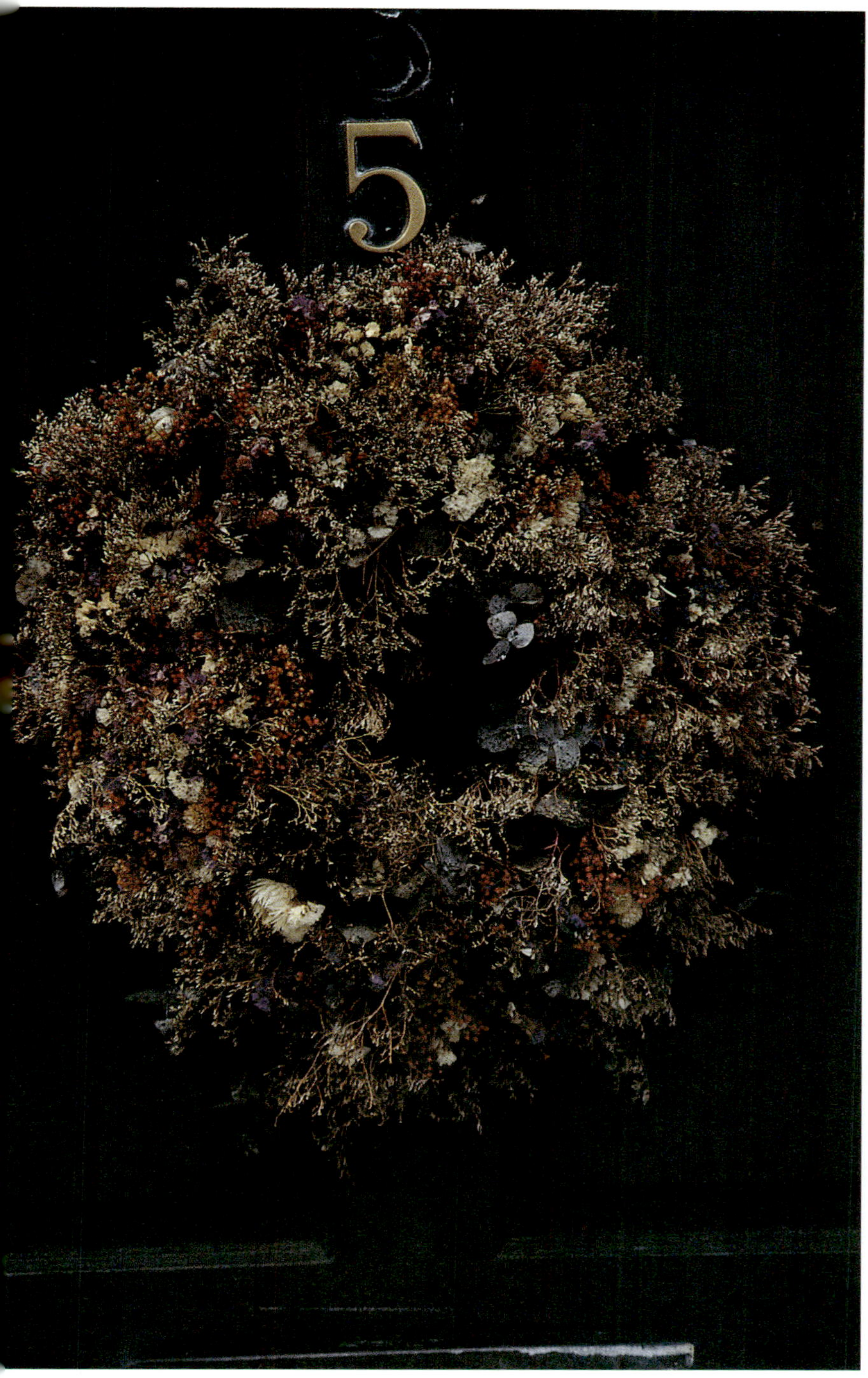
5

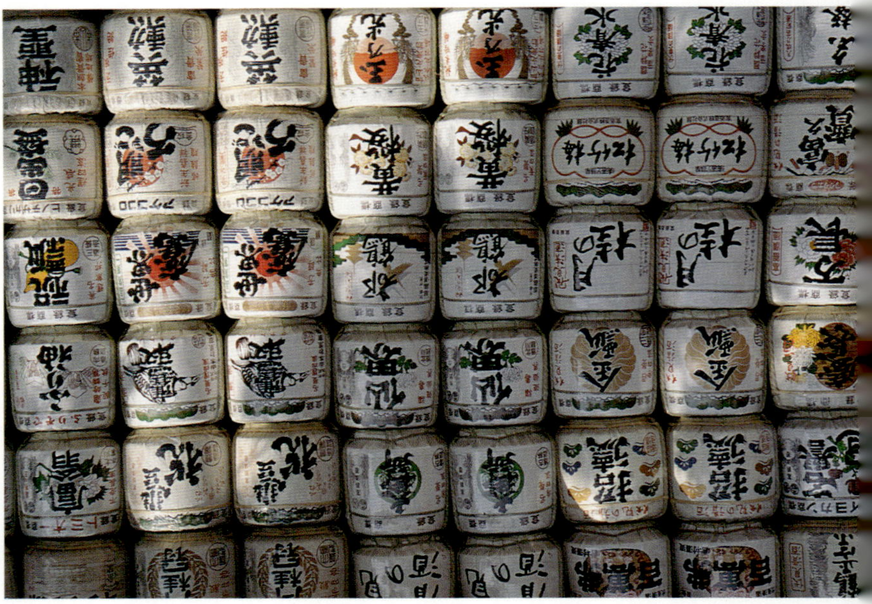

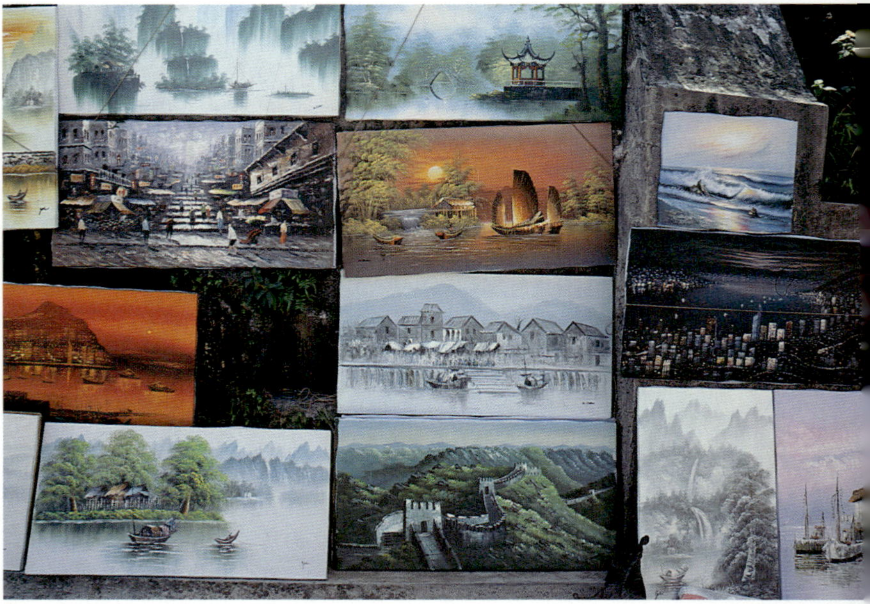

– H –

Page 133

The white architectural detail against the sky and the fire hydrant against a dark background were both exposed properly without any problem by the REBEL X/XS's multi-area metering system.

Page 134

The portrait mode is ideal for all sorts of pictures of people, and requires nothing from the photographer other than composing the photo.

Page 135

The ideal lens opening for rendering detail is usually several stops down from wide open. Here a telephoto zoom was perfect for capturing detail in this wreath without getting too close.

Page 136

Photos like these which rely on fine detail for interest must be taken with really sharp lenses such as the Canon L series.

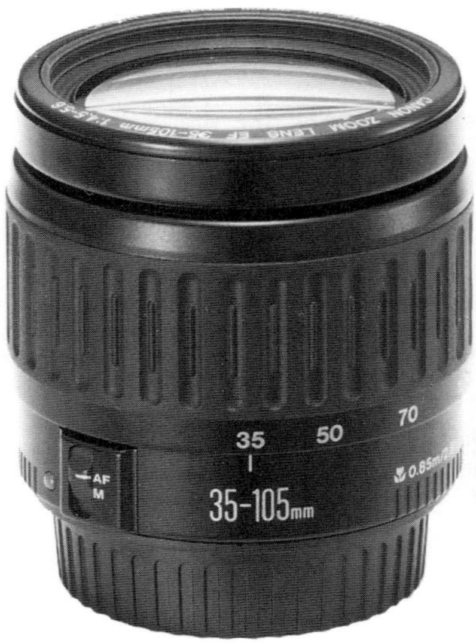

Canon EF 35-105mm f/4.5-5.6

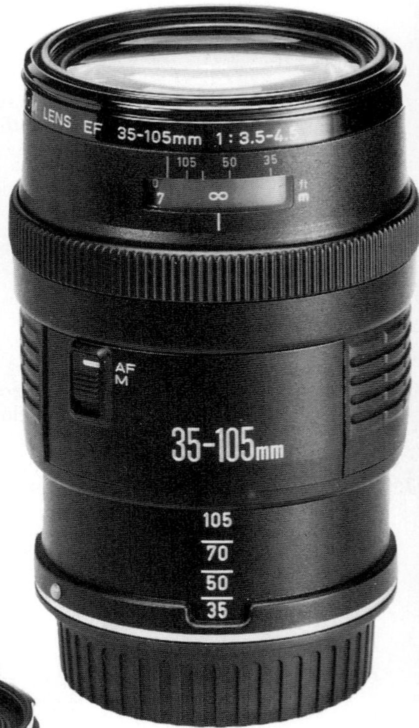

Canon EF 35-105mm f/3.5-4.5

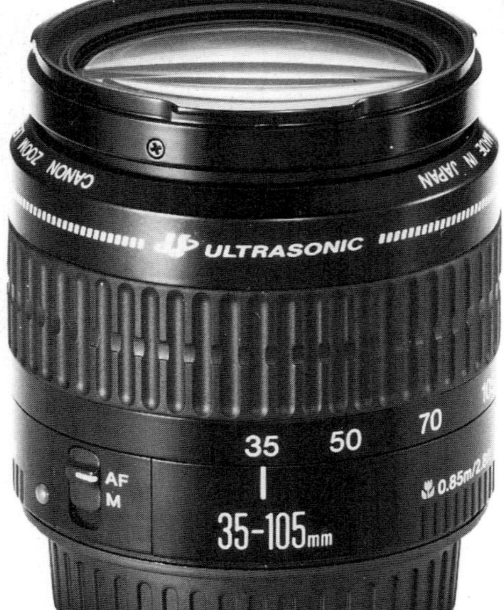

Canon EF 35-105mm f/4.5-5.6 USM

Canon EF 35-350 mm f/3.5-5.6 USM

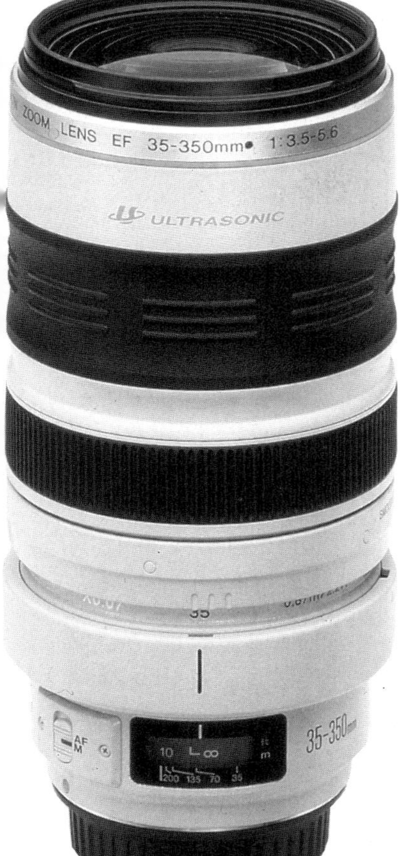

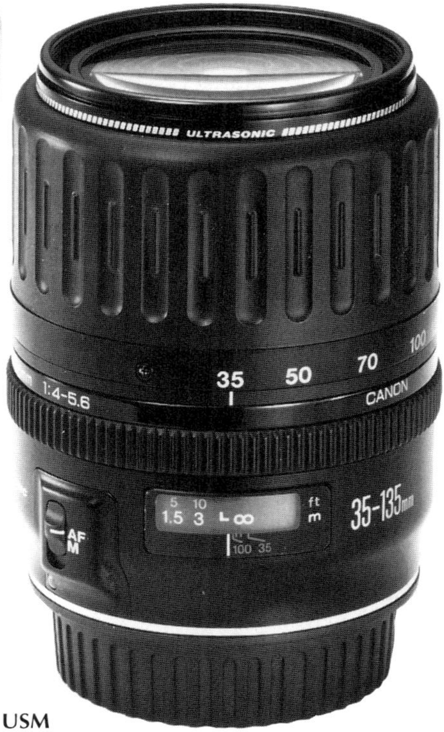

Canon EF 35-350mm f/4.0-5.6 L USM

Canon EF 35-135mm f/4.0-5.6 USM: The triple zoom has become the standard because it is particularly compact and lightweight. Its optical design uses 14 elements in 12 groups. This also includes a molded aspherical lens. Fast internal focus allows a focus adjustment from infinity to 3 feet (1 m) in only 0.5 seconds. Manual focusing is possible when the AF feature is turned off. As is true of other lenses of the most recent generation, the distance and the image-reproduction scale are reported to the camera's microprocessor resulting in an automatically controlled operation in close-up or portrait mode. The smallest subject areas are 24.7 x 37.1 inches (61.8 x 92.7 cm) to 8.5 x 12.8 inches (21.3 x 32 cm) at a distance of 3 feet (1 m). A reduction of the distance by a factor of 0.25 in macro mode changes the values of the subject area by the same factor. The zoom has a length of about 3.5 inches (9 cm). and weighs just 15 ounces (425 g).

Canon EF 35-350mm f/3.5-5.6 L USM: This super-zoom lens covers the largest focal length range of all the Canon zoom lenses. It ranges from the wide-angle all the way to the super-telephoto range. This was achieved by a separate adjustment microprocessor in the lens and a multiple group design comprising 5 lens groups, all of which move when the focal length is changed. However, the movements of each group are very short because each lens group exhibits an optimal index of refraction. Focusing takes place via a rear component focusing system which is run smoothly and rapidly by an ultrasonic motor. It allows sharp focusing in the wide-angle range down to 27 inches (0.67 m). In the greater telephoto range the close-up limit is 6.6 feet (2.2 m). This allows the smallest imaging field of 6.6 x 9.9 inches (15.5 x 24.7 cm).

Two UD glass elements reduce achromatic aberration and ensure sharp reproduction over the entire range. The lens is surprisingly compact, has a length of less than 7 inches (17 cm), weighs 48 ounces (1350 g) and may even be used for handheld shots, if supported with a rifle stock or hand grip.

Telephoto Zoom Lenses

Until recently, heated debates among proponents and opponents of zoom lenses still raged. Numerous quality improvements on lenses with variable focal lengths have reduced the problem to the question of maximum aperture (speed) versus convenience. Fixed focal lengths will always be available for special problems but a user-friendly zoom lens is quite welcome even in professional circles. The advantage of framing a subject in an ideal manner without changing camera position is tempting. However, many photographers forget that the relationship between foreground and background changes rather dramatically considering a distance of 60 feet (20 m) and a focal length of 200mm or 24 feet (8 m) and a focal length of 80mm. This is not obvious based on the main subject but based on the size and sharpness of objects at different distances in the background. Many photographers think and see in focal lengths. They have a 50, 100 and 200 view. They know from the very beginning how the picture will look and how to represent the foreground relative to the background. A zoom lens makes this learning process more difficult but it opens up creative possibilities such as the so-called zoom effect, a radial blur.

Because it is convenient, the focal length range from 80 to 200mm has become the most favored. Canon has added to this: At one end of the spectrum is the 50mm and at the other the 300mm telephoto lens. There is a total of ten zoom lenses covering focal lengths from 50 to 300mm. Four of them carry the L designation, and two are equipped with new, inexpensive USM motors. Most lenses, with the exception of the EF 80-200mm f/2.8 L and the two new USM lenses have a push-pull zoom system.

The decision of what lens to buy depends on different requirements. The easiest criterion would be the quality group. A professional certainly will look at L lenses with more careful consideration; an amateur photographer will probably make a decision based on his or her budget.

A decision regarding the focal length range is more difficult. The focal length range of 50-200mm is certainly interesting for those who want to get along with the smallest number of lenses. Supported by a wide-angle lens, one may cover the entire range from 24 or 28 to 200mm with two lenses. The close-up range at 3.75 feet (1.25 m) at 200mm allows capture of a butterfly at a convincing size because (at 200mm) the size of the subject area is 5.3 x 8 inches (13.3 x 20 cm). A special macro setting and a distance of 3.6 feet (1.2 m) provides a subject area which (at 200mm) is not much bigger than a post card and (at 50mm) is still approximately 16 x 24 inches (40 x 60 cm). An wide aperture should not be used with a macro setting. A reduction by at least two f/stops from wide open is recommended. The type of "macro" setting on telephoto zoom lenses is a technical by-product of the lens design which may also be utilized in autofocus mode. There are two focusing ranges which prevent a time-consuming search for sharpness from infinity to the close-up range each time a picture is taken. On one hand, there is the normal range from close-up - between 6 feet, 5.5 feet, 4.5 feet and 3.6 feet (2, 1.8, 1.5 and 1.2 m) - to infinity, and on the other hand is the expanded range from macro - mostly 4.5 feet (1.5 m), rarely 1.5 feet (0.5 m) to infinity.

Their weight from 18 ounces (500 g) to 25 ounces (700 g) is acceptable. They are convenient to carry and easy to handle. The only disadvantage is their maximum aperture (speed) - based on the viewpoint of photographers who like to emphasize the particularly photogenic boundaries of light. Considering a focal length of 50mm, the f/3.5 maximum lens aperture is not exactly overwhelming; and considering a focal length of 200mm, a f/4.5 maximum lens aperture is barely adequate. An exception is the Canon Zoom EF 80-200mm f/2.8. Those who have a standard lens (maximum aperture at 50mm f/1.8) and want to stay at a reasonable cost, should consider the 100-200mm f/4.5 A lens.

A photographer who is not afraid to set up a tripod once in a while and has the time and patience will find the EF 100-300mm f/4.5-5.6 USM an ideal lens. Even the close-up setting of 4.5 feet (1.5 m) with a direct 6 times larger scale of reproduction is convincing compared with the standard lens. If the L is added, the overall quality of the 50-200mm lenses is improved by a calcium fluorite lens and that of the 100-300mm lenses by an additional UD lens, and corrected apochromatically.

Both 70-210mm lenses and the two 100-300mm L zoom lenses have a so-called macro setting with only minimal differences regarding scale of reproduction. With the shortest focal

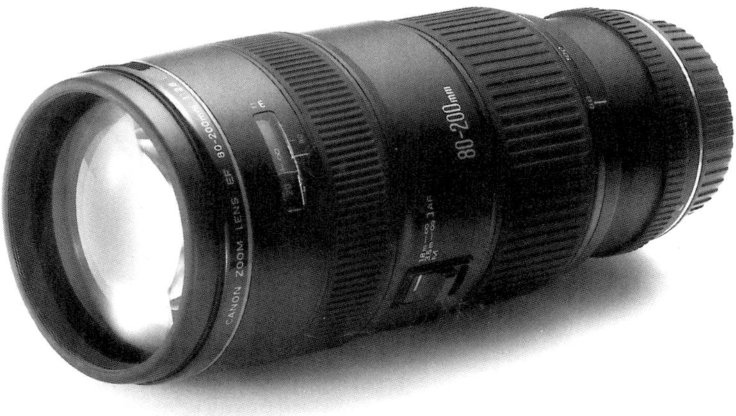

The fast EF 80-200mm f/2.8 L is an excellent lens for low-light photography or for isolating the subject by using a wide aperture opening.

length setting the subject is somewhat larger than a piece of letter-size paper and with the longest setting somewhat smaller.

The EF 70-210mm f/3.5-4.5 USM is likely to become the standard lens among the many zoom lenses. It may eventually replace the current 70-210mm lens. It is surprisingly compact and has a length of 4.9 inches (12.1 cm).

Canon EF 80-200mm f/2.8 L: This lens takes on an exceptional status due to another quality leap. Its rotary zoom ring ensures particularly precise adjustment. The aperture, which remains constant over the entire focal length range, and the image quality appealing to the highest professional expectations make this the lens for all situations and conditions. Three UD lenses reduce aberrations in this focal length range to a previously unattained minimum, including chromatic errors. The focusing speed of this Apo lens may be enhanced by preselecting one of the two adjustment ranges (5.4 feet [1.8 m] to infinity or 10.5 feet [3.5 m] to infinity). It is fast enough to still reproduce sharp images even at dusk or in rooms with low light. The AFD motor ensures superfast adjustment in 0.5 seconds over the entire focusing range.

Canon 70-210mm f/3.5-4.5 USM: This compact 5-group design is distinguished by fast internal focusing. This push-pull zoom

Canon EF 100-200mm f/4.5 A

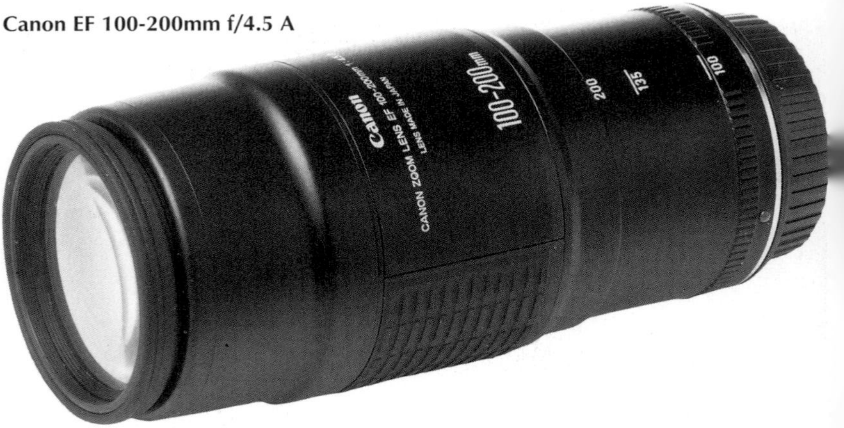

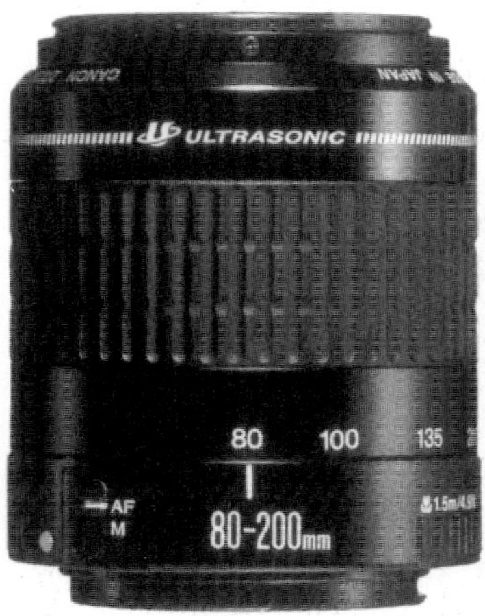

Canon EF 80-200mm f/4.5-5.6 USM

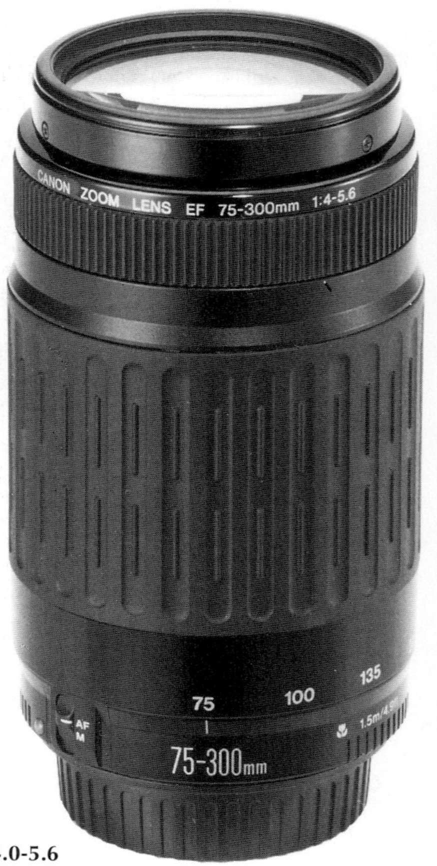

Canon EF 75-300mm f/4.0-5.6

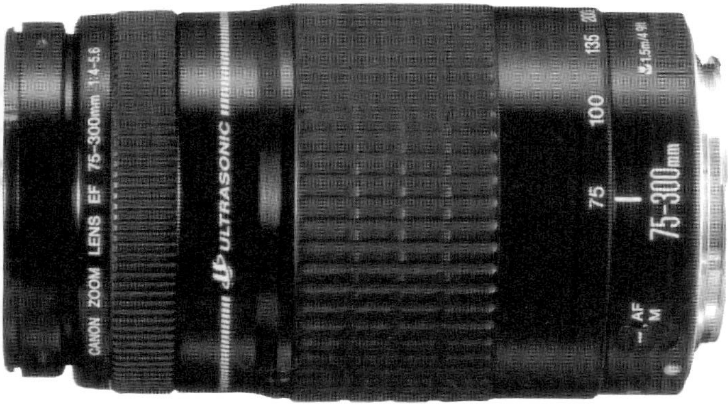

Canon
EF 75-300mm
f/4.0-5.6 USM

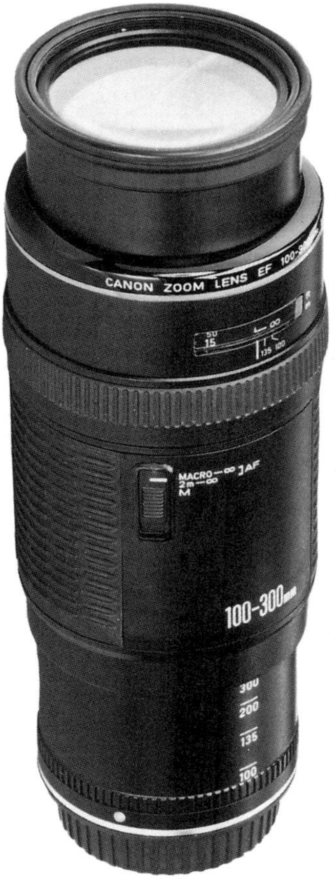

Canon EF 100-300mm f/5.6 L

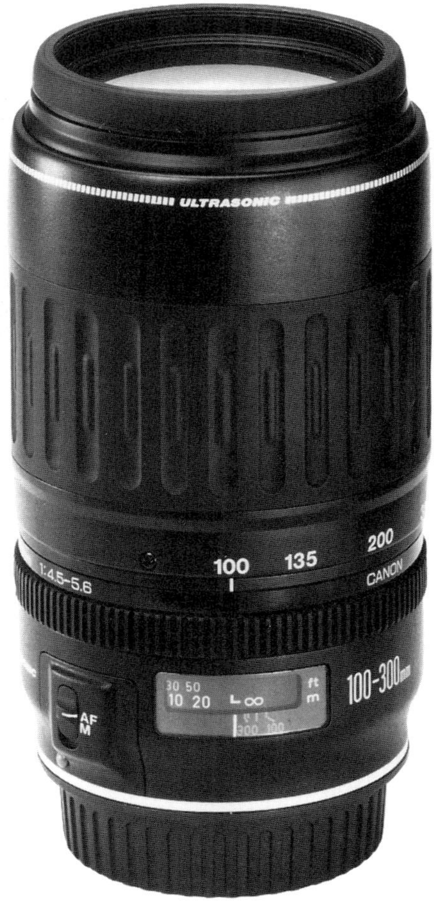

Canon EF 100-300mm f/4.5-5.6 USM

system is comprised of 14 elements in 10 groups. The focusing speed from infinity to 4.5 feet (1.5 m) is only 0.5 seconds. Manual focusing is possible without deactivating the AF mode. Depending on focal length, the lens has a length between 4.8 inches (121 mm) and 6.8 inches (170 mm). Its weight is about 19 ounces (550 g). The zoom system is one of the new lens designs which also reports the distance setting (scale of reproduction) to the camera's computer and has a particularly good effect on portrait and close-up program modes.

Canon EF 75-300mm f/4.0-5.6: This zoom lens allows an inexpensive beginning into the telephoto realm. Particularly lightweight plastic materials ensure its low weight at 17. 6 ounces (500 g), 30% lighter than the EF 100-300mm f/5.6. At a length of 4.8 inches (12 cm) it may be used quite comfortably for free-hand shots. The optical system consists of 13 elements in 9 groups. The shortest focusing distance is 4.5 feet (1.5 m).

Canon EF 100-200mm f/4.5 A: This inexpensive push-pull zoom lens may be adjusted only by moving the zoom ring. Manual focusing is not possible. The 3-group design uses 10 elements in 7 groups. The focusing speed for the entire focusing range is 0.7 seconds and the shortest shooting distance is 5.7 feet (1.9 m). The lens has a length of 5.2 inches (130 mm) and a weight of 18 ounces (520 g).

Canon EF 100-300mm f/4.5-5.6 USM: A very compact lens that offers exceptionally fast autofocusing due to its newly designed optical system with only 3 inner moving elements. The complete optical construction consists of 13 elements in 10 groups. The size of the lens is 4.75 inches (12.15 cm) long with a maximum diameter of 2.9 inches (7.3 cm). The weight is 19 ounces (540 g) and the angle of view covered by this zoom lens is 24 to 8 degrees.

Canon Extender EF 1.4X and EF 2X

Canon extenders are optical accessories which are placed between the camera and the lens to extend the effective focal length of the main lens. The numbers 1.4x and 2x indicate the

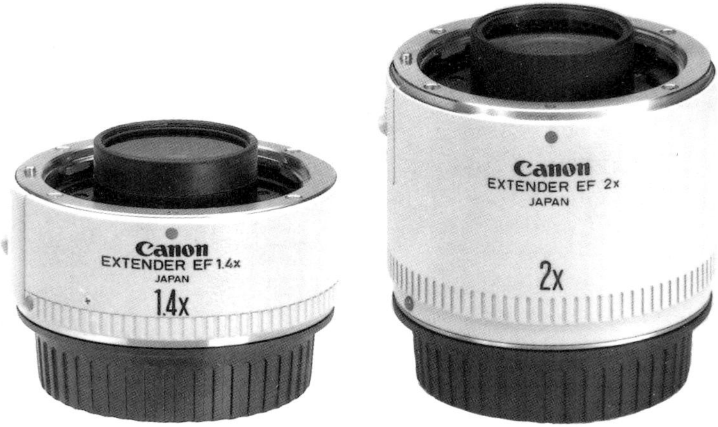

Canon's two EF Extenders: the 1.4x on the left and the more powerful 2x on the right.

factor by which the focal length is increased. This focal length extension produces a reduction of speed (or effective aperture). In the case of Extender EF 1.4x this is one f/stop, in the case of EF 2x, two f/stops. All functions governing aperture and autofocus control are maintained. However, if the aperture of the lens attached to the converter is less than f/5.6, the autofocus system won't function properly and the lens must be focused manually.

Although some after-market extenders or teleconverters have inexpensive low-quality optics, Canon converters are high-quality lens systems, specifically designed for use with Canon telephoto lenses. They are only slightly less expensive than an EOS Rebel X body but they add tremendous versatility to a lens outfit.

Special Lenses

Canon EF 50mm f/2.5 Macro: Macro lenses are designed for flat-field reproduction and high performance in the close-distance range. The 50mm Macro features particularly high resolution, excellent contrast and optimal image-area flatness. The minimum focus distance is 9.2 inches (23 cm); at this point a subject is recorded at half its original size (a 1:2 reproduction ratio) on the film.

Canon EF 135mm f/2.8 Softfocus.

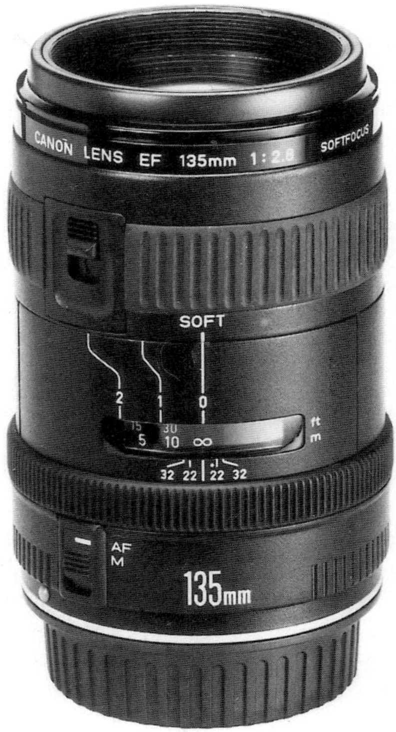

When pictures are taken of flowers, insects or other small subjects in nature, the aperture priority and auto depth of field features (DEP and A-DEP) of Rebel cameras come in handy. However, using these features will not eliminate the problem of shallow depth of field (which is barely 6 mm at f/11 and a scale of reproduction of 1:2). This is inherent in close up photography, but with proper technique, it can be reduced to an acceptable degree. For example, blossoms can be framed so that the largest part of a blossom is parallel to the film plane so that depth of field is not a critical factor in the final outcome. The same applies to a beetle. It is best photographed directly from the top or the side so that the largest area is parallel to the film plane. Also, with all close up work, use of a tripod is recommended.

Canon offers the Macro EF Converter as an accessory for use with this lens. This converter, which is connected between camera body and lens, permits shots at a scale of reproduction between 1:4 and 1:1 and compensates for the spherical aberration in the close-up and macro ranges.

The EF 50mm f/ 2.8 Macro is also suitable as a universal lens in all shooting ranges. The AFD motor allows automatic focusing from infinity to a scale of 1:0.5 in only 1.5 seconds. Manual focusing is also possible. The lens has a length of 2.5 inches (63 mm) and a weight of 10 ounces (285 g).

Canon EF 100mm f/2.8 Macro: This fast telephoto lens was designed specifically for macro shots up to a scale of 1:1 without additional intermediate rings or the life-size converter. A focus-limiting switch permits the selection between two distance ranges. One is within the macro range of 12.4 inches (0.31 m) and 22.8 inches (0.57 m). The other goes from 22.8 inches (0.57 m) to infinity. The autofocus motor covers this distance in exactly one second. The smallest subject area is 0.1 x 1.4 inches (12 x 36mm). A system of 10 elements in 9 groups provides a viewing angle of 24 degrees. The lens has a length of 4.2 inches (105.5 mm) and a weight of 23 ounces (650 g).

Canon EF 135mm f/2.8 Soft Focus: This lens offers a soft focus effect in addition to normal sharp focus. The degree of soft focus can be adjusted continuously. Focusing should take place after the amount of softening has been selected. The resulting soft focus effect is a function of the selected aperture and softening index setting. The effect is most pronounced with a soft focus setting of 2 and a lens aperture of f/2.8; at f/5.6 the soft focus effect is lost completely. For this reason, the lens performs best when used in the aperture priority mode. While the lens' telephoto perspective is noticeable in landscape shots, the 135mm focal length is not too long for portraits. It ensures a soft and clean separation between subject and background.

The 135mm f/2.8 Soft Focus lens consists of 7 elements in 6 groups. The AFD motor can adjust the focus from infinity to 3.9 feet (1.3 m) in 0.39 seconds. The lens has a length of 4 inches (10 cm) and a weight of 13.7 ounces (390 g)

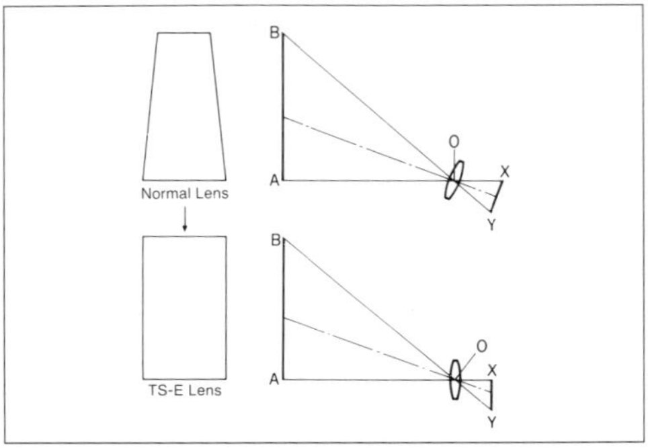

This simple diagram illustrates how a Tilt-Shift (TS-E) lens eliminates the need to tilt the camera upward when photographing a building, thus eliminating perspective distortion.

Perspective Control Lenses

Shift lenses allow the correction of the infamous converging verticals or distorted parallel lines which form when the film plane and the subject plane are not parallel. This is the case whenever, for example, large buildings are shot and the camera must be tilted upward in order to capture the entire view. Without this tilting the foreground becomes too dominant and only part of the building is in the picture. By shifting a TS lens out of the optical axis this view may be adjusted in the desired direction.

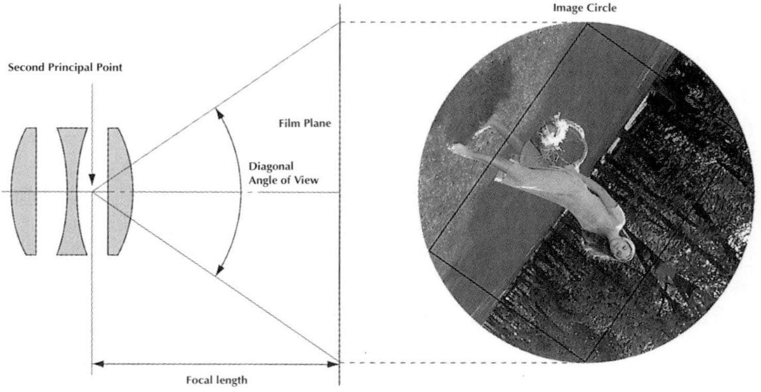

The larger the image circle of a Tilt/Shift (TS) lens, the greater the adjustment potential for perspective control.

Tilt-Shift Lenses

These special Canon EOS lenses come in three focal lengths: EOS TS-E 24mm f/3.5 L, TS-E 45mm f/2.8 and TS-E 90mm f/2.8. All three lenses exhibit excellent image quality. Outstanding, however, is the TS-E 28mm f/3.5 L lens. The L indicates that Canon has taken special pains concerning the optical system in order to ensure maximum contrast, resolving power and brilliance of color rendition.

All three lenses can be tilted by +/- 8 degrees and the (entire) optical system can be shifted by +/- 11 mm; 4 mm of this scale are marked in red on the super-wide angle lens only. With maximum shift vignetting may occur in this red range. A series of exposures should be taken in this critical range because the severe shift may result in aberrations.

Accessories

The accessories listed below are compatible with all Rebel cameras unless specified otherwise.

Focusing Magnifier

For extremely precise manual focusing, Canon offers a special focusing magnifier which is slipped onto the viewfinder eyepiece. The Focusing Magnifier S enlarges the center of the image by 2.5X. It may be folded up for normal viewfinder use. The kit includes the magnifier and the Adapter S, a square adapter, which is mounted to the eyepiece. Those who already have a focusing magnifier for the Canon F 1 need only purchase the square adapter. Photographers who wear eyeglasses may adjust the loupe to correct their vision within a range of -4 to +4 diopters.

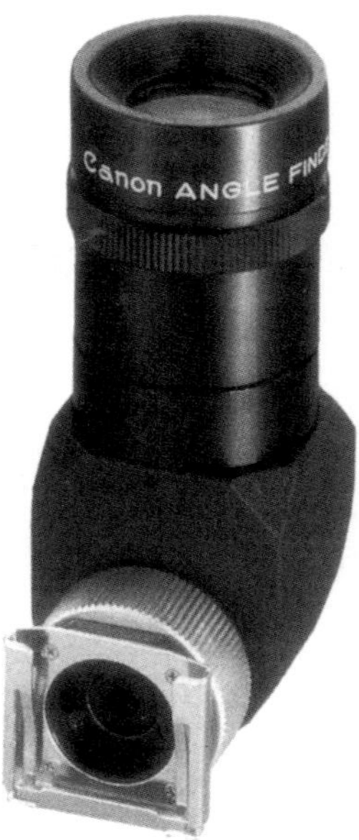

Right Angle Finders A-2 and B

By using an Adapter S the Right Angle Finder A-2 can be snapped onto the Canon EOS viewfinder eyepiece. Unlike the focusing magnifier, this finder permits viewing of the entire viewfinder image at a viewing angle of 90 degrees. However, the image is reversed left to right. The finder may be rotated so that it may be looked into from either side of the camera, or from the bottom. The optical system consists of 6 elements with a total magnification of 0.97x. Its weight is only 4.2 oz. (120 g).

Right Angle Finder B provides an unreversed image. This finder's technical capabilities are the same as those of the A-2 model. Both models feature (dioptric)

Canon Right Angle Finder B

eyesight correction in the range of +2 to -4 for those who wear eyeglasses. This finder also weighs 4.2 oz. (120 g).

Eyesight Correction Lenses

There are 10 different eyesight correction lenses to adapt the viewfinder image to the photographers visual requirements. The viewfinder has an inherent correction of + 1 diopter. The corrective lenses made by Canon are identified not by the diopter value of the lens itself, but their value in combination with the camera's +1 diopter viewfinder system. For example, a lens designated +4 is actually +3 alone, but gives a +4 correction on the camera. A special eyepiece, which fits even when the corrective lens is attached, keeps stray light out of the viewfinder eyepiece.

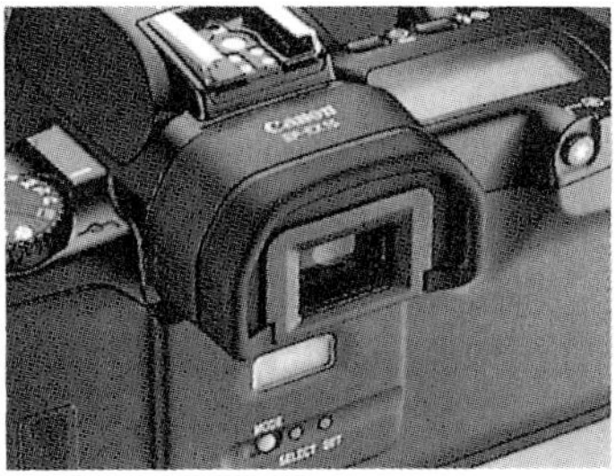

The Eyepiece Extender EP-EX15 increases comfort, but decreases image magnification.

Eyepiece Extender EP-EX 15

This extends the eye's distance from the viewfinder by 1/2 in. (1.5 mm). At the same time the viewfinder image size is decreased by 0.5 X.

Grip Extension GR-70

This grip extension with padded strap is designed for people with larger hands who find the standard grip on Rebel models prior to the X/XS too small.

Grip Extension GR-80TP

A particularly recommended REBEL X/XS accessory, this grip includes a built-in tripod for close-up, self-timer and slow shutter speed shots. Although not actually designed for other Rebel models, it will work with them fairly well.

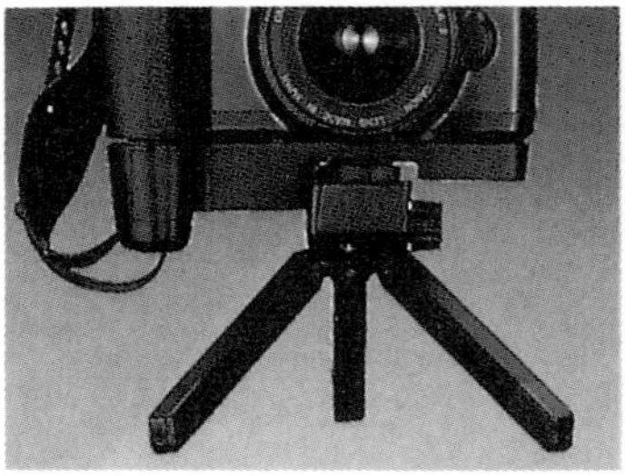

The Grip Extension GR-80TP is the first camera grip with a built-in tabletop tripod. Those with larger hands may prefer this grip due to its larger size.

Remote Release RS-60E3

This new cable release is available for the REBEL X/XS only. It plugs into the camera's remote control socket and is intended to prevent camera shake when the shutter is released. It is especially useful for macrophotographs and long exposures with a tripod.

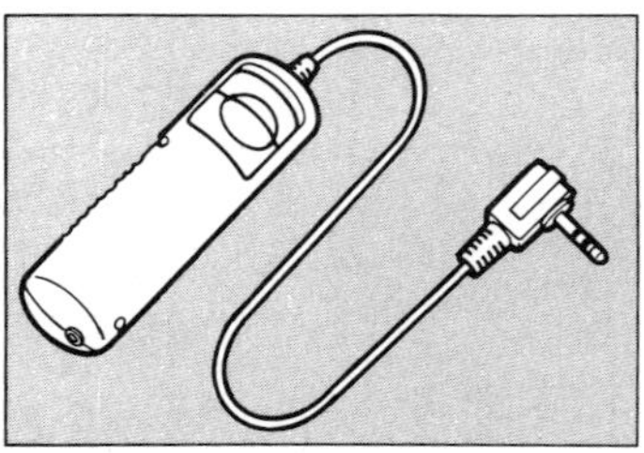

Remote Release Cable RS-60E3

Off-Camera Shoe Cord

This 2 ft. coiled cord has a camera adapter on one end and a flash adapter on the other. It enables the photographer to use a Speedlite flash off camera (for example, on a flash bracket) while still maintaining all dedicated flash functions.

Camera Cases

Canon offers an assortment of fitted cases to accommodate several different lenses mounted on the various Rebel cameras.

Camera Bags

A camera bag such as one of the Domke® models is often a better choice than an everready case due to the added flexibility it offers. A number of sizes and styles are available to hold extra lenses, a flash unit, accessories, film, and this book! Domke bags

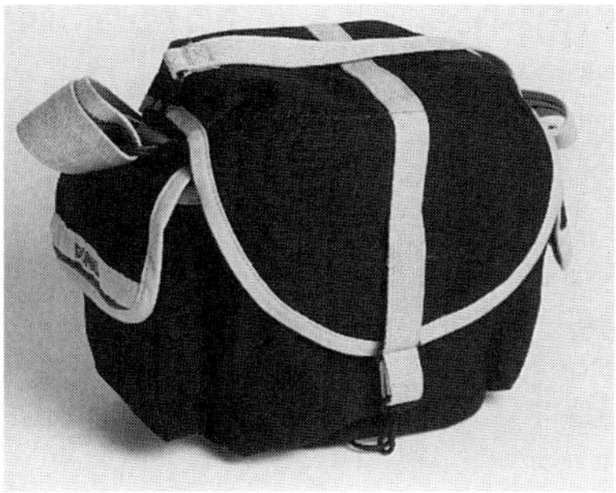

Domke F3X Super Compact Bag

were designed by a professional news photographer and are comfortable to carry and highly accessible in the field

There are many other brands, including the hard shell cases which resemble a suitcase. A waterproof case of this type is ideal if you're boating or traveling in the tropics or desert because they are well-sealed against water, humidity and dust. However, they may not be the ideal choice if you are going to walk for any distance with your equipment. Even with a shoulder strap, they are not comfortable to carry. A "fanny pack" like the Orion II AW from Lowepro® or the F-5XB Shoulder and Belt Bag from Domke® are a good choice for hiking, backpacking or cross-country skiing.

Besides style, there are other things to consider when purchasing a camera bag. Think about the amount of equipment you intend to carry and your picture-taking style. Choose a bag which is larger than you currently need, so it will hold a second flash unit or any new lenses acquired later.

Make sure that the zippers are covered by overlapping flaps so that water cannot enter from the top. A completely water-proof bag cannot be made, but it should at least be adequate to keep the equipment dry in rain, snow or dense fog. The bottom of the bag should be reinforced so it can be carried with a heavy load. Equipment dividers should be padded to protect valuable equipment from banging around. Well-designed, Domke patented dividers have sewn-in bottoms to eliminate "wandering" equipment and to make equipment changes from one bag to another quick and easy.

Filters

Filters can be used to enhance or correct the way an image will appear on film. Purchasing even a few filters and using them properly can make a big difference in the final outcome of your photography. Experimenting with the many special effect filters available from manufacturers such as Cokin® will add hours of enjoyment and may result in many interesting and unusual photos.

Only circular polarizing filters can be used with the REBEL cameras' AF system. Canon offers these filters in four different sizes (48, 52, 58 and 72mm). Unfortunately, the use of polarizing filters is complicated by using zoom lenses because many have a front ring which rotates when the lens focuses. Therefore, the effect achieved by rotating the filter is changed. In the case of some lens units, the front lens group is drawn into the barrel to such an extent that, at some distance or focal length settings, adjusting the filter becomes impossible. In this instance the Cokin® Filter System offers advantages. Cokin offers a large number of acceptable adapters and intermediate rings for use of their filters on Canon EF lenses.

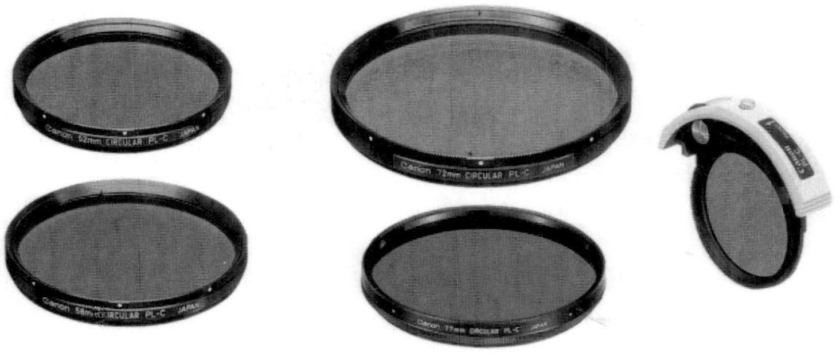

Canon makes circular polarizing filters in a number of sizes.

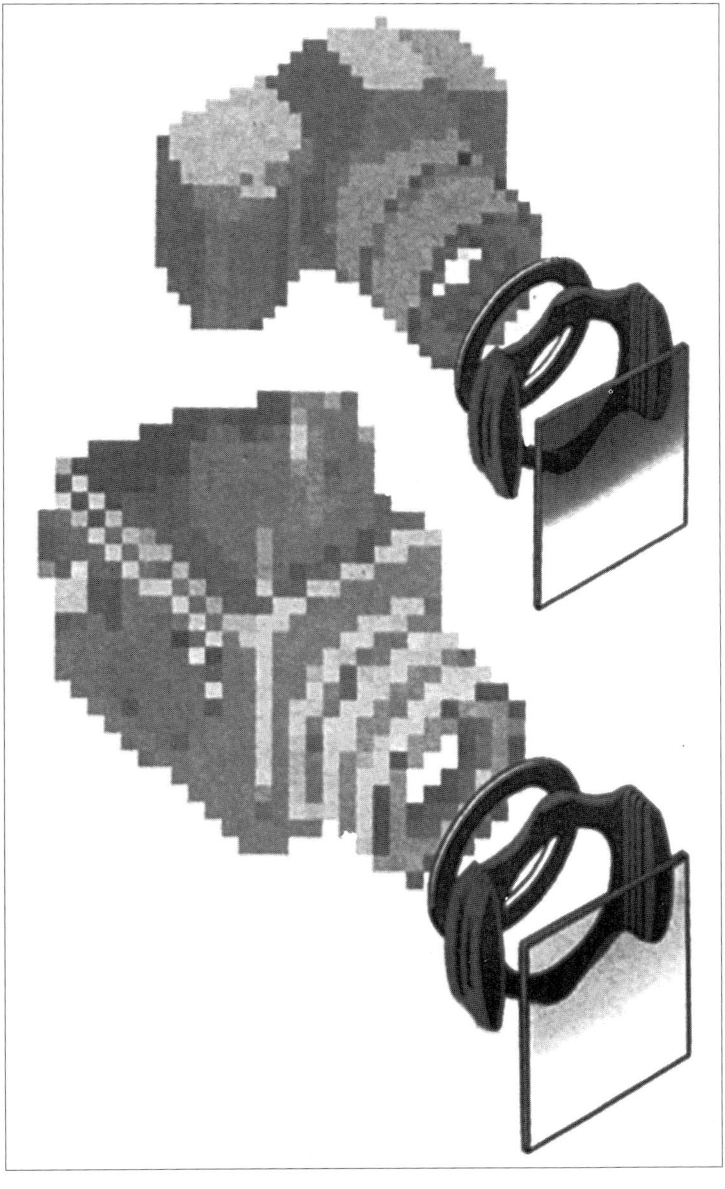

The Cokin® Creative Filter System. Photo courtesy of Cromofilter, SA.

General Purpose Filters

Polarizing Filters (circular)
Polarizing filters can eliminate distracting reflections on non-metallic surfaces such as water, glass, polished stone, wood or varnished surfaces, as well as dyed surfaces. Also, grasses, plants and (in particular in southern countries) plants with leather-like leaves not only reflect visible light but also UV radiation which the film receives as blue light. In these situations, polarizing filters offer warm, spring-like green colors. The effect is strongest at an angle between 30 and 40 degrees relative to the reflecting surface. Greater focal lengths enhance this effect significantly. Distance views are improved in particular. The result may be controlled visibly in the viewfinder.

Graduated Neutral-Density Filters
Like polarizing filters, these are a "must" for landscape photographers in order to reduce intense contrasts produced by the sky. Water, sky, snow and sand or other light-colored surfaces can also be darkened with these filters. Colorless subjects (such as sky) benefit from colorization and darkening. Cokin makes many different filters of this type.

Skylight Filter
Protects against UV radiation in the mountains and at the ocean and adds a slight overall warming effect to the photo. Like all filters, it should be used only in conjunction with a lens hood to prevent flare caused by light reflected from the two surfaces of the filter. Skylight filters are often left on the lens at all times, which is not true with other filters, as a safeguard against scratching the front element of the lens.

Filters for Black and White Photography

Yellow Filter
This filter is used to produce a tonally correct sky. It is a must to obtain correct tones in sunny snowscapes.

Green Filter
This enhances the gray-scale differentiation of greens, and darkens red, blue and magenta. It is useful at the seaside to reproduce the sky in the correct gray-tone and make brown or tan skin appear even darker. Freckles become more noticeable in portraits.

Orange Filter
This filter darkens blues. White clouds stand out vividly against the sky. Views of distant objects are enhanced. Its effect may be increased dramatically by adding a polarizing filter.

Red Filters
With this filter, blue sky turns deep black, clouds are offset distinctly and everything red will become considerably lighter. The same applies here as for all other black and white filters, subjects of the same color as the filter become lighter, the complementary-color subjects becomes darker.

The Flash System

The Built-in Flash

Small flash units built into cameras have become much more powerful in recent years. By integrating the flash unit's control system with that of the camera, picture-taking techniques previously used only by professionals are now automated. For example, professionals and amateurs alike have become more interested in using flash due to features such as programmed fill flash. All the tedious computations and adjustments have been eliminated. The convenience of always having a flash unit at hand and ready to enhance a shot is very much appreciated by REBEL S/SII/XS photographers. But that does not mean that off-camera flash units are no longer useful.

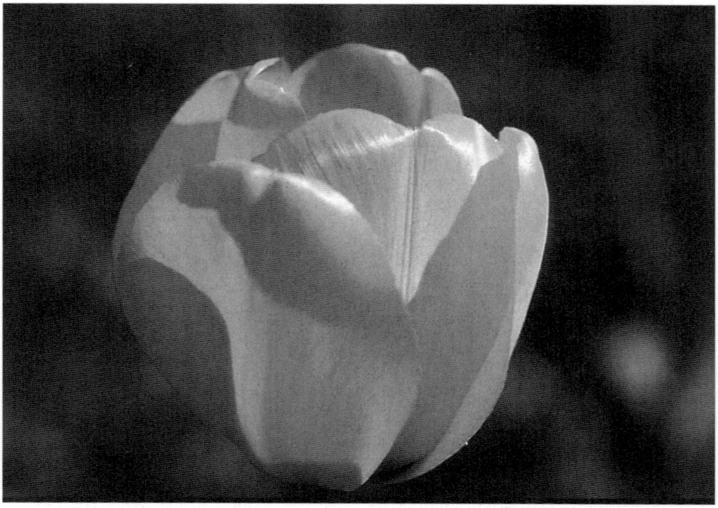

Many REBEL series cameras feature a built-in flash unit which is useful with the automatic program modes for better illumination of a wide variety of subjects.

The REBEL S/SII/XS cameras feature a built in flash unit with a guide number in feet of 40 or a metric guide number of 12. (A guide number is a function of the film speed and all guide numbers in this chapter refer to ISO 100.) This is not very powerful although it may illuminate the viewing area of a 28mm lens. However, this built-in flash unit should not be underestimated. Under poor lighting conditions or even in darkness it ensures adequate illumination. A photo opportunity will not be missed because the camera was not ready at the decisive moment. In addition, the flash recycling time is less than two seconds.

This built-in mini flash unit is even more important for fill flash shots than flash-only shots. Those who take photographs with fast fixed focal length lenses or with fast film will appreciate the creative touch of flash, as well as the shooting distances possible with fill flash. With a 400 speed film and a telephoto setting, the shooting range is 84 feet (28 m) and at ISO 1000 it is almost 150 feet (50 m) at f/2. This allows the photographer to light up an entire building or hall with his mini flash unit. This is the reason

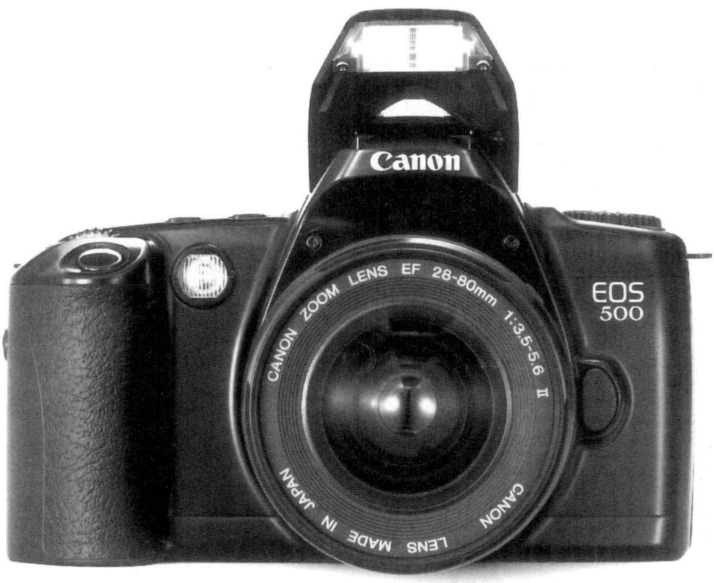

The built-in flash of the REBEL XS will pop-up automatically in certain modes, and can be activated manually, as needed, in other modes.

Middle

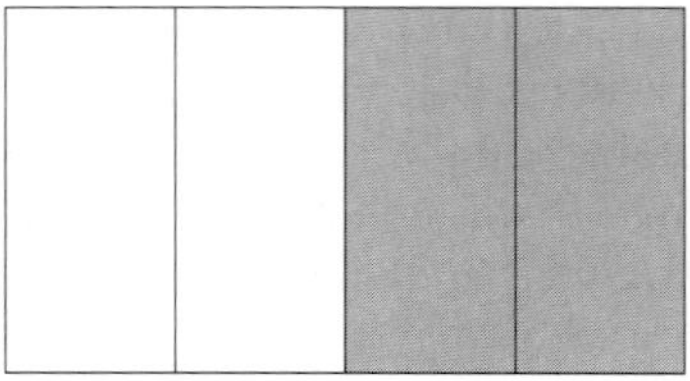

Right

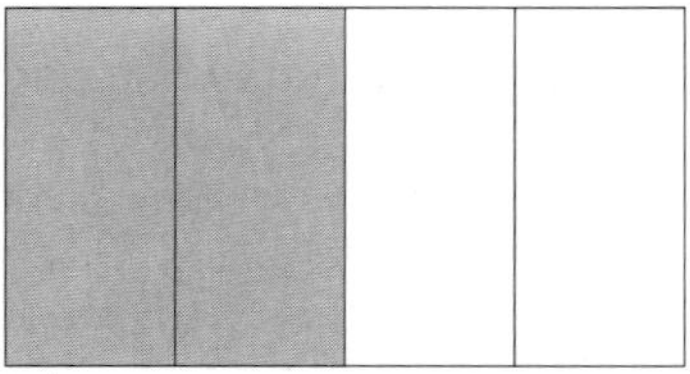

Left

The multi-zone metering for flash gives the active AF metering zone first priority, just like the metering system for existing light. The surroundings are also analyzed and given consideration.

why a photographer should feel comfortable making frequent use of this built-in flash. When telephoto or zoom lenses are used, shadows may occur at distances of less than 4.5 feet (1.5 m). In this instance the lens partially obstructs the path of the flash. This makes a Canon EF 28-50mm f/3.5-5.6 USM standard zoom lens an excellent choice because it has been designed specifically for all EOS models with built-in flash units. This lens maintains a constant length and full flash exposures may be taken at a distance as close as 3 feet (1 m). Sometimes the shadow problem may be handled simply by removing the lens hood.

Fill Flash Pictures

Considering the use of flash, there is no difference between flash (when the flash is the main light) or fill flash. In combination with daylight, fill flash performs two almost contradictory functions. The least noticeable function is the use of flash to increase the contrast, thereby making color pictures more brilliant and colorful; here, the flash will be the main source of light. Photographers who take pictures with programmed subject-specific modes or Av mode may add the function of the built-in flash unit in such situations.

Better known, however, is the other function of reducing high or excessive contrast between light and shadows to an acceptable degree. The mini-flash is highly effective in this program mode and its light factored in with automatic exposure modes. External Speedlite flash units may also be controlled automatically by the subject-specific programs. When combined with these external flash units, the REBEL cameras offer even greater flash performance.

Fill flash is quick to apply and easy to learn. One image effect, the glamour character of the early 1950s may not be everyone's desired result, but it is at least worth experimenting with. Those who have been disappointed by faces that are too dark in reproductions will be thrilled with the results of using fill flash. Mixing fill flash with daylight is one of the simplest and most effective methods of achieving extraordinary results with an unusual use of light.

Generally, all backlit subjects are good candidates for fill flash. The most beautiful backlighting occurs early in the morning and late in the afternoon when light grazes a subject but is still quite intense. In these instances, fill flash will enhance the mood in a particularly effective manner even when the background is very bright. This is not the only positive effect. Printing will be simplified considerably by the increased color and detail in the shadow areas, in most instances the image effect will be enhanced considerably.

Flash may also be used as artificial sun in order to improve color rendition. By using flash, low-contrast subjects in the shade or under a cloudy sky suddenly receive color. The sky or background appears even darker and more dramatic.

If the camera's built-in flash unit is used exclusively, the aperture priority and manual modes should be used and the flash added manually. When the shortest sync speed display of 1/90 blinks, the subject will be exposed correctly but the background will be overexposed. With an aperture value of f/2.8 and a film speed of ISO 100 the built-in flash unit will cover a shooting distance up to 18 feet (6 m). When used as main light, the flash only reaches 12 feet (4 m).

Many of these flash techniques may also be employed for time exposures. In this instance, the flash and the existing daylight or ambient light will complement the pictures which have areas in focus, and other areas out of focus.

Canon Speedlite Flash Units

Both the built-in and shoe-mounted Canon Speedlite flash units feature two automatic operating modes: A-TTL and TTL control. In TTL mode, only the main subject is illuminated precisely. The correct exposure is achieved by metering the light reflected by the film plane. Convenient A-TTL metering automatically compensates for contrast between the main subject and the background so that both image areas will complement each other in the final exposure. The Speedlite flash units may be used in combination with almost all automatic and subject-specific programs. In some instances, a thorough knowledge of flash technology is recommended in order to be able to plan a desired result ahead of time. The same applies to the use of flash in manual operating modes.

The Speedlites are compact flash units which are designed specifically for use with EOS cameras. They are attachable units with a hot-shoe contact. In order to assure that the flash unit has been slid onto to the shoe properly, the foot has an additional securing ring. It must be screwed on tightly, otherwise the securing pin on the foot may not engage the flash shoe.

The Speedlite 430 EZ, the current top-of-the-line model among the Canon system flash units, has a guide number between 82 and 142 in feet (25 and 43 in meters). The guide number is a function of the film speed and generally refers to ISO 100. This value for light yield, divided by the shooting distance, results in the aperture value required for correct exposure. The guide number, divided by the aperture value informs the photographer of the maximum distance at which a subject will be illuminated by the flash unit. However, the guide number is also affected by the shape of the reflector which allows an adjustment of the angle of illumination to the lens viewing angle. This explains why the same flash unit, even though it emits light with identical maximum values at the flash tube, may have different guide numbers, the lowest values refer to the wide-angle range and the highest values to the telephoto range.

The Speedlite's zoom head reflector is automatically set to match lens focal lengths of 24, 28, 35, 50, 70 and 80mm when used with EOS lenses. In the case of zoom lenses the reflector position also follows focal length changes. Manual adjustment is required with non-EOS lenses or for special effects.

Frontview
Canon Speedlite 430 EZ
1. Swivel/Tilt Flash Head
2. Infrared Pre-flash Illuminator
3. Autofocus Assist Light
4. Locking Pin
5. Sensor
6. Battery Compartment
7. External Battery Pack Connection
8. Locking Ring
9. Synchronization Contacts

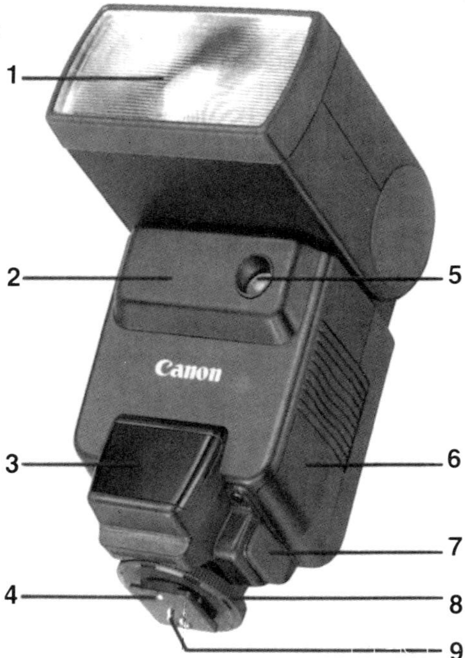

Rearview
1. Release Button for Head Tilt
2. LCD Screen
3. Mode Change Button
4. Control Button for Manual Modes
5. Ready Light
6. 1st/2nd Curtain Sync Control
7. LCD Illuminator
8. Manual Reflector Zoom Control
9. On/Off Switch

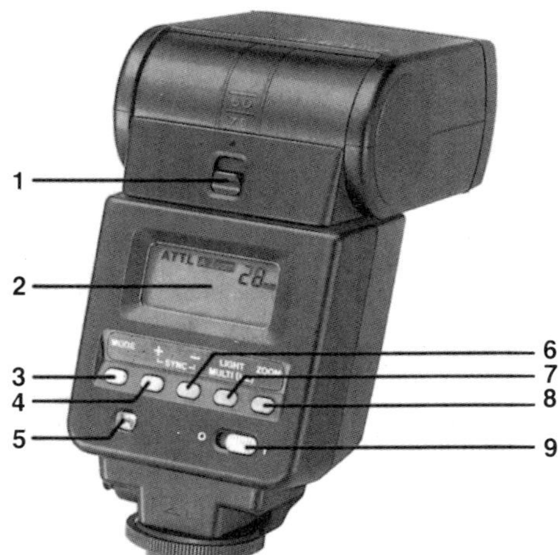

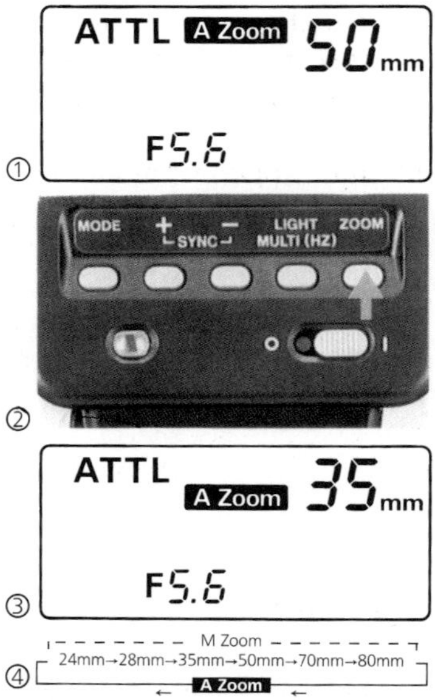

When used with Canon EF lenses, the Canon Speedlite 430 EZ's zoom head automatically adjusts from 24mm to 80mm to match the focal length of the lens in use.

A green ready light on the back of the flash indicates that the camera has been switched to flash mode and may be fired. The indicator lights when 70% of the full capacity has been reached after a super-fast charging cycle. The change from green to red indicates that the flash unit has been fully charged. By pressing the illuminated ready light on the flash unit a test flash may be fired. The AF control indicator in the viewfinder will blink if there is insufficient light.

When you have finished shooting, the flash unit should be switched off, however, it is easy to forget this while shooting. If you are shooting intermittently at a long event, the Speedlite's automatic battery-saver circuit comes in handy. This automatically shuts off the unit to eliminate battery drain (with the 420 EZ, after approximately five minutes; and with the 430 EZ, after about 90 seconds). The 420's monitor display begins to blink about 30 seconds before the flash unit switches off. A light touch on the shutter release or a turn of the main switch will turn the flash back on.

All flash functions are displayed on the LCD panel on the back of the flash. The AF assist light on the front of the flash allows the

REBEL camera's autofocus to operate in darkness. By focusing on the pattern projected by this light the camera determines the shooting distance. If it is greater than the shooting range of the pre-flash, the AF control indicator will blink in the viewfinder below the image. Normally, this should not happen within a range of 2.7 to 24 feet (0.9 to 8 m) because this is the unit's working range. When the AF control indicator blinks, the finger should be taken off the release and, if possible, one should go closer to the subject. A correctly exposed and sharp flash exposure is ensured only when a renewed touch of the release does not cause the indicator to blink.

The 430 EZ's data monitor displays a +/- sign for plus or minus correction. The gray button on the extreme left is used to activate different operating modes.

Flash with Automatic Program Control

The REBEL X/XS offers multi-zone metering for flash pictures and works with four zones. Again the active AF metering zone is given first priority, the surroundings are also analyzed and given consideration.

Initially, it is hard to remember all the programs and their features. For practical reasons, one should initially concentrate on one or two methods: use either P or Tv flash mode only. Then, step-by-step, one may explore other programs, each of which offer effective creative alternatives.

Shooting with any REBEL camera and flash is the easiest when everything is set for automatic operation (green zone): The lens is on AF, the camera on the green rectangle, the flash unit on A-TTL. All the photographer has to do is aim at the main subject through the AF metering field, lightly touch the release and observe the green numbers and symbols at the lower image edge where information regarding exposure time is displayed. Normally, the camera works with flash at a sync speed of 1/90. If the range of the flash is exceeded, the shutter speed and aperture indicators will call for a change of distance.

Flash Using Shutter Priority Mode (Tv)

In Tv mode the shutter speed is selected by the photographer. However, this speed must not exceed 1/90 second. Otherwise, only part of the image area would be illuminated. Times slower than 1/90 may be used. The flash unit is set to A-TTL and connected. When the shutter release is pressed, the aperture value, determined and set by the flash unit based on the pre-flash, will appear in the viewfinder.

Flash Using Aperture Priority Mode (Av)

Some still think that the light of an electronic flash will destroy the entire mood of a picture. Of course, there are many cases when it makes sense to reach for high-speed films and not use the flash unit. But once the eye has been trained to recognize the details of using light, even those situations can often be enhanced with a touch of flash, resulting in technically improved, more expressive photos.

One way to achieve this is the aperture priority mode (Av). The camera is set on Av mode and the Canon 430 EZ or 420 EZ flash unit is switched to A-TTL. By lightly pressing the release the required shutter speed is determined for the standard aperture value of f/5.6. Should a different aperture value make more sense for the task at hand, it may be adjusted now and the release again pressed lightly.

The shutter speed which is adjusted automatically in Av mode results from the existing total amount of light. Flash is added to this basic brightness. It is of no consequence for a technically perfect flash picture whether the exposure will be 1/30 or 30 seconds, but there is a world of difference from the viewpoint of creativity. The flash may act as the main light and be used in conjunction with time exposures for special effects. The photographer may enhance the existing ambient mood or use lighting skills to create an intense, effective mood.

Here is a common practical problem: a portrait taken in the living room with an evening mood. By setting the camera to Tv, the flash sync speed is too fast and only the flash light is registered. The ambient light is much too weak to register at 1/90. In

Av program mode the exposure time appropriate for the ambient light is determined. The flash illuminates only the foreground in order to fill in light for correct exposure with the set aperture. This picture has captured a portrait radiating the mood of its environment.

This flash technique is suitable not only for indoor shots but is even more effective and impressive outdoors. In early dusk, for example, when shooting with a high-sensitivity film. With the Av setting, a mood-enhanced picture is obtained. A touch of flash light has added color to the picture within a range of 90 to 120 feet (30 to 40 m).

The portrait example is best implemented with the use of a monopod in order make the foreground and the background as sharp as possible. However, this is not always necessary. If a picture is to be taken of a sidewalk musician, the photographer may want the subject to appear more abstract and dramatic. Then the aperture is reduced to extend the total exposure time. Following the flash exposure, the camera will be held in the hands, or intentionally moved. The result will be a correctly exposed background with motion blurs complemented by a sharp flash image to create an exceptional mood.

Should this result still not be interesting enough, colors may be enhanced by mounting a filter on the camera or the flash unit. If a filter is used on both the camera and the flash unit, two complementary filter colors can be used. In this way the background or the flash subject may be covered separately with a color tint. There are no limits to the photographer's imagination.

Stroboscopic Flash Techniques

The flow of motion may be fixed in several individual images, all of which appear in one frame. With Canon Speedlite 430 EZ and 420 EZ units, such stroboscopic effects may be created automatically. The maximum number of flash exposures is a function of battery power and doubles up to 10 flashes per second when an external battery pack is used.

The procedure for taking strobe exposures is as follows: first the camera must be set on M. The exposure should last at least one second but may exceed 30 seconds using the Bulb setting.

The aperture is selected manually. The Mode button on the flash is used to enter M. By pressing it again, Multi 1 Hz will be displayed. Now the exact number of flashes per second may be programmed by pressing the Multi button. The Canon Speedlite 430 EZ allows programming of up to 10 exposures per second. The 420 EZ allows up to five. Of course, this high-speed flash sequence requires considerable power. Therefore, such flash exposures can be made only at 1/4, 1/8, 1/16 and 1/32 the maximum power. The flash unit's display will indicate the greatest possible shooting range for the set camera aperture. This information applies only when the ready light on the flash unit lights up in red.

TTL Automatic Flash Program

The EOS Speedlite units feature novel and normal flash programs such as the combination mode of M on the camera and TTL on the flash unit.

The manual adjustment of aperture and shutter speed will only be required for a few subjects, for example, when precise aperture or sync speed are desirable. If the camera is set to M, the flash unit will automatically switch to TTL. Of course, the flash unit's LCD will indicate this. It also displays the flash unit's working range applying to the film loaded in the camera and the standard aperture of f/5.6. Because a change of the aperture will affect the working range, these values will be immediately changed with each new setting.

Soft Light with Bounce Flash

It is true, small flash units have small reflectors and hence a relatively acute angle of reflection. Consequently, light is more direct and covers a small area. When aimed at the subject, this flash creates deep, harsh shadows. The EOS Speedlite unit's versatile tilt and swivel head may be used to modify this effect. Better results are obtained when the light makes a detour by first bouncing off of a wall or ceiling. The spatial character provided by illumination does not suffer noticeably and the shadows become softer. The EOS metering systems always measure light reflected by the subject and are therefore equally effective with bounce flash and in A-TTL mode.

The metering preflash is visible when bounce flash is used, whereas an infrared flash is used in other modes. The reflector is automatically adjusted to a focal length of 50mm, but manual override is possible. This flash technique requires that the information displayed in the viewfinder be observed carefully. Performance limits may be reached relatively quickly due to the total distance to be covered by the flash light. Bounce flash offers advantages in many picture-taking situations. For example, the unattractive red-eye effect can be prevented. Red eyes are an unpleasant side effect when the flash unit is relatively close to the optical axis of the lens. When a portrait is to receive particularly soft illumination, the reflecting surface should be physically as close as possible to the flash unit. For a clean illumination of large rooms it is best when the ceiling or wall is at a distance of 6 to 9 feet (2 to 3 m). The reflector's wide-angle setting reduces total brightness and, at the same time, improves light quality.

Notes

Notes

Notes

Notes

Notes